The Ideology of Democratism

The Ideology of Democratism

EMILY B. FINLEY

OXFORD
UNIVERSITY PRESS

OXFORD
UNIVERSITY PRESS

Oxford University Press is a department of the University of Oxford. It furthers
the University's objective of excellence in research, scholarship, and education
by publishing worldwide. Oxford is a registered trade mark of Oxford University
Press in the UK and certain other countries.

Published in the United States of America by Oxford University Press
198 Madison Avenue, New York, NY 10016, United States of America.

Library of Congress Control Number: 2022939679

ISBN 978–0–19–764229–0

DOI: 10.1093/oso/9780197642290.001.0001

3 5 7 9 8 6 4 2

Printed by Integrated Books International, United States of America

CONTENTS

PREFACE

Is democracy antidemocratic? If you apply the standards of a hugely influential modern understanding of what democracy ought to be, this question is not as paradoxical as it may seem. According to this understanding of popular government, which forms part of a larger view of human nature and society, the practices of actual democracies fall far short of, or egregiously violate, what is considered to be "real" democracy. This view is not confined to a small minority of theorists, and it is not of recent origin. It has been a powerful and growing influence in America and leading Western European nations and their colonial satellites for a couple of centuries. It has long been prominent in universities and intellectual circles, and it is today more widespread than ever—so ubiquitous, in fact, that its views are a prominent ingredient in public debate whenever issues of democracy or related issues are raised. This view of democracy informs a wide range of demands for reform that often extend far beyond politics. This understanding of democracy has become something like a new view of life, a replacement for old Western beliefs and practices, and in some instances appears to have taken on a religious dimension. The research behind this book provides overwhelming evidence for the view that a certain imaginative belief in democracy has emerged that has all the earmarks of an entire ideology and that is, moreover, perhaps the dominant political belief system in modern Western society. So compelling is the evidence for this view that it is surprising so few have been aware of this hugely influential ideology and that nobody has undertaken a comprehensive study of its features. It is as if the ideology in question has been assumed by its advocates and many sympathizers to be self-evidently true and that it has, as it were, been able to hide in plain sight.

This book investigates the underpinnings and major thrust of what appears to be yet another political "ism." Considering the enormous influence of this belief system, it needs to be examined with care. The name I give this post-Enlightenment understanding of democracy is "democratism." While I am not the first to use this term for the phenomenon in question, this book is, to my knowledge, the first attempt to offer a systematic description, analysis, and assessment of the ideology of democratism.

At its core, democratism is a hypothetical or ideal conception of democracy that is only tenuously connected to the actual, historical desires of real popular majorities. Rousseau was a pioneering figure in elaborating a new conception of democracy that theoretically calls for rule by the people but eschews popular sovereignty in practice. Rousseau labels the ideal expression of the popular will the "General Will." While Rousseau coined the term and gave it powerful expression in *The Social Contract*, many others have consciously or unconsciously incorporated this same fundamental concept into their understandings of democracy. Democratism can perhaps best be summed up as the belief that democracy is real or genuine only to the degree that it reflects an idealized conception of the popular will. The president of Freedom House was oriented by this democratist conception of democracy when he declared popular majorities a "threat" to democracy. How could a popular majority threaten democracy, one might wonder? When democracy morphs conceptually in the imagination from a *type of government* into an abstract and ahistorical ideal, its historical manifestations may be considered false, not "real democracy," or not democratic enough. One of the abiding features of democratism is the belief that true democracy can be accomplished once certain institutional mechanisms are put in place. It is always just over the horizon.

Because the general will is an ideal, a leader or group of leaders must bring it to life practically. Rousseau's *Social Contract* is, again, paradigmatic. An all-knowing legislator is Rousseau's solution to the seemingly intractable problem of escaping business-as-usual politics. Leading without coercing, omniscient and all-capable, the legislator is the deus ex machina of *The Social Contract*, setting the new political system in motion. Those who conceive of democracy according to the democratist perspective rely on a legislator in one form or another to midwife a new, truer Democracy into existence. Because of its prima facie commitment to democracy, democratism is often reluctant to acknowledge its dependence on a legislator or vanguard to encourage the "right" democratic norms. One of the paradoxes of democratism and one of the indicators of its ideological nature is the need for an elite to coax the general will—whatever name it might go by—from the populace.

Calling for greater power to the people and fewer mediating institutions between the people and government, democratism has every appearance of being highly democratic. Heavy use of abstract concepts from the democratic lexicon has helped democratism largely escape notice as an ideology and as fundamentally antidemocratic. It will likely come as a surprise to many to see notable champions of democracy such as Thomas Jefferson and the school of thought known as deliberative democracy included in this book as examples of an ideology that, to a greater or lesser degree, rejects popular sovereignty. Subtle assumptions about the need to alter inherited norms and cultural practices guide the ostensibly democratic thought of democratists. Careful examination reveals that what may at first seem like reasonable reforms are in fact proposals for dramatic, even revolutionary changes to a people's social norms and ways of life. Democratism glosses over the ways in which it expects to transform a people's practices and even psychology, focusing instead on the technical aspects and new procedures. Yet the adoption of the new "democratic" system is dependent on the people accepting it and practicing it, much more so than on the correct political architectonics, as the history of political revolution and lesser political change reveals.

To what extent is democratism's ideal of democracy connected to actual democracy as a form of government? If it is found to have little in common with our traditional notion of democracy as "rule by the people," then it is worth investigating this new conception of rule and asking if it is desirable or legitimate. Part of this will entail asking if democratic idealism is a fruitful way of conceiving democracy, or if such idealism inherently encourages undemocratic, even dangerous political practices. If democratism is not a system that depends on the people's actual, historical will, then on what does it base its legitimacy? These are questions that this book investigates through a careful examination of this ideology's leading representatives, the democratists.

The original idea for this book was sparked by an observation that the vast majority of democratic scholarship in recent decades is oriented by a shared normative assumption about democracy, namely the belief that real democracies are more or less legitimate as they conform to an ideal of democracy. This assumption is rarely spelled out, but it underlies almost all normative questions about democracy in political science and public discussion. Furthermore, because a democratic ideal is held to be normative, it is assumed that all countries of the globe must be striving toward it, even if it is not apparent that they are doing so. The assumption is that in undemocratic countries most of the people, if they were able to think rationally and clearly about their interests, would choose something like Western-style democracy, and specifically "democracy" as the elite representatives of this ideology conceive of it. It seemed to me that this democratic idealism represented a type of enchantment that Max Weber thought had disappeared from the Western imagination. Weber was, of course, correct in the sense that scientific rationality had replaced an earlier Christian and spiritual interpretation of life, but in another sense the world remains very much enchanted. This book argues that the modern Western world is enchanted with an imaginative vision of democracy that at times is almost indistinguishable from religious belief. And like religious belief, it has its apostles, who define the democratic orthodoxy, and also its heretics, who must be managed and censored.

I began this book in the summer of 2016, before it was clear that a new form of populism was beginning to take shape in the United States and many European nations. Since then, it has been interesting to see new manifestations and expressions of what I have taken to be the ideology of democratism. If anything, it has become more pronounced and overt. It is routine to hear about this or that policy or action being urgently needed in order to "save democracy," for example. Yet increasingly, it seems, democracy must be rescued from itself. It must be saved even from popular majorities. The term "populist," paradoxically, is now often used to indicate those who allegedly wish to destroy democracy. "Populists" are often derided as "authoritarians" or "fascists." The democratist ideology has created the framework for this otherwise perplexing phenomenon, equating populism with what would seem to be its opposite: authoritarianism. Those who interpret democracy as an ideal believe that its correlation with the will of actual majorities need not be perfect or even approximate. Censorship, military action, or other seemingly undemocratic activities may be needed to coerce an unwilling or ignorant population into accepting what the democratists consider to be a more genuine expression of democracy. Even elections may be considered outmoded institutions if they do not produce results that would further the democratist ideal. Perhaps democracy proper—the actual rule by the people through some form of representation—is an outdated form of government, inappropriate for extended territories or particular peoples, and another type of rule is warranted, say, some form of aristocracy (from the Greek, "rule by the best") or oligarchy ("rule by the few"). But democratism does not openly declare the desire for another form of government; it presents itself as supremely democratic and its contributors as the mantle-bearers of true democracy. The evidence must be weighed as to whether democratism represents a variant of democratic thinking or the opposite and to what extent this modern, visionary conception of popular rule overshadows the older concept of democracy as actual, rather than hypothetical, rule by the people.

ACKNOWLEDGMENTS

This book would not have been nearly as enjoyable to write and to revise without the enthusiastic support I received from so many around me. On our first date, my now-husband coaxed me into a conversation about epistemology and about the ideas I was just beginning to work out for my book. Since that first date, you have always encouraged me, Brian. Always pushing me to go to conferences, attend or give lectures, teach courses, and, above all, to keep writing. You have never faltered in your support, which has often meant lugging our entire family across the country for extended periods of time or for weekend "getaways" with three kids and an academic conference. None of this would be possible without you. Thank you.

At The Catholic University of America, Claes Ryn spent untold hours discussing the ideas of this book, offering suggestions, and reading drafts at the eleventh hour. The courses that I took with you alerted me to the indispensability of the imagination in questions of life and politics, to the need for continual and careful revision (a lesson that I am still learning), and also to the idea that a work is never quite done—it can always be expressed differently, improved, cast in a different light. That last lesson is one I am only now beginning to appreciate.

Phil Henderson, thank you especially for your comments and direction on the chapter on Wilson and on the topic of the Bush Doctrine. Patrick Deneen, I am grateful to you for generously offering advice that proved very helpful in getting this book published.

The providential friendship that began my very first week of graduate school with Lucie Miryekta has played no small role in the course of my intellectual development. Our conversations about the eternal questions that would go until the wee hours of the morning, from the basement on Blair Road to the California wineries, were formative. I turned to you for help making connections when I was too sleep-deprived or spent to carry on, and you never failed to lead me to the heart of the matter.

Though its faults are mine alone, so many colleagues and professors have provided the intellectual village from which this work was brought forth. I would like to thank Alison McQueen for her selfless mentorship at Stanford for two years. The direction you provided me for deepening my engagement with Rousseau was especially invaluable. Marek Chodakiewicz, I would like to thank you for generously allowing me to attend your course on Russian history at the Institute of World Politics and for shaping the trajectory of my intellectual pursuits. Ryan Holston, thank you for having numerous conversations with me about deliberative democracy, for generously sharing your own work on the topic with me, and for reading an early draft of my chapter on the topic. Justin Garrison, thank you for your mentorship over the years, beginning when I was your teaching assistant. I appreciate your commenting on an early draft of the chapter on Jefferson and for offering constructive advice. David Hendrickson, I would like to thank you for reading a version of the chapter on Jefferson. As an expert on the man and someone whom I cite in this book, I consider myself very fortunate to have received your feedback. Matthew Cantirino, I appreciate your reading versions of the chapter in which I define democratism and for offering helpful commentary. I have gleaned many insights from your own impeccable writing and work. Eric Adler, thank you kindly for offering publishing advice when I reached out to you.

I consider my encounter with Rajan Menon at a conference nearly providential. Thank you, Dr. Menon, for reading a version of the chapter on Maritain and for suggesting that Oxford University Press might be a natural home for a book like mine. It turns out that you were right, and I am grateful for your introduction to David McBride. David, I am grateful to you as my editor, for your advice, for taking a chance on my manuscript, and for finding reviewers. I am also grateful to my anonymous reviewers, whose comments and criticism helped me to strengthen the manuscript considerably.

I would like to thank the librarians at the Catholic University of America Mullen Library. When I moved away from the area, you were kind enough to continue mailing hard-to-find books to me so that I could finish my research. That service was indispensable.

I especially want to thank my father, who first instilled in me a love of reading and a love of political philosophy. And thank you for reading over chapters of this manuscript and offering your advice and, most of all, encouragement.

I also want to thank my mother, who always encouraged me to broaden my mind and whose support I have always enjoyed.

Thank you to my mother- and father-in-law, Joanne and Drew, for always taking an interest in my work and success. Thank you for your tireless help with the children for extended periods and giving me the gift of time to spend on intellectual work. Words cannot adequately express my gratitude to you.

Rousseau Sets the Tone

Introduction

It seems appropriate to begin by analyzing a person who was of central inspiration to the entire ideology that is about to be examined. He may indeed be a paradigmatic figure for democratism. Jean-Jacques Rousseau "set the world in flame," Lord Byron said.[1] Referring to him as the "apostle of affliction," Byron joins many others who have seen fit to use religious language to describe the philosopher who has become more of a prophet. The sociologist Robert Nisbet calls Rousseau "the man of the hour" and "the saint of saints" and says, "He offers absolute power in the form of divine grace, of the community of the elect."[2] Along these same lines, Jacob Talmon criticizes Rousseau's "Discourse on Inequality," calling it "that Gospel of Revolution."[3] Robespierre, however, was sincere in calling Rousseau "divine."[4] Ernst Cassirer, also an admirer, summarizes Rousseau's political project along these lines: "The hour of salvation will strike when the present coercive form of society is destroyed and is replaced by the free form of political and ethical community—a community in which everyone obeys only the general will, which he recognizes and acknowledges as his own will. . . . But it is futile to hope that this salvation will be accomplished through outside help. No God can grant it to us; man must become his own savior."[5]

Rousseau's ostensibly secular philosophy of democracy has led many to conceive of his project in religious terms and has inspired a corresponding quasi-religious faith in the type of democracy he envisions. At the heart of Rousseau's political philosophy and no doubt informing the ersatz religion of democracy that he arguably founded is the concept of the general will. This was surely on the mind of Nisbet when he referred to the "absolute power" Rousseau offers. Cassirer specifically mentions the general will as the vehicle for our political salvation. Rousseau suggests as much. This chapter examines the ways in which Rousseau's understanding of the general will, perhaps *the* concept orienting his

The Ideology of Democratism. Emily B. Finley, Oxford University Press. © Oxford University Press 2022.
DOI: 10.1093/oso/9780197642290.003.0001

philosophy of democracy, guides the democratist interpretation of democracy in general and the popular will in particular.

In this chapter, I highlight those aspects of Rousseau's political thought that are reflected in the modern, conflicted understanding of democracy that I identify with democratism. This book takes seriously Rousseau's assertion that a singular "great principle" guides all of his works.[6] "All that is challenging in the *Social Contract* had previously appeared in the *Essay on Inequality*; all that is challenging in *Émile* was previously in *Julie*," Rousseau insists. I draw on these and other works and find that in them is indeed a guiding principle, the same that guides democratism. To demonstrate that Rousseau's political philosophy is paradigmatic of what I here identify as a comprehensive political ideology, I must paint with somewhat broad brush strokes. To go into great detail and to analyze the many nuances of any one aspect of Rousseau's thought will ultimately detract from the major purpose of this book. Like other chapters, this chapter has the limited aim of establishing a particular thinker's connection to democratism. I touch on the concepts of the legislator and Rousseau's understanding of education as they fit within his political philosophy, but the concept on which this chapter focuses most attention is the general will.

My interpretation of Rousseau's general will is certainly not the only one. Many would agree, though, that for Rousseau the general will is *the* voice of the people and is the source of political legitimacy. Precisely how it is to be elevated and discerned is a matter of debate—and one of the subjects of this book. Rousseau offers hints about how to tease the general will from the merely aggregated, historical desires of the people, but he does not offer many details.[7] According to Judith Shklar, the general will is "ineluctably the property of one man, Jean-Jacques Rousseau. He did not invent it, but he made its history."[8] Rousseau seems to have given expression to an idea already in currency and one that would outlast many of the particulars of *The Social Contract*. "By turns celebrated and condemned, the general will in its history *after* Rousseau stirred passions as few ideas, concepts, words, or metaphors have," write James Farr and David Lay Williams.[9] Farr and Williams mention Rousseau's influence on some of the French revolutionaries, such as Abbé Sieyès, who invoked the general will "to elevate the Third Estate from 'nothing' to sovereign," as well as the *Declaration of the Rights of Man*, which proclaims the law to be "an expression of the general will."[10] They note his influence on many thinkers, including Kant, Fichte, and Rawls. This book seeks, among other things, to illustrate that his influence extends well beyond the narrow realm of political philosophy and can be detected in myriad and unexpected ways in modern interpretations of democracy and politics in the broad sense.

Rousseau and the Social Contract Tradition

To illuminate the connection between Rousseau's political philosophy and democratism, it will be helpful to place Rousseau in the context of the social contract tradition that preceded him. Rousseau emerged in the wake of a new brand of humanism—very different from humanism of a more classical type—which set the tone for Enlightenment and later thinking about life and politics. This new humanism revolutionized the West's philosophical anthropology and transformed its understanding of self, family, and community. Modern humanism proposed that the person be understood first as an individual, apart from the traditional social and spiritual nexus that for so long had been at the foundation of Western political philosophy. In the first book of Aristotle's *Politics*, he says that every polis is a species of association, composed not of individuals but of smaller associations, the smallest being the household.[11] It was not until a new humanism followed by the Enlightenment that political philosophers began to imagine political society composed of individuals as the primary building blocks. This new understanding of personhood and its relationship to politics harbored the seeds of political revolution and found concrete expression in strains of thought derivative of the Reformation, which had stressed a direct relationship between God and the individual. Church authority, especially that of Roman Catholicism, represented the antithesis of individual autonomy as humanism now understood it. As might be expected, the doctrine of the divine right of kings was challenged. The ultimate culmination of this new political role of the individual was the French Revolution in 1789.

One of Rousseau's predecessors in the social contract tradition, Thomas Hobbes, was among the first major political philosophers to reimagine political order as an expression of the desires and consent of the individual.[12] Hobbes witnessed the political instability that unfolded in the wake of crumbling Church authority and corresponding royal authority and responded with a philosophy of the Leviathan state. Meaningful association and political order are possible only under the rule of an absolute sovereign, Hobbes insisted, a conclusion he drew from his belief that human existence is *bellum omnium contra omnes*. Driven by fear of violent death and a corresponding desire for power over others—a *libido dominandi*—the sole hope for a stable political order must lie in an all-powerful state. Yet Hobbes lays the groundwork for Rousseau's understanding of a general will. The people, Hobbes says,

> reduce all their wills by plurality of voices unto one will; which is as much as to say, to appoint one man or assembly of men to bear their person; and every one to own and acknowledge himself to be author

of whatsoever he that so beareth their person shall act or cause to be acted in those things which concern the common peace and safety; and therein to submit their wills, every one to his will, and their judgements to his judgement. This is more than consent or concord; it is a real unity of them all in one and the same person.[13]

While Hobbes states that an all-powerful sovereign is the only way to ensure stability and security in the polis, his understanding of a commonwealth as an "artificial man" or organic body united in spirit and will suggests that he imagines each individual's will to be commensurate, in the end, with the will of the sovereign. Like Rousseau's general will, as we will see, unity in the Hobbesian commonwealth derives from a shared identification of the people with the sovereign, which is their multitude of wills united not just in practice but also in a metaphysical sense. Hobbes calls the Leviathan a "mortal god," whose great and terrible power is able "to conform the wills of [the people of the commonwealth] all to peace at home and mutual aid against their enemies abroad." In this sovereign "consisteth the essence of the commonwealth," and each individual must consider himself also the author of the sovereign's actions.[14] In many ways this anticipates Rousseau's understanding of the general will as the complete and perfect expression of the people's highest will, such that each citizen can identify completely with the general will if he or she reflects on the true general interest of the society.

   John Locke further oriented Western political philosophy away from the associational basis that had earlier informed its thought and toward the individual as the basic unit of social organization. The Lockean understanding of liberty, central to modern political thought in the West and especially in the Anglophone world, is based on his belief that the individual is primary. For Locke, concepts of property and ownership guide much of his thinking about politics. Liberty, according to Locke, is the ability to dispose of one's person and property as he or she sees fit, so long as this exercise of freedom does not infringe on the same right of others.[15] The individual's primary source of rights is his or her right to self-*ownership*. Liberty in this sense, for Locke, is the natural state, interrupted by perverse social institutions and hierarchies such as the Church and monarchy. The beneficiaries of these traditional institutions rely not on their own productive labor, the source of social and economic value, according to Locke, but on socially constructed power dynamics founded on inherited wealth, birth, and superstition. For Locke, productive labor is an expression of human freedom and also conducive to it. The universal impulse to mix one's labor and generate property confers a certain spiritual equality among persons and implies individual sovereignty. The desire to protect the fruits of one's labor is, according to Locke, a major impetus behind the social contract. "The chief end [of civil society]," Locke says, "is the preservation of property."[16] The commonwealth has the power to punish transgressions, make laws, and make war and peace, "and all this for the preservation of the property of all the members of that society."[17] Locke develops this image of human nature through a hypothetical "state of nature," in which the primary characteristics of human nature are freedom, equality, and rationality.

Rousseau follows the Hobbesian and Lockean social contract traditions, imagining the individual as the metaphysical cornerstone of a new political order.[18] Hobbes's Leviathan state is not entirely compatible with the later Enlightenment's quest for radical personal autonomy, while Locke's social contract supposes material conditions that would facilitate social hierarchy, seeming to perpetuate many of the old ways that had been institutionalized with the help of a system of inherited wealth.[19] Rousseau's novel contribution was to propose a political philosophy that would provide the protection and order promised by the Leviathan state while preserving individual freedom and also equality. The problem of political theory, according to Rousseau, is to "[f]ind a form of association that defends and protects with all common forces the person and goods of each associate, and, by means of which, each one, while uniting with all, nevertheless obeys only himself and remains as free as before."[20] Rousseau hopes to satisfy the Enlightenment demand for emancipation from the bonds of tradition and political hierarchy and also the establishment of perpetually peaceful life in community. As the Romantic movement unfolded, the Enlightenment epistemology and language of reason gave way to a new vocabulary of authenticity and freedom and stressed the importance of an undifferentiated political system. Political order was to be neither an organic, historically evolved kind of order nor a deliberate rational construct, but had to be, if it was to be legitimate, a product of wholly free choice.

While Rousseau challenges many of the Enlightenment's assumptions, he ultimately shares its fundamental epistemology. His emphasis on radical autonomy supported by a socially atomistic anthropology is largely consistent with Enlightenment voluntarism and rationalism. Cassirer is correct in saying that "Rousseau belongs, in spirit, with the rationalist individualists whom he is supposed to have overcome and denied."[21] Rousseau adopts an ahistorical approach to political philosophy, employing a theoretical "state of nature" framework to imagine what is politically normative while also preferring the individual as the primary political unit. At the same time, he inspires and taps into a growing desire for communal existence based in an idea of equality and freedom rather than traditional social distinctions. *The Social Contract*, according to Rousseau, outlines a political theory that resolves the tension between radical individual autonomy and meaningful community:

Since the alienation is made without reservation, the union is as perfect as possible, and no associate has anything further to demand. For if some rights remained with private individuals, in the absence of any common superior who could decide between them and the public, each person would eventually claim to be his own judge in all things, since he is on some particular point his own judge. The state of nature would subsist and the association would necessarily become tyrannical or hollow.

Finally, in giving himself to all, each person gives himself to no one. And since there is no associate over whom he does not acquire the same right that he would grant others over himself, he gains the equivalent of everything he loses, along with a greater amount of force to preserve what he has.[22]

While the ghost of Hobbes's Leviathan lingers, Rousseau also points toward a new understanding of sovereignty that emphasizes its *popular* source. Individual autonomy is preserved at the same time as absolute community is established because all individuals willingly unite in the social compact; none gains over anyone else, and liberty and equality are preserved. All are supposed to benefit by joining. The entire community forms a new "common superior" that is commensurate with the will of each individual: "each person gives himself to no one."

Rousseau, to a greater degree than Hobbes or Locke, stresses a nonrational or transcendent aspect of the social contract, but his understanding of political order as a deliberate contract belies a similar epistemological commitment to Enlightenment rationalism. Robert Derathé says that "Rousseau is a rationalist aware of the limits of reason."[23] Rousseau relies on both rationality and the primitive voice of nature or the conscience as the forces that will move the people to join the social contract. His own imaginative conception of civic life under the general will illustrates, for example, the importance of the nonrational in his political theory. To believe that the general will is possible and ought to serve as a normative guide to politics is to have a certain *faith* about what is ultimately possible. Politics, and specifically democracy, according to Rousseau, cannot be reduced to something so banal as the rational calculations of self-interested actors but is a moral and transcendent experience. Exiting the state of nature "produces quite a remarkable change in man," Rousseau says. "It substitutes justice for instinct in his behavior and gives his actions a moral quality they previously lacked."[24] Rousseau's understanding of the general will, so central to his thought on democracy, helps further illustrate this tension between rationality and intuition or spirituality in his thinking.

Origins of the "General Will"

Rousseau differentiates between the will of all, an aggregate of the will of all persons, and the general will, which reflects the people's highest collective will in an ideal sense. Unfortunately, he never gives a clear definition of the general will, despite the concept's centrality to his political theory. There are two dominant interpretations of the general will: those who view it as a procedure for generating a political will and those who view it as "an expression of a prior commitment to substantive values."[25] Those who view it as procedure look to Rousseau's guidelines for eliciting the general will. Those who advance the substantive interpretation of the general will, Williams says, look to Rousseau's remark that "[w]hat is good and conformable to order is so by the nature of things and independently of human convention," for example.[26] While I agree with Williams that the general will represents an ideal, or is "derived from Rousseau's commitment to metaphysically prior values," it seems a false dichotomy.[27] As I argue in this book, procedures play no small part in shaping outcomes and already imply substantive commitments. This idea will be important in chapter 4, which analyzes deliberative democracy and the role of "procedural norms." Rousseau asserts that the deliberation of "a sufficiently informed populace" under the right circumstances (that citizens "have no communication among themselves," for example) will result in the general will.[28] In Rousseau's mind, these procedures are *part* of the ideal of the general will and are, in some ways, inseparable from its substance. "[T]he general will is always right," Rousseau says, "and always tends toward the public utility," *so long as* the procedures are followed.[29] In the absence of proper procedure, the general will is impossible.

The notion of an ideal political will—rational or mystical—over and above the people's apparent will lies at the heart of a dominant Western conception of democracy, here termed "democratism," and I argue that such a bifurcated understanding of the people's will can be traced back to Rousseau's articulation of the general will. One of the underlying, if silent, assumptions of democratism is the idea that the people's will, *properly expressed*, is a normative ideal toward which historical democracies must strive.

The concept of the general will, however, predates Rousseau, and tracing its conceptual origins, which reside in theology, will help shed light on this complex and significant concept. Patrick Riley points out that the seventeenth-century French priest and rationalist Nicolas Malebranche contrasts the "general will" with the "particular will" in a way that anticipates Rousseau's conception. In *Traité de la nature et de la grâce* (1680) Malebranche says that it is in the capacity of "him whose wisdom has no limits" to discern the most fruitful general laws. On the other hand, "to act by *volontés particulières* shows a limited intelligence which cannot judge the consequences or the effects of less fruitful causes."[30] To intuit or interpret the general will is to possess a "broad and penetrating mind."[31] Pascal, too, says the particular will "involves disorder and self-love," and "not to 'incline' toward le général is 'unjust' and 'depraved.'"[32] For Malebranche and others, a general will is a godly will for its ability to see the whole and to anticipate the abiding needs of humanity over and above narrow, fleeting passions. For Rousseau and thinkers such as Diderot, the general will retains its original theological connotation of wholeness and perfection, but instead of being attributed to an infinite and omniscient God, it becomes a rational and ahistorical ideal.[33] Rousseau and others substitute for the will of God an abstract will of humanity universally accessible through reason.

The parallel between an ostensibly secularized concept of the general will and its original theological meaning is striking. Many later thinkers who invoke the concept retain its original normative connotation that the general is to be preferred to the particular. It is around the time of Malebranche that the term "transforms from the divine into the civic."[34] Riley says that Malebranche's use of these terms is "not very different from Rousseau's characterizations of volonté général particulière in Du Contrat Social (above all when Rousseau argues that volonté général, in the form of general laws, never deals with particular cases)."[35] For Malebranche, God must legislate through His general will "'and thus establish a constant and regulated order' by 'the simplest means.'"[36] The Italian scholar Alberto Postigliola, in "De Malebranche à Rousseau: Les Apories de la Volonté Générale et la Revanche du 'Raisonner Violent'" draws an interesting comparison between Rousseau's notion of the general will and Malebranche's. In Malebranche is "the universal and sovereign divine reason, which acts through general wills . . . that conform to general laws which it establishes itself"; in Rousseau is "the sovereignty of the moi commun which is exercised through general wills . . . which yield a [system of] legislation."[37] For Postigliola, Rousseau, "having appropriated Malebranche's notion of justice (understood as a rationalist and 'geometrizing' generality')[,] committed the 'unforgivable' error of forgetting that the 'general will' of a people lacks 'the divine attribute of infinity.'" Rousseau's error "consisted precisely in using the epistemological categories of Malebranche . . . while continuing to speak of a generality of the will which could not exist in reality as 'unalterable and pure' unless it were the will of an infinite being. . . . In the Rousseauean city, generality cannot fail to be finite, since it can be no more than a sort of finite whole, if not a heterogeneous sum."[38] Postigliola's criticism might similarly apply to kings claiming divine right. God's will as mediated through the king will necessarily become finite, as the king himself is. Rousseau's concept of the general will, which also requires mediation, would seem not immune to the charge that his system is another variant of divine right, with the concept of Humanity divinized and the legislator coronated.

Rousseau's conception of the general will bears a close resemblance to Malebranche's characterization of God's will. "It is not difficult to see in Malebranche's theological formulation a foundation for Rousseau's secularized discourse, with the question of salvation replaced by the common good," Williams observes.[39] The theological origins of the general will help to explain the trappings of religion that accompany many modern philosophies of democracy, including Rousseau's. A civil religion is essential to Rousseau's theory of democracy with the legislator playing the role formerly reserved for a king enjoying divine right. This is perhaps why many of the democratists examined in this book find spiritual meaning in the cause of democracy and why the Catholic thinker Jacques Maritain, for example, unites the things of God and Caesar in a way that would not have occurred to earlier Christian thinkers.

The so-called democratists that I identify in this book often do not acknowledge the metaphysical assumptions behind their conceptions of the popular will. Their theories of democracy rely to a greater degree than is acknowledged on faith—faith that the general will as imagined may be realized, even in the face of seemingly great historical obstacles. These thinkers often assume that the people are capable of transcending personal perspectives, historical circumstances, and human shortcomings such as selfishness and the desire for power in a way not unlike the divine. *Vox populi, vox Dei.* That the general will has its conceptual origins in metaphysics and theology complicates some of the later democratic theories that rely, consciously or otherwise, on this paradigm.

Scholars who have drawn a connection between Rousseau's general will and earlier theological ideas of the concept do not address the political and practical implications stemming from its secularization. Riley, to be sure, draws attention to Postigliola's concerns. And while Williams recounts Riley's analysis of the general will's theological origins and sees clearly a connection between Rousseau's general will and the general will that Malebranche attributes to God, Williams does not suggest how this might complicate our understanding of Rousseau as a *political* thinker. If, despite Rousseau's secularization of the concept, the general will is mystical and ultimately spiritual rather than political and historical, then we have reason to doubt that the general will can serve as a valuable guide to politics. There is no reason to believe that the collective will of the people can act in the way that we would imagine a divinity ought to act. Democratists, however, are adamant that, as Joshua Cohen states, a "free community of equals . . . is not an unrealistic utopia beyond human reach, but a genuine human possibility, compatible with our human complexities, and with the demands of social cooperation."[40] Cohen puts this idea to work in his philosophy of deliberative democracy. He mentions the general will's conceptual origins only in a footnote, but there he contends, "The theological background of the notion of a general will in the idea of universal grace underscores the need for a non-utilitarian, aggregative interpretation of the common good."[41] For Cohen, as for others, the theological roots of the general will are not a hindrance to its political conceptualization or implementation, and perhaps are even an asset. I argue, however, that the secularization of a spiritual and theological concept may be deeply problematic as a normative guide for politics. It also may help explain why aspirations for democracy that rest on a Rousseauean conception of the general will are so often hypothetical and unattainable in practice.

Rousseau's General Will

The formal procedures that are to guide the emergence of the general will help reveal its substance. Rousseau describes few specific measures when he introduces the concept in *The Social Contract*, and so those he mentions must be treated as significant. "If, when a sufficiently informed populace deliberates," Rousseau says, "the citizens were to have no communication among themselves, the general will would always result from the large number of small differences, and the deliberation would always be good."[42] The two criteria, that the populace be "sufficiently informed" and that citizens abstain from communication, constitute what might be considered the republican and democratic elements in Rousseau's philosophy of the general will. Yet they are frustratingly vague. The meaning of an informed populace is debatable, but it would seem that Rousseau has in mind at least some basic knowledge of the subjects of deliberation and also that citizens be "informed" in the moral sense of heeding one's individual conscience—the reason that citizens must have no communication among themselves. Any influence on the individual other than his or her own intuition or reasoning would result in *la volonté de tous*, "the will of all," merely the sum of individual interests and private opinions.

Partial associations fostering communication promote inequality and stifle freedom, Rousseau believes: "For the general will to be well articulated, it is . . . important that there should be no partial society in the state and that each citizen make up his own mind."[43] The general will must apply equally to all citizens and be in the best interest of the whole of society. Rousseau seems to borrow this idea from the earlier, theological conception of the general will. God establishes "laws which are very simple and very general," Malebranche had said.[44] For Rousseau, all human beings, especially those of "simple morals," are able to discern the general will. It is a universal. Rousseau is not clear about precisely *how* citizens access the general will, but it seems to be through something like the conscience, as Williams suggests.[45] It is this law written on the heart that enables citizens to intuit or reason the general will. Williams claims that "an objective or even transcendent conception of justice is part of the core meaning of the general will."[46] In order to access this universal, Rousseau indicates that it is necessary to shed the accumulations of history and culture and listen to an inner voice. One of the reasons that Rousseau distrusts "learned men and orators" is their tendency to lead us away from this inner voice through refined language and sophistry.[47] "Man's first language, the most universal, the most energetic, and the only language he needed before it was necessary to persuade men assembled together, is the cry of nature," Rousseau says in the "Discourse on Inequality."[48]

Preventing communication is important to the formation of the general will because, according to Rousseau, it encourages citizens to heed the voice of nature or reason rather than social prejudices. To consult one another or to consult social norms for guidance would result in a fracturing of the body politic into so many divided interests and loyalties. It is in this criterion that we gain a better understanding of Rousseau's definition of freedom. That citizens exercise a *free will* is essential to the unfolding of the general will. But this freedom is precarious: "Myriad obstacles threaten it [free will] from all imaginable angles."[49] The corrupting forces of ambition, money, and seeking public approval represent "a constant threat hovering over Rousseau's republic and the governance of the general will."[50]

Rousseau's understanding of freedom is a complicated one. At one point in *The Social Contract* he states, "[T]he philosophical meaning of the word *liberty* is not part of my subject here."[51] But in an important way it *is* part of his subject. Rousseau takes for granted a particular understanding of liberty that is sharply at odds with other, earlier conceptions of the term, and this is important for understanding the revolutionary implications of his political philosophy. For Rousseau, traditional social custom and norms, religion, and even family life represent obstacles to liberty as he interprets it. Such norms are based in illegitimate power relationships. "Since no man has a natural authority over his fellowman," Rousseau says, "agreements alone therefore remain as the basis of all legitimate authority among men."[52] Instead, "obedience to the law one has prescribed for oneself is liberty," Rousseau says in *The Social Contract*.[53] This amounts to emancipation from the "slavery" of all-consuming appetites. Paradoxically, it is through obedience to one's own law that one also participates in the general will and there finds a virtuous life. Virtue, Rousseau says, is "merely [the] conformity of the private to the general will." Yet despite his belief that traditional social mores and taboos are illegitimate sources of moral authority, Rousseau still believes that civil society tempers the instincts and passions that otherwise constitute freedom in his state of nature. Indeed "sublime virtue" is required to distinguish the general will from the private will, Rousseau says.[54] While all persons are *capable* of discerning the general will—"it is necessary simply to be just to be assured of following the general will"—presumably not all possess the exquisite virtue required to do so. Thus, Rousseau devises an elaborate substitute for the old society, complete with the civilizing forces of a public censor, civil religion, and legislator, all of which must help "make virtue reign."[55]

The General Will and the Legislator

Rousseau observes that for the general will to be realized, the people must already be what they are to become through it: "the effect would have to become the cause."[56] The general will requires virtuous people for its discernment and instantiation, but the general will is also supposed to help create a good body politic. To resolve this paradox, Rousseau introduces the legislator, who is to institute the new system that will enable the people to realize their highest moral potential. Rousseau gives the legislator divine qualities: "He who dares to undertake the establishment of a people should feel that he is, so to speak, in a position to alter man's constitution in order to strengthen it. . . . [H]e must deny man his own forces in order to give him forces that are alien to him."[57] The legislator is all-powerful and all-knowing. He is "in every respect an extraordinary man in the state."[58] This calls to mind the description Hobbes gives of "that great Leviathan, or rather, to speak more reverently, of that *mortal god*," the sovereign.[59] According to Rousseau, ordinary citizens lack the ability to see the general and abstract good, which exists apart from partial and personal interest, and it is the duty of the legislator to supply this virtue to the people. To effect this change in the people, who cannot understand what is ultimately in their interest, Rousseau says that the legislator must persuade them by nonrational means. Rousseau's legislator is to perform a sleight of hand similar to Plato's "noble lie" that helped to establish his famous republic.[60] With "recourse to an authority of a different order, which can compel without violence and persuade without convincing," the legislator will deceive the people into adopting the social contract.[61] He will put "in the mouth of the immortals" his decrees, Rousseau says, because like the bronze- and iron-natured citizens in Plato's ideal republic, ordinary citizens would otherwise be unable to accept what might seem to them to be nothing other than a change of power.[62] As if to prepare the way for the legislator in *The Social Contract*, Rousseau draws the reader's attention in the "Discourse on Inequality" to the Roman people's emancipation from the Tarquins: "[A]t first it was but a stupid rabble that needed to be managed and governed with the greatest wisdom, so that as it gradually became accustomed to breathe the salutary air of liberty, these souls, enervated or rather brutalized under tyranny, acquired by degrees that severity of mores and that high-spirited courage that eventually made them, of all the peoples, most worthy of respect."[63]

Many democratist interpretations of democracy incorporate some aspect of the Rousseauean idea of a legislator without using the same language. Woodrow

Wilson abstractly names this figure a "leader of men." Jacques Maritain conceives of a global senate of nationless legislators. But others, such as the deliberative democracy theorists, assume the function of a legislator in their theories of democracy without indicating a particular person or group. The procedures that guide discussion or thinking about politics are meant to encourage from the people the right ideas, effectively playing the part of an impersonal legislator. In general, democratism assumes that a legislator, in whatever form it takes, will set up a new system. Citizens, recognizing the superiority of the new system over the old, are expected to maintain it freely—albeit with the hefty support of elaborate institutional mechanisms. All of the thinkers examined in this book share a fundamental assumption about the need for a legislator of one sort or another to bring about the ideas of the philosopher—who represents the primary architect or "legislator." The philosopher's legislators, in the form of persons or impersonal procedures, are imagined to be able to bring forth abstract and objective justice in a way reminiscent of Malebranche's God. Precisely *how* the legislators are to bring the new system into being is often left vague. Rousseau describes the "recourse to heaven" that the legislator must have, but democratism generally has little to say about the impetus behind the people adopting the new system.[64] It is difficult to imagine a "noble lie" borne out in practice, especially in a political system claiming to be democratic. For democratists, therefore, the focus tends to be on the new procedures rather than altering psychology. The presence of the legislator—primary and secondary—is a source of tension within Rousseau's theory of democracy. The legislator is a decidedly undemocratic presence in what is to be a political system dependent upon the wholly free will and choice of the citizens. Paradoxically, democracy, according to those who advance this theory, requires *undemocratic* means for its institutionalization, revealing one of the central paradoxes of democratism.

The Idea of Education

Rousseau believes citizens must be prepared for the type of political order he envisions. His lengthy exposition on education, the *Émile*—which he considered his "greatest and best book"—relates to his *Social Contract* in the way that Aristotle's *Nicomachean Ethics* relates to the *Politics*.[65] It describes the type of character and instruction necessary for a person to be fit for the type of political order that Rousseau envisages. Rousseau describes in great detail the measures that the tutor is to take to ensure Émile's proper upbringing and his eventual fitness for participation in democracy, and the book culminates with Émile being introduced into political society.[66] Like a creature in a pre-civil state "given over to the single feeling of his own present existence, without any idea of the future," the child represents for Rousseau a blank slate, though one in whom nature reigns.[67] Émile is meant to be a "general" child in this sense. Rousseau does not take into account the ways in which nationality, religion, culture, custom, temperament, and personality might affect the child's disposition and ultimately formation as a man and a citizen. Rousseau operates ahistorically in the *Émile* as he does in *The Social Contract*. Setting his treatise on education and his treatise on politics essentially outside of history eliminates the obstacles that would arise if one were to consider the impact of particular experience and identity on one's political beliefs and worldview. Hence Rousseau says in *The Social Contract*, "What makes the work of legislation trying is not so much what must be established as what must be destroyed."[68] Education, broadly understood, functions similarly to the legislator. F. C. Green points out that "state education in citizenship beginning at childhood" is important for the emergence of the general will. This rather than the mystical legislator is Rousseau's "real solution" to the challenge of implementing the general will, Green says. "[H]ow the private will of the individual citizen should conform to the general will," according to Green, is the great issue of education for Rousseau.[69] The purpose of education, like the legislator, is to elevate citizens toward realization of the general will, a task that citizens alone are not up to.

That the tutor must guide and cultivate the child's supposed natural inclination toward spontaneity and authenticity is one of the tensions within the *Émile* that reflects one of the overall tensions within democratism. To have a tutor elicit what ought to come naturally suggests that whatever behavior may emerge is a learned behavior. Rousseau is so detailed in his treatment of the child's education that he even stipulates the proper bath temperature for the boy, believing such minute details to impact the child's final proclivities. The "guided spontaneity" of the *Émile* reflects the "natural" emergence of the general will in *The Social Contract*. A tutor or legislator is tasked with overseeing the psychological and moral transformation of another. "Education" as an abstract concept does not have the antidemocratic appearance of the legislator and instead suggests self-transformation, but behind the Rousseauean understanding of this concept a hierarchy is nonetheless present.

The mystical and omniscient legislator presents a stumbling block to those looking to Rousseau's philosophy for a model of democracy, which is perhaps why thinkers such as Green focus on the role of education more broadly and play down the legislator as extraneous to Rousseau's central purpose. The devices of education and the legislator are reminders that the people, on their own, are unable to discern the general will and require institutional guidance of one sort or another. Concrete examples will make this clear in the following chapters. Thomas Jefferson, for example, assumes that education of a certain type can enlighten citizens and turn them away from "monkish ignorance" and superstition.[70] Woodrow Wilson compares the work of a "leader of men" to that of a mechanic: in order to shape the public's will he "must know what his tools can do and what they will stand."[71]

Rousseau's Philosophical Anthropology

Rousseau tells of a road-to-Damascus conversion in which "suddenly I felt my mind dazzled by a thousand lights; crowds of lively ideas presented themselves at the same time with a strength and a confusion that threw me into an inexpressible perturbation." It was at this moment, Rousseau recalls, that he realized the key to his political philosophy: "that man is naturally good and that it is from [our] institutions alone that men become wicked."[72] It is because of our underlying natural goodness, he believes, that we are all capable of participating in the general will. This denial of Christian Original Sin, which prompted Archbishop Beaumont of Paris to ban Rousseau's works, is the "fundamental principle of all morality," Rousseau says in a response to the archbishop. If "there is no original perversity in the human heart," then manipulating or altering institutions and external circumstances can ameliorate what has seemed to be an intractable problem of human existence.[73] In *The Social Contract* Rousseau writes, "Men are not naturally enemies, for the simple reason that men living in their original state of independence do not have sufficiently constant relationships among themselves to bring about either a state of peace or a state of war. It is the relationship between *things* and not that between men that brings about war. And . . . this state of war cannot come into existence from simple personal relations, but only from *real relations*."[74] In this sense, Rousseau anticipates Marx's philosophy of historical materialism by nearly a century. External—that is, material—conditions drive the acquisitive and self-centered impulse. In the *Second Discourse* Rousseau says, "The first person who, having enclosed a plot of land, took it into his head to say, 'This is mine,' and found people simple enough to believe him, was the true founder of civil society."[75] It is "by accident" that natural human goodness degenerates.[76] Historical circumstances and social institutions, however, need not affect human flourishing. Altering the way in which human beings assemble in community can to a great extent restore our original goodness, Rousseau believes, and then perpetuate it through the new political order. This is the idea of the general will.

Just as happy families are all alike, "truth has but one mode of being," Rousseau avers.[77] To exhibit civic virtue, recall, is to follow the general will and to distinguish it from the private will.[78] The best society seems to be the one in which the private and public wills are indistinguishable. Society must be politically and morally homogeneous, Rousseau assumes. The criterion that human beings must dissociate from one another in order to discern the general will indicates Rousseau's belief in a shared Good, true for all people and each political community. While perhaps some diversity of expression is permitted, in order for citizens to find the "point of agreement among all [of their] interests" it is necessary that in each person is a fundamental inclination toward the universal Good. According to this logic, desires that incline away from the *general* and toward the *particular* will are rooted in *amour propre*. This harkens to Malebranche's assessment of God's will, which is wholly good and general, as opposed to the limited and selfish wills of individuals. Ultimately for Rousseau, human beings cannot be motivated by different aspirations, values, and creeds and still come together in a shared conception of what is normative. Such expressions of particularity, he believes, necessarily detract from recognition of the general, shared good that is true for all persons. "Either the will is general," Rousseau says, "or it is not."[79]

Rousseau anticipates the potential problem for freedom that his philosophy implies and assures readers that to diverge from the general will is to act irrationally and against one's *true* self-interest: "We always want what is good for us, but we do not always see what it is."[80] To be free, he insists, is to conform to the general will. It is impossible to genuinely will anything contrary. The general will is ultimately identical with the will of each individual, if only deep down. Rousseau explains using an analogy to the body: "As soon as this multitude is thus united in a body, one cannot harm one of the members without attacking the whole body." Individuals united into a body politic become a single sovereign in a mystical sense, and "since the sovereign is formed entirely from the private individuals who make it up, it neither has nor could have an interest contrary to theirs."[81] To desire what is contrary to the general will is, effectively, to enslave oneself to base passions, to *amour propre*. Rousseau's body metaphor is reminiscent of that of St. Paul, who reminds the Corinthians that "there are many parts, yet one body."[82] However, according to Christianity, this unity is spiritual and transcendent in the mystical body of Christ. Rousseau imagines that this type of mystical unity is possible immanently and politically, an idea that Hobbes had articulated the century before. For Rousseau, to be free is to partake in this unity and submit to the general will.

Rousseau and other democratists assume that all rational or reasonable persons are, in theory, universally able to access and appreciate this general will and that those who choose not to must "be forced to be free."[83] Implicit is that all persons ultimately share in the same basic social and political desires, in the same way that all Christians share in the same eternal goal. God composed the body, Paul says, so that "if one member suffers, all suffer together; if one member is honored, all rejoice together."[84] Rousseau's understanding of the civic body and the general will are in many ways the secularization of Christian concepts. If the general will is indeed a theological and metaphysical concept rather than a political one, then finite human beings are not equipped to discern it, as Postigliola had pointed out. And not only might human beings be ill-equipped rationally to comprehend a general will, but their interests might not overlap in such a way that a general will would be possible even theoretically. A "general will" in Christ is possible for Christians because, as Bertrand de Jouvenel points out, they are part of a mystical body, not a social body.[85] One of the beliefs of democratism is that a mystical union in a general will of some sort is possible, either through rational agreement about an *a priori* conception of the common good or through "overlapping consensus" about that which is normative.[86]

Democratism comes down to the fundamental belief, in agreement with Rousseau, that human beings are naturally inclined toward *Christian* love for one another. De Jouvenel's critique of socialism sheds light on this aspect of democratism. Monastic communities work, he says, because "the members of the community are not anxious to increase their individual well-being at the expense of one another," unlike communities that are not foremost oriented toward God.[87] For Rousseau and other democratists, human beings *are* capable of this kind of infinite and self-denying love, and they are, moreover, capable of directing it toward political ends and, finally, the state. But is it possible to channel infinite, Christian love toward finite, political goals? Or is the nature of public policy such that it is always a mix of good and evil, depending on context, whom it impacts when and in what unforeseen ways—all phenomena that stem from the perspectival and limited nature of human activity? Rousseau admits that "falsity is susceptible to an infinity of combinations" but seems not to consider that truth may also be of this quality.[88] The general will is presumed to be an unmixed good, but it is, in the end, a political ideal, not a divinity.

Rousseau and Gnostic Thinking in Democratism

Rousseau's portrayal of humanity as essentially good eliminates from it those qualities that would make the prospect of radically changing political existence seem hopeless. This skewed characterization is one of the prominent features of what the philosopher Eric Voegelin identified as a form of gnosticism (from the Greek word *gnosis*, "knowledge"), which he regarded as one of the preeminent ideological forces in the modern Western world. A primary ingredient of this modern gnosticism is an abiding dissatisfaction with existing social and political reality, which is combined with a belief that human effort can permanently change existence. Voegelin says that the gnostic intellectual assumes the role of prophet. This person claims to have the ideological formula for altering "the structure of the world, which is perceived as inadequate."[89] In order to make such an undertaking appear possible, Voegelin contends, the gnostic presents a vision that excludes essential features of reality and the human condition, to the point of distortion.[90] Rousseau reimagines the history of human social relations and unveils what to him has been a hidden truth. "O man, whatever country you may be from, whatever your opinions may be, listen: here is your history," he begins the *First Discourse*.[91] Assuming the role of the legislator and pedagogue for his reader, Rousseau points to material conditions as the wellspring of social ills and believes that by reuniting persons in community in a way that is "natural," man can recover his lost freedom and equality. Rousseau presents asocial and prepolitical man as good, full of pity and compassion. "[N]othing is so gentle as man in his primitive state," he says.[92] At the same time, in society "each finds his profit in the misfortune of another," and "we find our advantage in the setbacks of our fellowmen."[93] One extreme is a product of man's unadulterated "nature"; the other, civil society. Having presented these opposite extremes of human behavior as products of material circumstances, Rousseau makes plausible the idea that social reorganization could return human beings to their "natural" state of goodness. His idea of the general will provides the solution. Rousseau gives the formula for correction: "Remove from [private] wills the pluses and minuses that cancel each other out, and what remains as the sum of the differences is the general will."[94] Attributing his notion of the human condition to nature, "which never lies," Rousseau presumes knowledge that has heretofore been kept secret. By adopting his political arrangements, it is assumed, human beings can dramatically alter social and political life.[95]

This "gnostic" element in Rousseau's political philosophy seems to reflect something of his own dissatisfaction with life and his desire for people and circumstances to change. He had a tendency in many of his autobiographical writings to blame those around him, friends and strangers alike, for his loneliness, bouts of paranoia, and unhappiness.[96] "[M]y ills and my vices came to me very much more from my situation than from myself," Rousseau writes in a letter to Malesherbes.[97] He finds greatest peace when he is alone on the island of St. Pierre, for example. Considering himself "the most sociable and loving of men...cast out by all the rest," Rousseau blames his enemies—real or imagined— for his misanthropy and failures.[98] The "long train of miseries and misfortunes" in his life, Rousseau believes, are caused by machinations of his fellow human beings.[99] He accuses faceless rogues of being "false and perfidious," "iniquity," "vanity," and "animosity," and he finds their company "tedious and even burdensome."[100] Rousseau's lengthy apologia, *Rousseau, Judge of Jean-Jacques*, reveals the extent to which he feels victimized. "At least I am not to blame," he concludes after self-examination.[101] His encounter with a humanity he found so disagreeable may have informed his belief that, in the end, a legislator must transform and perfect it, which would mean awakening humanity's essential goodness. On the one hand, Rousseau sees great evil in particular human beings with whom he comes in contact. On the other hand, he finds in humanity's nature general goodness. The feeling that "men are wicked" alongside the belief that, "nevertheless, man is naturally good" is characteristic of a side of the romantic sensibility which democratism in general exemplifies.[102]

A New Rousseauean Worldview

Carl Schmitt sees continuity between Malebranche, Rousseau, and modern liberalism, and believes that liberalism's fundamental defect is the "banishment" of the particular. Schmitt says that this defect can be explained with reference to Rousseau's embrace of the general at the expense of the particular.[103] It is paradoxical that liberalism should banish the particular, to borrow Schmitt's phrase, since the central claim of liberalism is that it allows individuality and authenticity. Democratism shares many of the features of liberalism as a worldview and condones its "banishment" of the particular.[104] Along with Malebranche, democratism holds that laws of a state driven by "mere experience of need, rather than wise foresight" are characteristic of the *volontés particulières* and are associated with "self-love" and "ignorance."[105] In various ways, the thinkers examined in this book uphold the view that politics must comprehend a general good and that the art of politics is devising, in one way or another, a system that will enable the general will to become manifest once and for all. Democratism presents the general will as something that *actually* exists or might exist and that ought to guide politics. However, if the concept is at heart theological or metaphysical, it raises doubts about its practicability, even normativity. It also suggests that its underlying framework is not democratic in the way that it claims, relying as it does on the authority and designs of a political architect or philosopher.

If, as Rousseau asserts, "undoubtedly there is a universal justice emanating from reason alone," then disagreement could arise only from a conspiracy against justice itself.[106] A person whose loyalty lies outside the general will poses a threat to communal harmony. The one who reverts to "his own forces" over those of the general will and the legislator is, according to Rousseau, "a rebel and a traitor to the homeland"; he "is not a moral person [*personne morale*], but a man," and may be put to death "as a public enemy."[107] It is along similar lines that Rousseau reasons in the *Reveries* that those participating in the conspiracy against him "ceas[e] to be human."[108] The Rousseauean anthropology bifurcates good and evil in such a way that particular individuals who defer to their own will over the abstract general will fall decidedly on the side of evil and cede even the right to life. Understanding Rousseau's use of the general will in light of its theological origins helps to explain, for example, the religious fanaticism with which the Jacobin revolutionaries persecuted skeptics of the Revolution. The general will, like the will of a perfect and benevolent God, appears sacred and inviolable. If truth has but one mode of being, then to dissent is to align with evil itself. Negotiation, compromise, and acceptance of a working agreement suggest a bargain with the devil. Upholding this quasi-religious view of the general will, democratists tend to couch political issues in spiritual language and treat military missions as crusades. This theme is analyzed in the chapters that follow. Wilson and Maritain are two figures who often invoked spiritual and specifically Christian language to describe earthly missions. Wilson's conflation of the secular and the spiritual, at times, seemed to motivate his more repressive domestic measures during the war and also his desire for "force without limit" in America's mission abroad.[109]

It is difficult to escape the conclusion that the general will, conceptually, suffers the fate that Rousseau says befalls natural-law thinking: "Writers begin by seeking the rules on which, for the common utility, it would be appropriate for men to agree among themselves; and then they give the name *natural law* to the collection of these rules, with no other proof than the good that presumably would result from their universal observance."[110] One of the major differences, however, between Rousseau's general will and Christian natural law is that traditional and orthodox Christians tend not to believe that natural law ought to be translated into a specific political order.[111] For Rousseau, a legislator can help midwife the general will into existence. This poses a problem, however, for democracy in the concrete. The legitimacy of the general will derives from its separation from government. "And yet," Bryan Garsten points out, "the generality of the sovereign, its distance from actual politics, was precisely what allowed it to be . . . or even insured that it would be, usurped" by politicians.[112] One of the persistent elements of democratist thinking is the belief that the people's will exists as an ideal that supersedes the people's actual, historically manifest will and that the philosopher can discern the true will and devise a way to implement it politically. Those claiming to work in service of the general will seem only to "have powers all the more formidable," Benjamin Constant avers, "in that they call themselves mere pliant instruments of this alleged will."[113]

Most political philosophers would concede Rousseau's influence on the West, but many do not or do not fully acknowledge the importance of features of his thought to which attention is being drawn here. Some have considered Rousseau a proto-totalitarian for his conception of the general will and the frightening prospect of being "forced to be free," but few locate the general will's potential for social harm in the secularization of the theological concept.[114] Too many thinkers fail to engage central themes in Rousseau's thought that not only pervade his work but ultimately hold it together. Nelson Lund writes in an introductory statement in *Rousseau's Rejuvenation of Political Philosophy: A New Introduction*, "Rousseau's presentation of his thought is deliberately paradoxical, frequently outlandish on its face, and packed with subtleties that invite careful thought."[115] It is common for interpreters of Rousseau to refer in a dismissive way to aspects of Rousseau's political philosophy that are difficult to reconcile with traditional notions of democracy as something that respects differences and divisions and eschews elitism. The legislator, the "noble lie," and the mystical general will—aspects of Rousseau's political philosophy that this book takes very seriously—are often glossed over as intentionally "outlandish" and "paradoxical." But these elements of thought actually make sense to Rousseau and are some of his most original contributions to political philosophy. This is the reason these elements have been chosen over others for careful examination and analysis. These themes give Rousseau's theory a special impact and coherence and help explain the meaning and great appeal of democratism and why so many political theorists, democratic theorists, and others have—knowingly or not—adopted these same elements into their own thinking.

The profound influence that Rousseau has had on a great many political, intellectual, and religious figures in the West is not always obvious. The idea of giving oneself "to no one" has inspired a vision that goes far beyond politics in the ordinary sense. Life, in its entirety, Rousseau suggests, can be transformed. His theory brings comfort and hope to those who wish to escape from the everyday, from the reality of divisions and inequalities in society and the messiness of actual politics. *The Social Contract* is much more than a political treatise. Its vivid account of a new society based on the hypothetical origins of humanity promises radical social and political change that would entirely transform human existence. If Rousseau's political philosophy is convincing, it is because it fits within an entire worldview, a reimagining of the basic terms of human existence.

Whether under Rousseau's direct or indirect influence or on their own, a great many thinkers and other figures have contributed to what is here called democratism and to the patterns of thought and imagination from which it is indistinguishable. Just how much influence Rousseau has exerted can never be ascertained, and it is not the purpose of this book to attempt such an assessment. The purpose is to identify the elements and enormous influence of an ideology that, if not unnoticed, has not been systematically analyzed and defined. It is high time for such an endeavor. Rousseau is playing a central role in this work because he is an early and paradigmatic representative of this mighty historical force. Going deeply into Rousseau is to come close to the heartbeat of democratism.

Toward a Definition of Democratism

Introduction

Democratism is framed within the democratic lexicon, but its defining feature is a longing for a new type of existence that has little to do with "rule by the people." It is a comprehensive framework for understanding life and politics that has profoundly influenced the imaginations of elected and unelected officials of the most powerful governing bodies in America and major Western European nations and their colonial satellites (hereafter referred to simply as "the West"). Despite its undemocratic overtones, the ideology of democratism has become largely synonymous with democracy itself. Democratism's vision, as the following chapters demonstrate, has much in common with the millenarian hopes of past and present religious sects in its visionary promises of an altogether new, democratic age. Like many other "isms," democratism indicates much more than a type of rule. The task of this book is not to analyze the merits or demerits of democracy as such. Instead, it tries to characterize and define a phenomenon that was assumed by Edmund Burke in 1790 when he derided the "democratists who, when they are not on their guard, treat the humbler part of the community with the greatest contempt, whilst, at the same time, they pretend to make them the depositories of all power."[1] Others have used the term to approximate at least some aspect of what I am here investigating.[2] James Burnham uses "democratism" to describe an "ideological conception of democracy" in which "the technical problem of government is to provide institutions and procedures designed to translate as directly, accurately, and quickly as possible the opinion of the popular majority."[3] Erik Von Kuehnelt-Leddihn, in his first book written under a pseudonym, occasionally uses the word "democratism" to denote the "democratic way of life" and also certain cultural and sociological phenomena of democracy, specifically its "totalitarian (all-embracing, all-controlling)" tendencies.[4] Von Kuehnelt-Leddihn, however, who emphasizes the "ochlocratic" or mob-rule impulse of democratism, and Burnham, who similarly sees in the

The Ideology of Democratism. Emily B. Finley, Oxford University Press. © Oxford University Press 2022.
DOI: 10.1093/oso/9780197642290.003.0002

ideology of democratism a dangerous tendency toward unmediated rule by the people, bring to light only what resides on the surface of democratism: an apparent morally or constitutionally questionable desire for direct rule by the people. One person who has used the word "democratism" with the awareness that it represents a larger view of life and politics is Claes G. Ryn. In *America the Virtuous* (2003), Ryn remarks, "At a time when the problems of democracy might seem to raise questions about its survival, a new ideology—which in one of its prominent aspects may be called democratism—puts great emphasis on democracy's superiority and missionary task." Ryn goes on to quote Allan Bloom, who acts as a representative of this democratist faith when he proclaims in *The Closing of the American Mind* (1987), "There is no intellectual ground remaining for any regime other than democracy."[5] Ryn, however, never sets himself the task of sorting out the meaning of democratism. This book seeks to define and illustrate this complex and often subtle ideology that rhetorically champions the will of the people but in practice cares little for popular rule.

The Visionary Element of Democratism

More than an elaborate philosophy or logic of a particular understanding of democracy, democratism functions at the level of the imagination as intuitions about morality, good and evil, human nature, the limits and possibilities of political programs, and other fundamental beliefs. Reasoned arguments, to be sure, support these assumptions, but these beliefs all hang together holistically at a deep imaginative level. Irving Babbitt (1865–1933), one of Rousseau's harshest critics, argued, "A great multitude since [Rousseau's] time must be reckoned among his followers, not because they have held certain ideas but because they have exhibited a similar quality of imagination."[6] According to Babbitt, the imagination is the primary faculty that guides our sense of what life is really like. Babbitt sees two kinds of imagination: the idyllic and the moral. Rousseau, according to Babbitt, exemplifies the idyllic imagination, the defining feature of which is the tendency to look toward some type of golden age, past or present, as one's motivating vision. When Jefferson laments that "every form of government" could not be "so perfectly contrived that the will of the majority could always be obtained fairly and without impediment," he is exhibiting the quintessential democratist tendency to long for a perfect, pure democracy.[7] It is no coincidence that those who have adopted the logic of Rousseau's general will and other aspects of the *Social Contract*—without necessarily having read anything that Rousseau wrote—also share to a great extent his impressions of human nature and many of his political conclusions.[8] For the democratist, "true" democracy is always just around the corner, following the widespread observance of a new political program. This, of course, finds different expression in different thinkers, as the chapters of this book show, but one constant is an abiding dissatisfaction with democracy as it has been practiced historically and the expectation that with the widespread adoption of new social practices and programs, a new age of peace and equality will be possible.

Democratism versus Republicanism

The first more or less comprehensive elaboration of the major tenets of democratism can be found in Rousseau's *Social Contract*. It celebrates a new type of "democracy" that has little in common with classical notions of popular sovereignty. While the Rousseauean kind of democracy may well have emerged from a genuine desire to reform society along more democratic, egalitarian lines, it puts forth a subtle new social and political hierarchy based not on birth, wealth, or religion but on conformity to the new understanding of democracy.

How does the democratist interpretation of democracy differ from, say, classical republicanism or republicanism of the American founding variety? These types of republicanism, after all, seem to share something in common with democratism.[9] Like democratism, republicanism does not look to the hoi polloi as a source of responsible government. Both believe that an elite of some kind ought to "refine and enlarge the public views, by passing them through the medium of a chosen body of citizens, whose wisdom may best discern the true interest of their country."[10] But the difference between Madisonian republicanism and Jeffersonian democratism is, for one, belied by the fact that Jefferson, whom this book identifies as representative of many democratist tendencies, took strong issue with the Federalist interpretation of republicanism and was notoriously at odds with other framers, such as John Adams. Jefferson, too, considered himself a republican, but of a very different sort. He argued that genuine republicanism is "government by its citizens in mass, acting directly and personally, according to rules established by the majority," and that the type of government codified in the U.S. Constitution did not meet that definition.[11] Jefferson and other democratists claim that representatives must merely channel the people's will rather than refine it or mix it with other aristocratic elements, as Madison, Adams, Hamilton, and others, following the classical thinkers, believed. However, as examples in this book demonstrate, democratism seeks to "refine" the popular will in subtle ways. Working to give expression to the people's will as it *ought* to be, democratism relies on various institutional means and theoretical devices to silence oppositional voices, dismissing them, in one way or another, as "undemocratic."

The difference between the democratist desire for a Rousseauean "legis-lator" of some sort to coax from the people its highest or general will and the desire of Madison and Hamilton, in the *Federalist Papers*, for example, to find institutional mechanisms to restrain majoritarian factions united against the common good, is not insubstantial. The former type of "republicanism," if democratism may be called that, rests on a philosophical anthropology very different from that of the latter type of republicanism. The republicanism to which Madison, Adams, Aristotle, Cicero, and others gave qualified sup-port is guided by the belief that human beings are very often attracted to evil. Institutions such as religion, the family, community, tradition, and social norms, at their best, curb selfish desires and mediate behaviors that would harm the common good. Democratism, on the other hand, believes that these institutions are part of the problem and must be replaced. In addition, ac-cording to the older type of republicanism, the people, especially acting en masse, are perpetually prone to making unwise decisions given the morally cleft nature of the human psyche. Therefore, an enlightened leadership class defined foremost by its *moral* superiority is needed to elevate the popular will toward its highest expression. These classically minded thinkers were open about their distrust of the unmitigated will of the majority, fearing fiery passions of the moment and self-serving interests. They believed that morally upstanding leaders must sway the people away from hasty, imprudent, or oth-erwise short-sighted decisions. Yet these figures *did* see a role for the popular will to exert its influence in governing. Even Aristotle was convinced that a government without at least the tacit support of its people could not survive. And a *good* government, Aristotle argued, would contain a prominent ingre-dient of popular rule.

Republicanism of the classical sort considered oratorical ability indispen-sable for statesmen to accomplish the task of elevating the populace toward the common good. Cicero, of course, is one of the prime examples of a re-publican translating oratorical acumen into political effectiveness. Jefferson was notoriously sheepish about public speaking, despite being a learned and highly capable writer, perhaps because he did not wish to place himself in this traditional republican camp. He and other democratists, beginning with Rousseau, associated effective oratory with demagoguery, assuming that flowery language was taking the place of superior reasoning. This is one of the reasons that in the *Social Contract* Rousseau forbade communication among citizens prior to their discerning the general will.[12] To allow citizens to ex-change ideas would be to permit those of keen rhetorical skills to sway the opinions of others unfairly and without merit.

Democratist Theory of Leadership

Rousseau, Jefferson, and other democratists believe that human nature is generally good. The people, when given the right information, will usually choose what is in the best interest of the community. Political leaders need not be the moral superiors of the people, and indeed according to most democratists, political leaders historically have often been the moral *inferiors* of the people. What is needed for the realization of true democracy, according to democratism, is for a new leadership class to emerge that will help to open the eyes of the people to the true or rational course of action, which should be self-evident but is not always readily apparent. When they discuss the concept of leadership, democratists emphasize its technical aspects—improving and standardizing the education system, removing existing leadership, and redesigning institutions. Because the existing leadership class and old system is held to be the culprit in preventing the emergence of true democracy, much of democratism's work entails the destruction of these institutions. The framers of the U.S. Constitution, to be sure, also believed that the right institutions could curb or shape the behavior of citizens, but most framers were not oriented by the normative belief in an idealized republic. Human nature, being what it is, will always thwart pursuit of the ideal. Instead, it is best to make do with certain givens, thinkers such as Hamilton and Adams—tracing their philosophical lineage back to Aristotle—believed. Many of them seemed to assume with Machiavelli that the statesman who looks to the ideal instead of the real will sooner bring about the ruin of his republic than the ideal city.

Quentin Skinner opens his *Liberty before Liberalism* with a quotation from Henry Parker, an influential member of the opposition to Charles I's regime at the outset of the English Civil War in 1642. Parker argued that " 'the supreame judicature, as well in matters of State as matters of Law' must lie with the two Houses of Parliament as representatives of the ultimately sovereign people. 'The whole art of Soveraignty' . . . depends on recognising 'that power is but secondary and derivative in Princes. The fountaine and efficient cause is the people, so that the people's elected representatives have a right to 'judge of publike necessity without the King.' "[13] Parker's views on the legitimacy of the sovereignty of the people as mediated through Parliament represents a classical republican view, one characteristic of Hobbes's pro-commonwealth adversaries and one that persists in the thought of the framers of the U.S. Constitution. This older understanding of republicanism did not call for the direct rule of the people as an abstract and undifferentiated body, as would be the case with the French revolutionaries, for example. Instead, Parker and others as diverse as Cicero, Locke, and John Adams gave qualified support to some form of representative govern-ment in the historical sense. That is, they took for granted that sovereignty rests with the really existing people through their actual, physical representatives in Parliament. But Rousseau adopts a decidedly different interpretation of popular sovereignty. He contends that the people are sovereign insofar as they represent the General Will, which at a deep and metaphysical level is identical with their own will. The people are to be represented not as various corporate bodies with diverse interests but as a single entity by the mystical Legislator.

Democratism and Absolutism

This new articulation of an ahistorical "democracy" (or "republic," as Rousseau termed it) has become paradigmatic for democratic thinking and inaugurated an entirely new tradition of "democratic" thought that, paradoxically, resembles the thought of one of republicanism's greatest adversaries. Hobbes famously articulates a new view of sovereignty in which the state as an abstract entity is sovereign. Recall that Hobbes argues in his *Leviathan* that the state "'is One Person, of whose Acts a great Multitude . . . have made themselves every one the Author' and that 'he that carryeth this Person, is called soveraigne.'"[14] "It is here, in short," Skinner points out, "that we first encounter the unambiguous claim that the state is the name of an artificial person 'carried' or represented by those who wield sovereign power, and that their acts of representation are rendered legitimate by the fact that they are authorised by their own subjects."[15] There is a clear parallel with Rousseau's General Will. Rousseau, too, contends that the multitude of people constitute one body and that they are "represented" by a Legislator—Hobbes's sovereign.

Rousseau's *Social Contract* is not typically considered compatible with Hobbes's *Leviathan*, for Rousseau stresses that the people are ultimately *free* and that the Legislator is merely a functionary serving the ontological role of bringing the popular will into existence. The people each follow their own will, Rousseau insists, which happens to coincide with the General Will when they obey their moral conscience. But Rousseau's concept of an abstract state that the people author not by the fact of their historical existence, including ways of life, traditions, and constitutions, but by their existence as a metaphysical en-tity places Rousseau's political philosophy alongside Hobbes's. Both are ahistor-ical thinkers that posit an abstract, quasi-divine will over and above the people. Rousseau contends that the people are "as free as before" because they are merely following the will that is in their corporate interest; hence they could really de-sire no other. Yet Hobbes also insists that the people living even under absolute sovereignty are "free" so long as they are not physically impeded from exerting their will.[16] Most twenty-first-century readers will react to this notion of liberty as Hobbes's political adversaries did in his own time and consider such a definition narrow to the point of absurdity. But why should Rousseau's understanding of liberty be any more reasonable? Rousseau insists that deep down, all people desire something he calls the General Will and to accept it is to be free. This unorthodox understanding of liberty could as easily be contested as Hobbes's as being hollow. Hobbes admits that while people enjoy a natural liberty so long as they are physically unimpeded, as subjects they are not free because they are subject to the king's will. But if Hobbes had said that the monarch, naturally having in mind the best interest of his subjects, renders his people free when they obey his benevolent will, would that have differed qualitatively from Rousseau's proposition that citizens are "free" so long as their expressed wills align with the General Will? Rousseau's infamous remark that some citizens may need to be "forced to be free" suggests that this comparison might not be an unfair one. Deploying the terminology of "liberty" and "equality" of classical republicanism, Rousseau is able to put a democratic veneer on what otherwise has remarkable kinship with Hobbes's theory of absolutism. Hobbes may have had it right when he said, "The word '*libertas*' can be inscribed in as large and ample characters as you want on the gates and turrets of any city whatsoever."[17] The power of abstract rhetoric over the imagination is evident in Rousseau's theory of "democracy" that ends up justifying a Hobbesian form of absolute sovereignty.

Education and Human Nature

Democratism's heavy use of abstract language helps to give many of its programs and theories the appearance of being commensurate with traditional notions of democracy and republicanism even when they are not. "Education" is one of the abstract terms that democratists often invoke. Without examining the tenets of the democratist understanding of what constitutes education, it might appear that democratism is in keeping with classical republicanism, which also stresses the need for an informed citizenry. Yet the democratist understanding of what constitutes a proper education is informed by a fundamentally different understanding of human nature. Democratism's belief that the people are generally good leads to the idea that the people must only be awakened through some form of enlightenment to their true and rational interests. Then, it is assumed, they will elect leaders representing the policies that correspond with those interests. It is always assumed that the people's best interests align with those valued by democratism. Politics is a matter of correct reasoning and judgment rather than a moral-ethical challenge, as it was for classical republicans. Classical republicanism held that education was important for soul-craft, which ultimately would affect the constitution of the polis. For Aristotle, for example, education was a training of the habits and cultivation of character (*ēthikós*) through right action. The *Nicomachean Ethics* is a treatise on education, specifically character formation and its relationship to political life. Democratism, too, believes that education is a prerequisite for a healthy polis, but unlike Aristotle, democratists do not believe that "none of the moral virtues [are] implanted in us by nature."[18] To the contrary, democratism tends to hold with Rousseau that man's destructive passions "have alien causes," and once those external sources of evil (bad institutions and traditions) are eliminated, a harmonious equilibrium can be restored.[19] Peace and amity are the norm, disrupted by corrupt institutions and bad actors. Contrast Rousseau's *Émile* with Aristotle's *Ethics*. Rousseau's lengthy meditation on education details the ways in which a tutor can elicit Émile's inborn goodness and reasonability. The *Émile* is something of a microcosm of democratism. It assumes that the child is naturally good but requires coaching to bring out his "spontaneous" goodness.[20] For republicans of the Rousseauean cast of mind, education takes on a distinctly romantic or Enlightenment flavor. Rousseau and Jefferson alike stressed the need for the people to be "sufficiently informed" in order to make wise choices, but while Rousseau emphasized the need to allow the impulses of the heart to flow unimpeded, Jefferson tended to stress the need for rational or scientific literacy among the population. This understanding of education, characteristic of democratism in general, more closely approximates Aristotle's notion of the "intellectual virtues" and their formation. Unlike the moral virtues, which must be developed through action, intellectual virtues may be taught. Assuming that moral action derives primarily from right reasoning, democratism focuses almost exclusively on rational thinking in one form or another as the primary goal of education. In this way, democratists are able to give the impression that those who will be overseeing education—the democratists themselves, we must presume—are simply technical experts rather than an intellectual overclass.

Claiming that the people are, on the whole, naturally good, democratism generally avoids the topic of democratic leadership, which turns out to be at the crux of its philosophy. The tension between the democratist desire for direct popular rule and the belief that a leading class of elites must reorient the people is in part a product of its philosophical anthropology. Because democratism assumes that the people are inherently good, it must account for the perpetual deviations from the state of freedom and equality that it claims should be the norm. So public officials, institutions, and other sinister forces are blamed. "The people cannot assemble themselves," Jefferson laments. "Their representation is unequal and vicious. Various checks are opposed to every legislative proposition. Factions get possession of the public councils. Bribery corrupts them. Personal interests lead them astray from the general interests of their constituents: and other impediments arise."[21] There is a strong conspiratorial element to democratism, as examples in the following chapters will show.

The Democratic Philosophy of History

Democratists imply that they can guide the people out of the quagmire of their broken democracies and to a new existence. The conviction that democratism's own initiates ought to lead society toward its teleological end is bolstered by belief in a democratic philosophy of history. The idea that history is pointing toward its end in universal Democracy has assumed various guises apart from democratism—famously as American Manifest Destiny and American Exceptionalism—but it is also one of the hallmarks of democratism. Indeed this linear narrative of history has permeated a great deal of modern democratic thought. Even Alexis de Tocqueville, a "democrat" at odds in many other ways with democratism, asserted that "to wish to stop democracy [is] to struggle against God himself."[22] The "gradual development of equality of conditions" is "a providential fact," Tocqueville stated in the introduction to *Democracy in America*. "It is universal, it is enduring, each day it escapes human power; all events, like all men, serve its development."[23] John Quincy Adams, similarly a democratic realist in other respects, declared in his famous "Speech on Independence Day" that the principles of the American Declaration of Independence are "the corner stone of a new fabric, destined to cover the surface of the globe."[24] The idea that democracy has been preordained not just as a political system but as a universal way of life is one that has held powerful sway over the modern Western imagination.

Democratists identified in this book, such as Woodrow Wilson, Jacques Maritain, and George W. Bush, adopt the Christian language of good and evil, light and darkness, and the providence of God to describe what they interpret as a world-historic battle for democracy. But the democratic philosophy of history need not take on overtly religious or millenarian language to describe what is essentially the same belief. Rousseau's confidence in the existence of a General Will, Jefferson's faith in the people, and John Rawls's belief that through a "veil of ignorance" people will almost invariably arrive at some form of liberal democracy as politically normative, all evince an underlying faith in democracy as historically inevitable given the right conditions—which democratism proposes to facilitate. The language of "waves" of democracy and democratic "backsliding" indicate that for many, democracy is the norm and other political and social forms are outmoded, awaiting evolution. In ways more or less subtle, much of modern democratic theory rests on this philosophy of history.

A Foreign Policy of Democratic Imperialism

Among democratism's foreign policy consequences is a tendency toward expansion and democratic imperialism. This comes into special focus in the chapters on Jefferson, Wilson, and war democratism. Oriented by the twin beliefs that politics can be ordered according to reason and that we are approaching the dawn of a new global democratic age, many democratists have called for the liberation of oppressed peoples in distant lands. Even the more sober-minded John Quincy Adams, again, reveals the modern democratist temptation to interpret history along progressive-democratic lines. The Declaration of Independence, he asserts, "was the first solemn declaration by a nation of the only legitimate foundation of civil government."[25] Echoes of this sentiment, which itself reflects the same basic assertion in the opening lines of Rousseau's *Social Contract*— "[M]an is born free, and everywhere he is in chains"—may be found throughout the speeches and writings of many prominent Western democrats, regardless of partisan affiliation.[26] The effect of delegitimizing other existing regimes is, as Babbitt points out, to promote a crusader mentality. In the case of revolutionary France, which had adopted the Rousseauean democratic imagination, "the will to power turned out to be stronger than the will to brotherhood," Babbitt avers, "and what had begun as a humanitarian crusade ended in Napoleon and imperialistic aggression."[27] The final chapter of this book examines the blurred line between humanitarianism in the name of democracy and armed intervention. "[T]he idealism and the imperialism," Babbitt proffered, "indeed, are in pretty direct ratio to one another."[28]

An expansionist and imperialist foreign policy is not the only possible consequence of democratic idealism. At the domestic level, democratism tends to invite the desire for greater power and control over those viewed as resistant to its beliefs. Rousseau is clear about this in the *Social Contract*. In a particularly chilling passage, he declares that any person who transgresses the social contract becomes "a rebel and a traitor" and "ceases to be a member" of the contract. "In that case the preservation of the state is incompatible with his own. Thus one of the two must perish," Rousseau says. "[W]hen the guilty party is put to death, it is less as a citizen than as an enemy."[29] He ceases even to be considered a "moral person" (*personne morale*), Rousseau says. While this may represent the extreme, Rousseau is merely taking democratism to its logical conclusion. Democratists profess the will of the people supreme but abstract from the notion of popular sovereignty an ahistorical ideal. They account for persons and groups in society that do not conform to the ideal as having abdicated their citizenship or status as full members of the democracy. It is assumed that those citizens who constitute the "real" people favor those same norms as the democratists themselves.

Those who do not agree with the democratists are derided as "extreme," "funda-mentalist," "authoritarian" or in some other way at the fringes. Jefferson referred to his enemies as "monocrats." These people may be safely excluded from dem-ocratic society, paradoxically, in the name of democracy.[30] This is particularly apparent during Wilson's wartime presidency, especially when he deployed the Committee on Public Information to suppress civil liberties and control dis-sent, but it is also visible in subtler ways, for example, in deliberative democ-racy. Deliberative democracy's numerous procedures and careful framing of acceptable discussion implies its desire for certain normative outcomes and the attendant need to exclude persons who fail to observe protocol. These persons can simply be dismissed as enemies, uninterested in "open" and "genuine" dem-ocratic debate.

Democratism and Democratic Legitimacy

It should be noted that it is not the intention of this book to suggest that the un-mitigated will of the majority ought to be politically normative but rather to in-vestigate a phenomenon that appears to be more elaborate and systematic than simply the hypocrisy of a few powerful actors. There is an unmistakable pattern among some of the most well-known "democrats" of the modern age vocally championing the will of people while at the same time working to undermine that will, whether consciously or otherwise. These so-called democrats are reluc-tant to admit openly that they do not wish to translate the popular will into leg-islation and instead hope to find ways for their own beliefs to become instituted. The comparison of the beliefs and actions of numerous of these figures reveals a common theoretical commitment to democracy but not the desire for its actual practice. It is important to investigate this phenomenon in order to understand the extent to which it is democratic, as it claims to be. Are the people, as they are historically constituted, actually sovereign? Or are they sovereign only in the ab-stract, pawns in an imagined dialectic of democratic history? If it is shown that there is very little deference to the popular will in democratism, then on what does this ideology base its legitimacy? These are important questions because Rousseau and those who have taken up his ideas in the intervening centuries claim to be advancing the only possible legitimate theory of politics. They also claim that it is democratic.

At the heart of the implicit or explicit philosophy of each of the thinkers examined in this book is an underlying belief in the rationality of political life. The challenge of politics for democratists (and many others) is foremost tech-nical and material, to be solved through a new politico-economic architectonics and an attendant education program that would promote rationality and hence an ability to appreciate the new system. As will become clear through examples in the following chapters, the elements of managerialism and scientism often result in authoritarianism of varying degree. It may be subtle, but the desire for strict control over institutional mechanisms and so-called democratic procedures stems from a desire to control the outcome, which, it is assumed, will be rational and just. If the outcome—egalitarian democracy—is just, then the means of arriving at that outcome ought not be impeded, according to those who hold this view. If indeed there exists a general will that "is always right and always tends toward the public utility," then it follows that those who refuse to obey the procedures or who otherwise find themselves at odds with what has been deemed to be the "general will" may be considered enemies and "violator[s] of the compact."[31] It turns out that in the democratist version of democracy there may be many people—perhaps even a majority—who cannot be counted as citizens but must instead be regarded as "incurables," to borrow the language of Jefferson.[32]

Implications for the Future

Democratism is expansive in its ambitions and expects that, sooner or later, the world will embrace democracy. While the electorate in America has tired of endless wars of liberation, it is open for debate whether those in power could once more drum up support for the "right" war of liberation. Or perhaps the elites will begin to conduct wars for democracy in superstitious ways, by proxy or by launching "color revolutions," for example. If democratism does not manifest as an actual democratic crusade, it will nonetheless wait in expectation for the "dominoes" of democracy to fall around the globe. Democratists also use tactics other than war, such as economic sanctions and trade incentives, for example, to encourage states to follow the political lead of the leading democratic nations. Orienting and guiding these specific foreign policy tactics is, again, the democratist philosophy of history, which expects democracy to sweep the globe as a matter of course. Western nations that use wealth and political clout to try to sway other nations toward democracy do so in part because of an underlying assumption that these coercive actions will move a nation incrementally closer to the democratic ideal. It comes as a great surprise when Western nations' overtures in the name of democracy fail or are rebuffed. It is especially troubling and perplexing to democratists when seemingly democratic nations turn away from democracy and Western norms associated with it. The very language used to describe this phenomenon, "democratic backsliding," reveals the progressive-democratic philosophy of history that undergirds it. Nations are assumed to be traveling backward in time when they turn away from the democratic way of life—however real or illusory it may have been in that nation in the first place.

If the ideology of democratism continues to replace the older understanding of democracy as rule by the people, then we can expect the concentration of greater and greater power in the ruling classes. That may include elected or unelected political officials or more nebulous but arguably more powerful interests, such as those that control our news and means of communication—the so-called Tech Giants and the corporate media. The proclaimed need for these bodies to have greater control, including over ideas, will invariably be couched in the language of protecting democracy. Because the democratic lexicon has been integral to the perpetuation of what, in many ways, is democracy's opposite, there is the risk that the original and literal meaning of democracy will no longer have significance or legitimacy, a trend already occurring. The traditional understanding of "rule by the people" will be derided as illegitimate—whether it goes by the negative "populist" or anything else—when the popular will does not align with the interests of the most powerful, albeit minority, interests. What is becoming increasingly clear is that the growing divide between the desires of popular majorities and those of powerful minority interests is untenable.

It is impossible to predict the ways in which this could manifest, but social and political unrest is a near certainty as democratism's lofty ideals clash with the reality of an increasingly oligarchic pseudo-democracy. Powerful minority interests will govern by administrative fiat, a method that Wilson pioneered, as emergencies, real or imagined—national security, environmental, public health, etc.—are invoked as urgent justification for circumventing the electorate. In this way, powerful elites and their chosen experts can claim to be acting in the name of democracy without actually observing its traditional practices. We can expect this trend to continue as the fissures grow between the concrete desires and ways of life of popular majorities and the competing desires and expectations of the ruling elite—elites who are perceived by many to be out of touch with the needs of ordinary people. Recently this discontent has found expression, for example, on the left in the form of international Black Lives Matter (BLM) protests and on the right in the protest against the results of the American presidential election at the U.S. Capitol on January 6, 2021. In an interesting turn of events, members of the left-wing BLM organization have marched alongside conservatives to protest COVID-19 vaccination mandates, which both groups contend is unconstitutional. These, alongside other indicators, such as the rise of Donald Trump at the expense of the Republican Party in America and the rise of other populist leaders in European nations, suggest that discontent has reached a critical mass and new political organizations are forming to try to cope with it.

A Democratic Spring in Democratic Nations?

Is a Western or American "democratic spring" unthinkable? It would seem ironic, but it is probably not outside of the realm of possibility for a democratic uprising of some kind to take place in a country in which a substantial portion of the electorate believes that democracy exists in name only. Jefferson's late fall from grace, with the removal of his statues and the discontinuation of the public observance of his birthday in his home county in Virginia, is yet another sign of America's waning faith in democracy. If it becomes clear that "our democracy" is merely an ideological projection, supported by abstractions and dreamy imaginings rather than actual practices, we can expect civil unrest to worsen. Prerevolutionary France in fact paid less in taxes than England during the same period, but gross inequities in the French tax system fomented indignation among the French peasants, who were forced to pay considerable sums while the nobles and clergy were largely exempt from taxation. The standard of living may be very high for most Westerners, but many nonetheless have noticed the formation of what appears to be a new caste system, headed by public officials who profit tremendously from their position in power. Sensing that a different set of rules applies to powerful and well-connected politicians and a wealthy elite—who at the same time proclaim everyone equal—voters are becoming cynical. Many have questioned the integrity of elections in nations once thought to be immune to the type of electoral manipulation that plagues countries of the third world. How to square democratic leaders' vocal proclamations that all are created equal and that the will of the people is supreme with an apparent political reality that includes a prominent ingredient of oligarchy? This book argues that this phenomenon is neither new nor limited to a handful of political elites but spans the modern era going back to the eighteenth century, cutting across nations, political parties, professions, and religious denominations. To understand the ideology of democratism is to understand this paradox and to be able to see with greater clarity otherwise perplexing political trends.

Thomas Jefferson and an Empire of Liberty

Introduction

This chapter looks to Jefferson as a possible source and illustration of the abiding confusion in the West about the meaning of democracy.[1] Like Jefferson, many democratic leaders are torn between a desire for direct popular rule and another, competing desire for the *proper* will of the people to be expressed. Jefferson is torn between a reverence for the common people and the belief that his own republican vision is the only valid one for the American republic.[2] This typical bifurcation of the popular will between its actual, historically manifest desires and an ideal interpretation of it is first outlined in Rousseau's *Social Contract* and is a hallmark of democratism.[3] While outwardly the people's champion, Jefferson nevertheless expresses a clear preference for an "enlightened" democracy that has many of the features of the democratist ideology.

It is time for a reassessment of this American framer and his understanding of democracy, which has greatly influenced not only American national identity but arguably the self-understanding of other democratic nations that have turned to Jefferson as a source of inspiration. This chapter tries to elucidate the paradoxical nature of democratism by focusing especially on the symbiotic relationship between Romanticism and Enlightenment rationalism in the thought of Jefferson. The first part of this chapter examines the tension between Jefferson's agrarianism and his progressive faith in scientific rationality with a view to illustrating this same dynamic within the logic of democratism. The second part of the chapter examines Jefferson's desire to expand the "empire of liberty" through the Louisiana Purchase. Jefferson's motives for territorial expansion and his policies toward Native Americans reveal practically some of the more sinister implications of his paradoxical understanding of democracy. An outspoken advocate of states' rights and federalism, Jefferson nonetheless sought territorial

The Ideology of Democratism. Emily B. Finley, Oxford University Press. © Oxford University Press 2022.
DOI: 10.1093/oso/9780197642290.003.0003

expansion and the removal of native peoples from the land, moves that concentrated greater power in the national government and trampled the rights of indigenous peoples. The concrete examples from Jefferson's presidency illustrate his commitment to a type of democracy that he does not always spell out. A look at his actions deepens our understanding of his theory. As with other thinkers examined in this book, Jefferson's use of benevolent-sounding abstract language tends to mask practical realities that undermine those very goals.

The idea that Jefferson is a contributor to a widespread ideology of democracy will no doubt alarm many. There are many sides to Jefferson and many different interpretations of this American framer. Because Jefferson never wrote political treatises, his political philosophy must be discerned through his letters—of which there are many thousands—his inaugural addresses, his *Notes on the State of Virginia*, and various other writings, including of course the Declaration of Independence. The fact that there are such a vast number of interpretations of Jefferson that are at odds with one another suggests that his thought is not always consistent. A writer and thinker as prolific and active as Jefferson is sure to hold different views at different times, some in competition. No person is simply one thing, and Jefferson least of all. One scholar observes, "Given the absence of a magnum opus by Jefferson and given the presence of thousands of his public and private letters, all scholarly efforts to present an integrative understanding of his political ideas are forced to employ an eclectic method," and finding "selective evidence" to support one's preconceived perspective on Jefferson is not difficult.[4] While that may be true to some extent, there is widespread evidence within Jefferson's corpus of a long-held commitment to what this book identifies as the ideology of democratism. This chapter approaches the study of Jefferson from multiple angles—examining his agrarianism, Enlightenment philosophy, religious belief, and statecraft—to demonstrate the presence of an essential unity in his thought *and* practice. When viewed in the light of democratism, Jefferson's philosophy appears less contradictory or eclectic and instead, like Rousseau's philosophy, guided by a unifying principle.

Jeffersonian Agrarianism and Faith in the Common Man

Jefferson's faith in the common people and his emphasis on equality has caused his love of republicanism to morph in the public mind into a love of democracy, and for good reason. Jefferson's definition of republicanism as "government by its citizens in mass, acting directly and personally, according to rules established by the majority," is akin to what we consider direct democracy, and that is the interpretation of republicanism to which he tenaciously adhered.[5] While he did not believe that direct democracy was possible beyond the small New England township, he did believe that the government ought to be as accountable and responsive to the people as possible. Jefferson historically has been associated with "Jeffersonian democracy" precisely for his seeming democratic instincts, evidenced in complaints, for example, that "our governments have much less of republicanism than ought to have been expected" and that "the people have less regular control over their agents, than their rights and their interests require."[6] Jefferson often commends the people's "good sense" and juxtaposes the corrupt populace of Old Europe with the "independent, the happy, and therefore orderly citizens of the United States."[7] At times he was fanatical in his faith in the people. In 1787 he said that should he be proven wrong that men cannot be trusted to self-govern, he would "conclude, either that there is no god, or that he is a malevolent being."[8] But Jefferson especially admired the agrarian lot of colonial America. If God had a chosen people, Jefferson famously opined, it would be "those who labour in the earth."[9]

Agrarians, according to Jefferson, are self-sufficient, dependent not "on the casualties and caprice of customers," as are merchants and tradesmen, professionals he openly disdains as harmful to the republic.[10] Jefferson finds simple virtue in the nature of agrarian labor and imagines that economic independence correlates with political independence. "Cultivators of the earth are the most virtuous and independent citizens," Jefferson writes to John Jay in 1785.[11] The yeoman farmer is for Jefferson the prime example of one who thinks for himself because he works for himself. Urban life, conversely, is inherently corrupting; these "sinks of voluntary misery" are full of transience and populated with those who would rather turn a profit than turn the soil.[12] Merchants "have no country," Jefferson decries. "The mere spot they stand on does not constitute so strong an attachment as that from which they draw their gains."[13] He insists that such city-dwellers cannot well exhibit the democratic virtues of liberty and equality.

Although certainly not alone in his fondness for the agrarian life, Jefferson differed from founders such as Adams and Washington, who, while also prone to agrarian encomia, do not look to this way of life as an exclusive source of democratic virtues.[14] Adams's and Hamilton's understanding of human nature as essentially divided between good and evil inclinations meant that they could not believe that even so wholesome an endeavor as husbandry could perpetuate virtue and freedom in the republic indefinitely. For Jefferson, the agrarian way of life to a great extent *creates* the material conditions that promote virtue and sustain democracy. Virtue is not, he asserts, difficult for most people provided they are nurtured by husbandry and rural life. "I think our governments will remain virtuous for many centuries; as long as they are chiefly agricultural," he writes to

Madison in 1787.[15] Framers such as Adams and Hamilton, while sympathetic to this view, believed that the Constitution must mitigate the effects of vice and faction, which they believed were permanent threats to liberty. The various constitutional checks and balances—checks which Jefferson believed unduly constrain the people's will—were in part designed to do this.

It is no coincidence that many have favorably compared Jefferson to John Locke and for this reason seen a significant influence of the latter on the American framing.[16] Jefferson's Lockean understanding of the role of productive labor, evident in his agrarian sentiments, greatly influenced his philosophy of democracy. Like Locke, Jefferson believes that one of the central purposes of government is to protect life, liberty, and property and that this is the core principle the various state constitutions "all cherish as vitally essential."[17] Jefferson often emphasizes the importance to democracy of men "enjoying in ease and security the full fruits of their own industry."[18] In his first inaugural address, he praises our "equal right . . . to the acquisitions of our industry" in America.[19] Like Locke, Jefferson finds in the apparently inherently egalitarian nature of productive labor evidence of equality as a natural right. The proper end of government, therefore, is the protection of our person and property, he reasons.[20] This is the social contract model of government, which holds that man "procure[s] a state of society" through "the exercise of [his] faculties." Society emerges through rational consent, this philosophy holds, and it is logical that persons would consent to leave the state of nature only if the new society can guarantee to protect the rights that existed in the pre-civil state. This new social state, Jefferson says, becomes one of man's "acquisitions," and one that "he has a right to regulate and control."[21]

Jefferson's vision of agrarianism seems to have been heavily colored by his understanding of government as a social contract and his belief that human beings are born free, equal, and rational. The productive nature of agrarian labor and the material self-sufficiency it provides the farmer suggest to Jefferson an attendant social and historical deracination, more in line with the sentiments of a dreamy idealist like Hector St. John de Crèvecoeur than the actual yeomanry. Crèvecoeur believed that the American farmer represented a "new man": he has left behind "all his ancient prejudices and manners" and received "new ones from the new mode of life he has embraced."[22] Jefferson's notorious disdain for traditional modes of life, especially those he associated with the "Old World," would support this notion. Those who cling to traditional beliefs are irrational, Jefferson says, easily held captives of "mystery & charlatanerie."[23] The lessons of those "ages of the darkest ignorance" are of little political value for Jefferson. Americans would do well to distance themselves as much as possible from the ways of their European forefathers. No political experiment could be "so stupid . . . so destructive of every end for which honest men enter into government" as those of our ancestors, Jefferson says in a letter to François D'Ivernois.[24]

Jefferson praises the pious husbandman who looks "up to heaven," and extols the virtues of steady industry, suggesting that he recognizes the agrarian way of life to be essentially a traditional one.[25] Yet he is very critical of traditional religion and systems of belief, even denouncing certain state constitutions as "poisoned by priest-craft."[26] Jefferson seems to ignore the traditional element of agrarianism and the deeply religious nature of most Americans, especially rural Americans. In the first half of the eighteenth century, the vast majority of the population attended church, and religious belief was on the rise.[27] How to square Jefferson's seeming unqualified belief in the virtue and capacity for self-rule of the American people with his condemnation of traditional believers, the people whom he accuses "of vulgar ignorance, of things impossible, of superstitions, fanaticisms, & fabrications"?[28] Many such people were the actual farmers at the time. Jefferson's praise for the rootedness of agrarian life suggests that on one level he understands this conservative view.[29] However, his belief that the American experiment proves there is indeed something "new under the sun" demonstrates that he sees in the American farmer a symbol or abstract representation of what he takes to be a "new man," an idea at odds with the continuity and traditional mode of existence that actual agrarians valued. It would probably have come as a great surprise to these farmers to know that they were looked upon as representing something entirely new rather than being an extension of a long line of farmers practicing more or less the same trade as their fathers and forefathers.[30]

Jefferson's idealized agrarianism was in part guided by his belief in America's providential role in history. Ernest Lee Tuveson, in his examination of what he sees as a millenarian tradition in American thinking, argues that Jefferson has a place among those who view America as "chosen."[31] According to Tuveson, the pastoral life is for Jefferson the apex of human moral achievement. If Jefferson views America as exceptional, it is because Americans largely belong to the class of agrarians. America is not a chosen nation but, as Jefferson says of the agrarians, a "chosen people." They are chosen because of their pastoral, innocent way of life, which Jefferson equates with an innocence belonging to the New World, which has made a decisive break from the corrupt Old World. Jefferson viewed agrarians as a stand-in for Americans in general; most Americans were farmers, after all. Disparaging those who make their living through commerce just as he condemns those who seem to him to sympathize with monarchy or orthodox religion, Jefferson imagines that America's essence is simple, moral, agrarian, and republican, and enlightened insofar as America is an entirely new nation, built not on tradition but on principles. Those who deviate from the American philosophy, as he understands it, belong in spirit to the Old World.

Jefferson, like Rousseau, intermingles nostalgia for an imagined Eden with the belief that human will and rationality can forge a new pastoral paradise. Jefferson's dreamy vision of a simple and virtuous rural existence recalls Rousseau's vision of natural man, who is "subject to few passions and self-sufficient."[32] Jefferson believes, with Rousseau, that human beings are naturally good, autonomous creatures who thrive without the accumulations of culture and tradition, commerce and consumerism. Cities, for Jefferson, represent the opposite of pastoral eudaimonia. "The mobs of great cities add just so much to the support of pure government," Jefferson complains, "as sores do to the strength of the human body."[33] Tuveson observes that Jefferson's belief that the agrarians represent the chosen people of God "echoes Rousseau's belief that 'dependance,' which 'begets subservience and venality,' is the 'natural progress and consequence of the arts.' "[34] Jefferson's paeans to the simple ways of the Native Americans reflects this Rousseauean naturalism.

Thus, it is perhaps not as paradoxical as it might at first seem that Jefferson should hold a romantic understanding of human nature and society and also an Enlightenment faith in progress through scientific rationality. Jefferson's romantic side, like Rousseau's, feeds into his Enlightenment beliefs, resulting in a political philosophy that expects "progress" toward a simpler way of life reflected in an imaginary past. Irving Babbitt sheds light on this apparent paradox. Both the Rousseauist and the Baconian, Babbitt says, reject the normativity of established practice and look toward some "far-off divine event": "Rousseau himself put his golden age in the past, but nothing is easier than to be a Rousseauist, and at the same time, like the Baconian, put one's golden age in the future."[35] Faith in an imagined future in which differences will be reconciled and the people will come together in a spirit of fraternity unites the romantic and the Enlightenment rationalist. "The differences between Baconian and Rousseauist, and they are numerous, are, compared with this underlying similarity in the quality of their 'vision,' unimportant," Babbitt says.[36]

Jefferson's commitment to agrarianism seems to have been more rhetorical and symbolic than substantive. It played a decisive role in his romantic-Enlightenment vision of a brand-new existence for America. The farmer, for Jefferson, is representative of a pure and simple nation. It was largely irrelevant to his enchanted vision that the yeomanry were traditionally religious and held the types of beliefs that he derided in his letters and private conversations. Jefferson abstracted from their roles as free farm-holders metaphysical traits of freedom and equality, equating these farmers with the nation he viewed as entirely new. For Jefferson, the American yeomanry did not represent a continuation of the age-old practice of farming, obviously predating the American "experiment," but a tabula rasa, simple and pure but needing to be gently enlightened in order to appreciate Jefferson's particular democratic vision.[37]

Jefferson's Philosophy of Education

Jefferson's paradoxical view of the agrarians is also evident in his belief that, for all of their simple virtue, they are still in need of education and reform of a particular kind. His understanding of reason orients his beliefs about the type of education that he believed could benefit his countrymen. Jefferson was adamant that reason must overcome superstition and that those subjects that emphasize reasoning and scientific inquiry ought to replace traditional disciplines such as theology and moral philosophy. Ethics "may be as well acquired in the closet as from Living lecturers," Jefferson said, and of moral philosophy, "I think it lost time to attend lectures in this branch."[38] Even subjects like religion can be evaluated and judged as true or not by appeal to one's reason alone. In a letter to Peter Carr in which Jefferson discusses which subjects are worthy of study, he advises Carr to "shake off all the fears and servile prejudices under which weak minds are servilely crouched. Fix reason firmly in her seat, and call to her tribunal every fact, every opinion."[39] For Jefferson, a real education means discovering for oneself what is reasonable and logical and what ought to be dismissed as mere superstition.

"Education & free discussion," Jefferson insists, can serve as the antidotes for "bigotry," "ignorance," and "Jesuitism"—the type of thinking he deplores.[40] With general enlightenment, "tyranny and oppressions of body and mind will vanish like evil spirits at the dawn of day."[41] Virginians in particular, Jefferson believes, are prone to old ways of thinking and would greatly benefit from "a general seminary of the sciences meant for the use of the state."[42] This would entail a system of primary schools and a university in Virginia "where might be taught, in it's [*sic*] highest degree, every branch of science useful in our time & country: and it would rescue us from the tax of toryism, fanaticism, & indifferentism to their own State."[43] Jefferson often proclaims the value of skepticism and the ability to discover for oneself the truth, but at the same time he believes that objective reasoning will naturally lead to his view of things. He fully expects that when reason is engaged, others will naturally be led to the same conclusions as he about politics. When the people are not so inclined, Jefferson admits that he feels he has a duty to "[sow] useful truths and principles among the people, which might germinate and become rooted among their political tenets."[44]

There is a part of Jefferson that, with Diderot, Voltaire, and other Enlightenment thinkers, "deplored the general taste" of the masses and distrusted their ability to rule.[45] Education, for Jefferson, can help to guide the thinking of Americans toward the beliefs that he holds to be true. He is careful to reserve his criticism for his political enemies and anonymous demagogues, but he nonetheless reveals an inclination to change the views of those people he otherwise lauds. One scholar argues that for Jefferson, education was "as critical to the long-term revolutionary effort of remaking society as muskets and manifestos were to the short-term effort of securing independence."[46] With other democratists, Jefferson believes that education, including the informal education of the people through their political leaders, ought to cultivate the kind of thinking that will lead the nation toward what he takes to be a genuine expression of republicanism. For example, he inaugurated government support of the sciences, dedicating himself, as one historian remarked, "to the application of science as the most certain means of national advancement and human happiness in the new republic."[47] While Jefferson ultimately hopes to improve the lot of agrarians through improvements in technique and machinery, it is unlikely that the yeomanry would have shared his desire for modernization and scientific advancement, especially through the vehicle of the state.

At the same time as he would wish to see scientific advancement, Jefferson demonstrates a wariness of established convention. In his letter to Carr, Jefferson famously writes, "State a moral case to a ploughman and a professor. The former will decide it as well, and often better than the latter, because he has not been led astray by artificial rules." Jefferson's penchant for rationalism and scientific thinking is motivated by his progressive belief that a scientific mode of thinking will contribute to a better future marked by general enlightenment. However, he also imagines a rustic past in which stultifying norms and conventions have not perverted humanity's natural good sense. In this respect, he puts himself squarely in the tradition of Rousseau's "Discourse on the Arts and Sciences" and *Émile*, which convey the idea that traditional academic disciplines and courses of study are detrimental to genuine knowledge. This idea is reflected in Rousseau's statement that, "I am perfectly sure that my heart loves only that which is good. All the evil I ever did in my life was the result of reflection; and the little good I have been able to do was the result of impulse."[48] Jefferson sees the plowman as wiser than the professor because, like Rousseau, he believes that those who have not been tainted by artificial conventions can simply follow their hearts and natural reasoning abilities. There is, again, a strong affinity between romantic and Enlightenment thinking. For Jefferson, as for Rousseau, the purpose of education is to help purify humanity.

Jefferson's twin romantic and Enlightenment proclivities explain why, for example, although remembered by some as "above all a farmer," he should at the same time hail Francis Bacon, Isaac Newton, and John Locke as "the three greatest men the world had ever produced."[49] His paradoxical view combines a preference for abstract reasoning with reverence for "natural man." Ultimately, however, Jefferson's desire to see a certain type of intelligence in power betrays his belief that the simple agrarian folk he admires must adopt or at least assent to more progressive, enlightened beliefs.

The "ward system" is Jefferson's plan to administer universal public education alongside direct democracy. What he considers "the wisest invention ever devised by the wit of man" was to divide counties into individual wards "5 or 6 miles square."[50] This apparent blueprint for decentralized democratic government, in which each member of the ward would have an "equal voice in the direction of its concerns," adds to Jefferson's reputation as America's archdemocrat.[51] However, there is another interpretation of this scheme. As an abstract proposal for a more pure democracy that Jefferson expects will be adopted universally, it fits well within democratist thinking. Hannah Arendt, in fact, likens this scheme to other rationally conceived revolutionary power-to-the-people programs: "Both Jefferson's plan and the French *sociétés révolutionaires* anticipated with an utmost weird precision those councils, *soviets*, and, *Räte*, which were to make their appearance in every genuine revolution throughout the nineteenth and twentieth centuries."[52] Intended to radically decentralize power and give full control of government to the people, these councils quickly became apparatuses of those at the top, as evidenced, for example, in Napoleon's takeover of the eighty-three departments created in 1790, which had been intended to decentralize power and provide local democracy throughout France. Napoleon co-opted administration, ensuring that his unified vision was enacted rather than the diverse intentions of local officials. The Russian soviets suffered a similar fate after the 1917 Revolution.

Although perhaps meant to provide direct democracy, revolutionary schemes premised on the Baconian belief that we "must begin anew from the very foundations" stem from the idea that society as historically constituted is inadequate and must be remade according to a better, more rational vision.[53] Such abstract planning is generally incompatible with decentralization, local control, and pluralism. Jefferson's belief that his scheme would be universally recognized for its superiority over the old way betrays not only the disconnect between the idealist planner and concrete reality but also the expectation that the new plan will be universally attractive. It reveals a conceit common to democratist thinking.

Jefferson's belief that the ward meetings "would at any time produce the genuine sense of the people on any required point, and would enable the state to act in mass" is not only highly idealistic but is also ultimately subordinated to his competing belief that democracy ought to take on the particular characteristics he believes appropriate. His micromanagement of a boy's boarding school in Virginia that was to be a preparatory school for his University of Virginia is telling of the level of control that Jefferson wished to exert over the minds of his countrymen. He believed, with Rousseau, that even the minutest details must be carefully managed by the visionary.[54] On its face, the ward system appears to be an instance of decentralization and direct democracy, but as a plan to reorganize society in accordance with a supposedly superior vision—Jefferson's vision—it betrays a desire for control and standardization ultimately incompatible with genuine democracy, which would hardly be democratic if it did not take into account existing conditions and practices.

Jefferson's imaginings about what might have been had his proposals been implemented reveals the dreamy, idealistic side of his political imagination. The ward system, he says, "would have restored to the citizen the freedom of the mind"; it "would have raised the mass of the people to the high ground of moral respectability"; it "would have compleated the great object of qualifying them to select the veritable aristoi."[55] Jefferson imagines that with some changes to the tax law, for example, "the farmer will see his government supported, his children educated, and the face of the country made a paradise by the contributions of the rich alone."[56] His philosophy of democracy relies heavily on the subjunctive, on what *might* have been, had the plan been implemented. Although he presents it as a tantalizingly simple task, such as changing the tax code, reforming existing institutions is not sufficient. Wholesale change is required. In the case of Jefferson's education schema, the entire program needed to be adopted for it to have the intended effect. "Jefferson avowed," Mark Holowchak writes, "that his reforms must be taken in toto, for Jeffersonian republicanism bespoke a systemic approach of education, and there was no system in place in Jefferson's day."[57] A uniform system would help to streamline thinking, presumably away from ideas about republicanism, religion, and politics that competed with Jefferson's own ideas.

Jefferson's hand in the creation of the University of Virginia reveals some of the practical consequences of his idealism. He had imagined an institution of higher learning where, according to Alan Taylor, "students would learn his notions of republicanism, rejecting the Federalism of northern schools and George Washington."[58] He hoped that scholarships would enable poor but deserving students to attend in addition to the wealthy. Yet the expensive buildings that Jefferson demanded, to the chagrin of the Virginia legislators, took all of the available money, leaving nothing for financial aid for students. The University of Virginia became the most expensive university in the nation, charging the highest tuition.[59] Jefferson's hopes of reforming and enlightening the most promising of his countrymen were dashed as the university took on much the same character as the college that he had tried in vain to reform, the College of William and Mary. The student body was composed mostly of the sons of wealthy, southern plantation owners. Unruly and "without shame," as one observer of the day lamented, the student body greatly disappointed Jefferson.[60] "The article of discipline is the most difficult in American education," Jefferson wrote in 1822. "Premature ideas of independence, too little repressed by parents, beget a spirit of insubordination, which is the great obstacle to science with us, and a principal cause of its decay since the revolution. I look to it with dismay in our institution, as a breaker ahead which I am far from being confident we shall be able to weather."[61] It is "jarring to read Jefferson write of 'premature independence' by the young and of postrevolutionary decay," Taylor observes, "for we associate him with confidence in people and progress." But, Taylor adds, "Jefferson was never entirely comfortable with people as they were."[62]

Because Jefferson views his countrymen through a romantic lens, he is often unable to accept them as they are. Eager to improve their thinking, he tried to establish a university that could accommodate these poor, rural folk, but his romantic thinking hampered his own efforts. Jefferson despairs that his university will have the intended effect and that future generations will accomplish what his could not, from emancipation of slaves to the realization of *true* republicanism.[63] He takes comfort in his advanced age sparing him "the pain of witnessing [the] consequences" of a dissipated and entitled youth taking up residence in the quarters he once envisioned housing future great leaders.[64] Because of his unrealistic expectations of the university—Palladian perfection, a disciplined and eager youth ready to abolish slavery—Jefferson's vision resulted in a university that was built at tremendous cost and unable even to offer scholarships to poor whites. The dissonance between vision and reality resulted not in falling short of the ideal but in a worse outcome than had Jefferson calibrated his vision to the constraints of reality.

Jefferson's "Empire of Liberty"

Jefferson's belief in an "empire of liberty" prefigures ideas that would become major impetuses behind the democratist foreign policy.[65] The Louisiana Purchase, his repeated attempts to acquire the Floridas, and his treatment of Native Americans illustrate his belief in the historical inevitability of democracy and also the paradox of trying to achieve democracy through force. Jefferson views democracy providentially, stating in his last public letter, "All eyes are opened, or opening to the rights of man. The general spread of the light of science has already laid open to every view the palpable truth, that the mass of mankind has not been born with saddles on their backs, nor a favored few booted and spurred, ready to ride them legitimately, by the grace of God."[66] He connects his desire to expand the country with a philosophy that puts America at the vanguard of democratic history. In this same letter, Jefferson says of the Declaration of Independence that it is "an instrument pregnant with our own, and the fate of the world."[67] For Jefferson, expanding the United States represents the natural course of events, an idea that would become popularly known as "manifest destiny." Acquisition of the Louisiana territory is "inevitable from the course of things," he believes.[68] Peter Onuf reads in the Louisiana Purchase the fulfillment of Jefferson's promises in his first inaugural address, which imagines a "transcendent" destiny for America. According to Onuf, the Louisiana conquest "was subordinated to a triumphalist narrative of liberation that focused on the 'natural,' irresistible extension of agricultural settlement and the progress of civilization."[69] Jefferson's desire to acquire the Floridas, a pursuit that became, according to Henry Adams, his "overmastering passion," similarly illustrates Jefferson's expansionist tendencies.[70] The Floridas, like Louisiana, were America's natural right and destiny. "We shall certainly obtain the Floridas, and all in good time," Jefferson writes in 1803. "In the meanwhile, without waiting for permission, we shall enter into the exercise of the natural right we have always insisted on with Spain, to wit, that of a nation holding the upper part of streams, having a right of innocent passage through them to the ocean."[71]

Jefferson's purchase of Louisiana (an offer he could hardly refuse, to be sure) represents not a repudiation of his philosophy in the name of political expediency but an illustration of his democratist philosophy. His justifications for his actions reveal the way in which democratists are inclined to interpret what would otherwise appear to be classic instances of territorial expansion—a desire of statesmen throughout the ages. However, conquest is not viewed by the democratist as merely that; it is couched within a larger narrative about natural rights and spreading freedom. This idea will be explored in greater detail in the chapter that examines the George W. Bush administration's foreign policy. Jefferson's "appetite for expansion," as Robert Tucker and David Hendrickson characterize his desire to acquire Louisiana and the Floridas, reveals the side of democratism that desires to spread its way of life.[72] This illustrates one part of the democratist paradox: wishing to spread democracy while avoiding the appearance of imperialism. Historian Walter McDougall suggests that the "[c]onstitutionally dubious" Louisiana Purchase "had ominous implications for the expansion of slavery and dispossession of Native Americans. . . . [N]obody asked the Creoles, Africans, and Indians beyond the Mississippi River whether they wanted to live under U.S. authority."[73] It can obviously be argued that any statesman would have done as Jefferson did when offered the Louisiana territory practically free of charge by Napoleon, but Jefferson demonstrates his commitment to a democratist perspective by justifying the acquisition of Louisiana and his desire for the Floridas as nothing more than helping nature take its course.

That Jefferson's theory comes into conflict with his practice—that expanding the territory of the United States *did* imply the classic notion of empire and that this action had repercussions for the liberty and self-determination of other peoples—illustrates the distance between the democratist theory of liberty and equality from its actual practice. An understanding of the inner logic of democratism could predict that the democratist, given power of this sort, might be inclined toward expansionist or undemocratic actions in the name of "democracy." Abstract proclamations about liberty and equality mean little in the face of actual political decision-making and the feeling that one can further the cause of democracy, even if it means taking steps that are undemocratic. Jefferson initially desired peaceful coexistence with Native Americans, but after the Louisiana Purchase he recognizes the practical difficulty of trying to assimilate them. One scholar contrasts Jefferson's cheerful first inaugural address, in which he says that "a spirit of peace and friendship generally prevails" among our native neighbors, with his later desire to see Americans settle "the extensive country remaining vacant within our limits" at the expense of the native inhabitants.[74] While Christian B. Keller sees in this dissonance Jefferson being "forced to submit philanthropic idealism to pragmatic necessity," it is also possible to read Jefferson's actions as being entirely consistent with his theory.[75] Jefferson sincerely believes that a wholly new democratic age is possible and that violence or undemocratic means may be required to get there. Toward the end of his life, he predicts in a letter to John Adams that all of Europe will soon "attain representative government, more or less perfect.... [T]o attain all this however, rivers of blood must yet flow, & years of desolation pass over." Jefferson nevertheless insists that "the object is worth rivers of blood, and years of desolation. For what inheritance, so valuable, can man leave to his posterity?"[76]

Jefferson's treatment of Native Americans reveals the sordid underside of his desire for an "empire of liberty." Determined to expand American territory and to civilize or oust native inhabitants, Jefferson greatly broadened federal powers during his presidency. He had formerly been opposed to the Trade and Intercourse Act, which regulated affairs with Native Americans, as an infringement of states' rights, but after he assumed office he was not shy about making use of it. Unlike Washington and Adams and the British before them, who "regarded the Indian tribes as foreign powers, with whom diplomatic relations were to be conducted according to traditional protocols," Jefferson took liberties that increasingly violated tribal sovereignty and acquired their lands through deception and salami tactics.[77] Commerce with the Indians was one of the major ways in which Jefferson envisioned "converting" them to the American way of life. Not only would they find agriculture and consumerism rewarding, but by living outside of their means they would be forced to sell their lands in order to escape debt, Jefferson predicted. Enclosed between white settlements, the Native Americans will, "for want of game, be forced to agriculture, will find that small portions of land well improved, will be worth more to them than extensive forests unemployed, and will be continually parting with portions of them, for money to buy stock, utensils & necessities for their farms & families."[78] Jefferson writes to William Henry Harrison, then governor of the Indiana Territory, that "to exchange lands" with the Indians, "we shall push our trading houses, and be

glad to see the good and the influential individuals among them run in debt. ...
[W]hen these debts get beyond what the individuals can pay, they become willing
to lop them off by a cession of lands. ... In this way our settlements will gradually
circumscribe and approach the Indians, and they will either incorporate with us
as citizens of the United States, or remove beyond the Mississippi."[79] Andrew
Jackson, whose Indian removal policies are notorious, acted on precedents that
Jefferson set. Jackson, in his message to Congress on the relocation of the Native
Americans, declared "that the benevolent policy of the Government, steadily
pursued for nearly thirty years, in relation to the removal of the Indians beyond
the white settlements is approaching to a happy consummation."[80]

The twin myths of manifest destiny and American exceptionalism, to which
Jefferson heartily contributed, as joined to a progressive-democratic interpretation of history have helped to inspire a foreign policy that is guided by idealistic visions of natural rights. These myths have helped many who share the
Jeffersonian imagination to reinterpret what would otherwise appear to be ancient methods of statecraft, characterized by territorial gains and the subjugation
of native peoples, as no more than the spread of liberty and democracy. "All our
liberalities to [the American Indians]," Jefferson writes to Harrison, "proceed
from motives of pure humanity only."[81] One can discern modern parallels in foreign wars of intervention ostensibly motivated by "humanitarian" and "democratic" goals. While claiming to spread freedom and democracy, to be creating a
more humane world, Jefferson is nonetheless willing to make use of violence and
other measures that undermine his goals.

Jefferson proclaims that the evolution of mankind toward liberal democracy
can be witnessed geographically, "from the savages of the Rocky Mountains" to
man in his "most improved state" in the coastal towns.[82] It is paradoxical that
Jefferson should look to the coastal towns for an example of man in his "most
improved state" given his disdain for commerce and cities in general. But while
Jefferson lauds agrarian life and occasionally praises the simple ways of Native
American life, he does so because he views these ways of life through a romantic and abstract lens. He believes that farmers, and to a lesser extent Native
Americans, are naturally good and uncorrupted by society. They are "unevolved"
or "premodern," representing a vision of the past uncorrupted by long-standing
social institutions. The abstract "people"—whether in the past, in a remote and
undeveloped place, or in certain forms in the present, such as the agrarians—are
thought to be good and simple but also in need of enlightenment in order to
move along the locomotive of democratic history. It is the present that is to be
lamented, according to the democratist, who, like Jefferson and other romantics,
projects on the past or on native peoples a vision of simplicity and harmony and
at the same time, like the Baconian, projects onto the future a vision of universal
enlightenment.

Jeffersonian Christianity and Democratism

Jefferson's near religious commitment to democracy and corresponding faith in the common people is well known. It should not be surprising, then, that his interpretation of democracy dovetails with his reading of Christianity. For Jefferson, Christianity, like democracy, is fully rational; the two, in fact, point toward one another. "Far from consigning religion and politics to separate spheres under the new republican dispensation," Onuf says, "Jefferson foresaw their ultimate convergence, for an enlightened, purified Christianity—the religion of humanity that Jesus had preached—constituted the only durable foundation for republican self-rule."[83] This would be the interpretation of Christianity and democracy of Jacques Maritain, a Catholic writing a century and a half later. Maritain, whose democratist interpretation of Christianity will be examined in a later chapter, similarly sees in Christianity the impetus toward democracy and argues that the two are complementary.

In the same letter to Carr in which Jefferson tells him to "fix reason firmly in her seat," Jefferson assures him that reason alone can lead him to the true religion. He tells Carr to read the Bible objectively as he would Livy and Tacitus and not to take anything on the authority or pretensions of the authors. Jefferson follows this advice in compiling the "Jefferson Bible." This compendium splices together those scriptural passages that Jefferson believed reflect true Christianity, shorn of all superstitions and miracles and compatible with empiricism and knowledge of the physical world.[84] Jesus, as Jefferson understands him, reforms the morals of humanity "to the standard of reason, justice, & philanthropy" and calls us to a religion of humanity.[85] Democracy, like Christianity, is still awaiting its final and perfect expression; only, as Justin Garrison points out, "the future state [Jefferson] has in mind is not found in some realm radically separated from this world, as is the case with traditional Christianity, but is instead located in this world, one that is supposed to be politically, rationally, and spiritually transformed by human hands."[86] Garrison points out that Jefferson's democracy contains its heretics, apostles, and martyrs precisely because Jefferson conflates democracy with a rationalist-Platonic Christianity.[87]

Jefferson's expectation that "the whole world will, sooner or later, feel benefit from the issue of our assertion of the rights of man" is part of a broader philosophy of history that not only envisions the American democratic way as the final stage of history but also sees in the American mission an eschatological imperative. Woodrow Wilson will take up this idea with even greater fanaticism, and Maritain, although a Catholic and one apparently in the Thomist tradition, will express similar beliefs. Guided by this narrative of history, Jefferson finds transcendent meaning in mundane political events. He sees, for example, the "Revolution of 1800" as having spiritual significance. "The regeneration of Rhode island" Jefferson interprets as "the beginning of that resurrection of the genuine spirit of New England which rises for life eternal." Reading this political event along biblical lines, Jefferson goes on, "According to natural order, Vermont will emerge next, because least, after Rhode island, under the yoke of hierocracy."[88] For Jefferson, nothing less than the hand of God helped to effect the change of power in American politics.

Jefferson's religious faith in democracy is on display when he suggests that apparent setbacks, even those of "the Dantons and Robespierres," must not cause the world to lose faith or America to waver from the "steady march to our object."[89] In his mind, there is a particular direction to history. When America appears to turn away from the type of republican thinking that he values, by electing his political adversaries, for example, he insists that such a state of affairs "is not a natural one." Jefferson believes that there is but one "natural" expression of democracy: his own idea of it. He explains the turn the nation has taken under current political leadership as owing to "the irresistible influence & popularity of Genl. Washington played off by the cunning of Hamilton which turned the government over to antirepublican hands, or turned the republican members chosen by the people into anti-republicans."[90] Jefferson often resorts to conspiratorial thinking when he believes that particular political or religious forces are derailing America from its preordained mission.

Jefferson especially views traditional religion as an obstacle to the republic he envisages. In the letter in which he writes that the fate of liberty in the world is bound up with America's fate, Jefferson expresses his hope that the rest of the peoples of the globe will "burst the chains under which monkish ignorance and superstition had persuaded them to bind themselves."[91] For Jefferson, orthodox Christianity represents an elaborate effort to deceive the masses. In a letter to Adams he declares that early Christian leaders "saw, in the mysticisms of Plato, materials with which they might build up an artificial system which might, from it's [sic] indistinctness, admit everlasting controversy, give employment for their order, and introduce it to profit, power & pre-eminence." Combining Plato's obscure philosophy with simple Christian truths, early Christian leaders ensured perpetual employment and riches for themselves and servitude of the masses, Jefferson proffers. Jefferson believes that individual reason must be engaged to rid Americans of false and superstitious religious beliefs that ultimately get in the way of the democracy of reason that he envisions.

Imagining that a conspiracy of elites stands in the way of democracy is one of the hallmarks of democratism. This type of thinking sees numerous, unnecessary obstacles thwarting what ought to be the people's natural will for reasoned democracy. Orthodox religion is often interpreted as a conspiracy against the people and a means of control, which is why many democratists insist that authentic Christianity is little different from a reasoned religion of humanity—which reflects many of the principles of democratism. This reasoned or "Platonic" Christianity revises traditional Christian concepts, transforming equality, for example, to mean absolute or material equality, and love of neighbor to mean diffuse love of humanity. Aspects of traditional Christianity and the Bible that do not square with Enlightenment rationality and empiricism are simply dismissed, explained as inauthentic and not a part of real Christianity. Jefferson suggests this when he tells Carr that he is "Astronomer enough to know how contrary it is to the law of nature" that the sun should stand still on its axis as recounted in the book of Joshua, and Carr should apply the same standard of reason to claims that Jesus "was begotten by god, born of a virgin, suspended and reversed the laws of nature at will, and ascended bodily into heaven."[92]

The vitriol that Jefferson directed toward "priestcraft" suggests that he, like the fifth-century Romans and so many others, felt that traditional Christian beliefs as interpreted by the Church were incompatible with his normative vision of politics.[93] Traditional Christianity seemed to command the loyalty of its believers in a way that threatened his Democracy of Reason. Jefferson's self-proclaimed "creed of materialism" is obviously antithetical to the Christianity that professes the divinity of Christ and looks forward to the Christian eschaton. It is not clear that these orthodox Christian beliefs can be reconciled with a political philosophy that puts its hope in *this* world, as Jefferson's does.

Jeffersonian Conceit

While Jefferson believes that the principles of democracy as he understands them are self-evident and discernable through rationality, he seems continually to discover people deviating from what ought to be the norm. While he is careful to reserve his real criticism for those in power rather than the people themselves, he suggests that those who disagree with him about the proper form of government are not simply in error but corrupt or malicious. This is one aspect of the democratist Enlightenment-romantic dynamic. It is expected that people are, on the whole, rational and good. When it becomes apparent that society is not pursuing the course envisaged as the only natural and reasonable one, the democratist blames a lack of proper reasoning or a few bad actors deceiving the people. In a letter to John Taylor in 1798, Jefferson describes the Adams administration as a "reign of witches" and expresses his faith in the people "recovering their true sight."[94] Adams, in Jefferson's mind, led the good people astray and deviated from the true principles of government. Jefferson's first inaugural address is also telling: "If there be any among us who would wish to dissolve this Union or to change its republican form, let them stand undisturbed as monuments of the safety with which error of opinion may be tolerated where reason is left free to combat it." That others might have a different idea about what is normative in democracy, for example, to what degree "the direct action of the citizens" is desirable and possible—something Jefferson suggests is an art rather than a science—is not a legitimate possibility in Jefferson's mind.[95] Jefferson's understanding of what constitutes republicanism is, for him, the final word.

At the core of democratism is an apparent faith in the people united with the insistence that they change in fundamental ways. Jefferson often exemplifies this paradoxical belief. Democratism claims that the principles of democracy are self-evident and discernable through rationality, but its elaborate prescriptions for changing existing norms and the contempt it has for existing institutions and opposing ideas suggest that it is but another manifestation of rigid ideological thinking. Jefferson exhibits an arrogance characteristic of democratist thinking when he looks forward to a time when his version of republicanism will be the only one. After his election to the presidency, he says, "I should hope to be able to obliterate, or rather," he corrects himself, "to unite the names of federalist & republican."[96] According to Richard Hofstadter, "abstractly, Jefferson accepted the idea of political division and the reality that opposition would be embodied in the form of parties; but concretely he could never see the legitimacy of any particular opposition in his own country."[97] Rather, Jefferson could not see the legitimacy of opposition to his own system of beliefs. David N. Mayer explains that "after the successful conclusion of the War of 1812, [Jefferson] reported with apparent delight the virtual annihilation of Federalism."[98]

Jefferson interprets 1776 and 1800 as two revolutions that attest to the power of reason to order politics. Anticipating what would become the dominant progressive narrative of history in the twentieth and twenty-first centuries, he imagines the American example, and specifically his administration's example, as profoundly important in the global dialectic of democracy.[99] "[N]or are we acting for ourselves alone," Jefferson says in a letter to David Hall in 1802, "but for the whole human race. [T]he event of our experiment is to shew whether man can be trusted with self-government. [T]he eyes of suffering humanity are fixed on us with anxiety as their only hope, and on such a theatre & for such a cause we must suppress all smaller passions & local considerations."[100] Nearly twenty years later, Jefferson expresses the same idea: "[A]s members therefore of the universal society of mankind, and standing in high and responsible relation with them, it is our sacred duty to suppress passion among ourselves, and not to blast the confidence we have inspired of proof that a government of reason is better than one of force."[101]

Like so many other democratists, Jefferson invites us to participate in an abstract and grandiose vision in which imaginative deference to The Cause overshadows historical considerations. In this way, the democratist encourages us to look past what might seem like obvious impediments if we were to examine the concrete steps necessary to pursue the vision. Those who would object to the democratist's vision are dismissed as self-interested, parochial, myopic, or otherwise unable to appreciate the more important goal of Democracy. While Jefferson himself is often taken up with local considerations, from Virginia politics to soil conditions, he always seems to set his gaze on the good of humanity and the fate of the world. Henry Adams says that Jefferson's provincial cares ultimately give way to a belief that "the world's ruling interests should cease to be local and should become universal."[102] Americans are foremost members "of the universal society of mankind."[103] Local matters are trivial in comparison to the transcendent mission that Jefferson sees as America's destiny. If the American experiment fails, Jefferson believes, the fate of self-government is sealed. It cannot exist anywhere if Americans cannot accomplish it. Jefferson's philosophy of history vacillates between the belief that America is simply a testament to the possibility of self-government and the belief that the American example will ignite in other countries a universal desire for democracy, creating a domino effect. Even in Jefferson's more modest moments, in which he simply lauds the American example, he nonetheless views the American founding as a world-historic event. He interprets the Revolution in France similarly and as ultimately compatible with the American Revolution. The regicide in France, Jefferson says, will inspire in other nations a "softening" of the monarchies, if not outright republican sentiment.[104] It seems enough for Jefferson that the Jacobins could proclaim the same abstract, universal principles as the Declaration of Independence. "It is unfortunate," he writes in 1795, "that the efforts of mankind to recover the freedom of which they have been so long deprived, will be accompanied with violence, with errors, and even with crimes. But while we weep over the means, we must pray for the end."[105] Rather than see the French Revolution fail, he says he would "have seen half the earth desolated. Were there but an Adam & an Eve left in every country, & left free, it would be better than as it now is."[106] It is perhaps for this reason that Henry Adams concludes that Jefferson "was a theorist, prepared to risk the fate of mankind on the chance of reasoning far from certain in its details."[107] Jefferson, like other democratists, believes that the means are radically separate from the end. Bloodshed may be a necessary, if unfortunate, avenue for the realization of liberty. "[W]hat signify a few lives lost in a century or two?" Jefferson asks in 1787 in reference to Shay's Rebellion. "[T]he tree of liberty must be refreshed from time to time with the blood of patriots & tyrants. [I]t is it's [*sic*] natural manure."[108] Envisioning a future in which inequality, strife, and injustice have given way to a new democratic existence, Jefferson and others are perfectly willing to accept and justify violence in the name of liberty and equality.

That Jefferson should for so long have been a herald of democracy perhaps reveals something about America's conflicted understanding of democracy. Torn between an idealistic desire for "rule by the people" and a competing hope for a certain normative outcome, many democratic leaders (with a lowercase "d") bristle against democracy's demand for consent. One can see the temptation, as Jefferson did, to decree the philosophical foundations of one's own political stance "natural" and "reasonable." However, we are right to suspect a contradiction between abstract natural rights and a reality that does not match. High, noble-sounding ideals and projections of a wholly different future seem to ring hollow as many ordinary Americans and others who are supposed to benefit from the democratic way of life feel that they do not have a meaningful impact on politics. Jefferson's belief that there is something new under the sun seems a product of romantic and Enlightenment optimism and the type of thinking that informs democratism. America, like every other nation, appears to be subject to the constraints and vicissitudes of history. To proclaim otherwise is not only naive but also potentially dangerous insofar as it contributes to unrealistic expectations that invite despair or revolt against reality itself.

As Jefferson demonstrates, democratism proclaims the highest democratic ideals of popular sovereignty, freedom, and equality, but in practice it inclines toward social engineering, inegalitarianism, expansionism, and a missionary zeal. Democratism is a comprehensive theory of democracy that, concretely, does not bear much resemblance to democracy in the classical or literal sense. It is often a cover for undemocratic practices. Tempering the will of the people may indeed be necessary, but the democratist is not so much interested in revising or improving this or that particular viewpoint or passion of the moment as in sweeping changes to widely held practices and beliefs. The democratist proclaims the will of the people sovereign but at the same time works to change those aspects of the popular will that do not fit within his or her own conception of what is normative. It is therefore difficult to assess the quality of the democratist's vision, since it operates under cover of rhetorical abstraction and obfuscation. To proclaim "all men created equal" and liberty and equality the highest ideals may be of great political value but detrimental to actual democracy, giving license to practices that are decidedly undemocratic, even authoritarian. Jefferson's proclamation "I know of but one code of morality for men, whether acting singly or collectively" exemplifies democratism's totalizing tendency. It precludes the possibility of those practical virtues that have sustained the American republic since its inception: compromise, negotiation, and toleration of opposing viewpoints and ways of life. Jefferson was outspoken about his desire to see the party of his adversaries "obliterated." He wished this, of course, in the name of what he took to be the common good and the will of the people. But his supreme confidence in his own interpretation of that code of morality reveals the same lack of political humility that bedevils the American republic today. Woodrow Wilson reveals this confidence elevated to the level of religious conviction. Understanding the ways that Jeffersonian democracy and Wilsonian democracy—ostensibly democratic traditions—relate and also the ways in which they fit within the broader ideological context of democratism will help to distinguish democratic illusion from democratic reality.

Woodrow Wilson

To Make the World Safe for Democracy

If Jefferson was an early American prophet of democratism, then Wilson was its messiah. From his time as president of Princeton to his time as president of the United States, Wilson put into practice many of the democratist ideals of which Jefferson only idly dreamed. While Jefferson, with his notion of an "empire of liberty," may have planted the philosophical seeds of armed intervention in the name of democracy, Wilson put the idea into practice. William McKinley, to be sure, had earlier introduced into U.S. foreign policy an idealism that held America responsible for the freedom and fate of other nations. McKinley first made use of the military to promote democracy abroad, but Wilson normalized the humanitarian cause as reason for military action across the globe. Throughout the nineteenth century preserving the Monroe Doctrine and cultivating America's image as a democratic leader in the world guided the foreign policy that would later morph into foreign interventionism.[1] John Quincy Adams's famous Fourth of July speech in 1821 represents the kind of exceptionalism myth that compelled belief among many until McKinley:

> America does not go abroad in search of monsters to destroy. She is the well-wisher to the freedom and independence of all. She is the champion only of her own. She will recommend the general cause by the countenance of her voice, and the benignant sympathy of her example. She well knows that by once enlisting under other banners than her own, were they even the banners of foreign independence, she would involve herself beyond the power of extrication, in all the wars of interest and intrigue, of individual avarice, envy, and ambition, which assumed the colors and usurped the standards of freedom. . . . She might become the dictatress of the world. She would be no longer the ruler of her own spirit.[2]

The Ideology of Democratism. Emily B. Finley, Oxford University Press. © Oxford University Press 2022.
DOI: 10.1093/oso/9780197642290.003.0004

Adams seemed to sense an incipient crusader mentality beneath the myth of American exceptionalism. The Spanish-American War in 1898 revealed that this myth had transformed from one that inspired well-wishing to one bent on liberation by force. In trying to democratize the Philippines and Cuba, America had chosen to ignore Adams's words and to pursue a new tradition of intervention abroad that would last for the next century and beyond. The Spanish-American War, many scholars argue, began a new and heretical tradition in America that went so far as to alter Americans' national self-understanding.[3] Going to war with Spain in order to support its Cuban colony's bid for liberation was the start of this new mentality in foreign policy thinking. Americans "accepted imperialism in 1900," Ralph Henry Gabriel says, and thereafter "enjoyed the mood of the conqueror."[4] In the words of Walter McDougall, Americans "allowed themselves to be swept by a hurricane of militant righteousness into a revolutionary foreign war, determined to slay a dragon and free a damsel in distress."[5]

McKinley's actions in 1898, supported by a public that had been encouraged by sensational accounts of the Cubans' desire for freedom, undoubtedly played a role in cultivating Wilson's own belief that the United States might help other nations in their bid for democracy. Unlike McKinley, however, Wilson interpreted the American mission through a theological lens, believing that democracy represented Good in a world-immanent battle against evil.

Wilson envisions history giving way to a new democratic age, characterized by universal peace among peoples and nations. America, Wilson says in a 1912 campaign speech, is the chosen nation, "and prominently chosen to show the way to the nations of the world how they shall walk in their paths of liberty." God presided over America's birth, and, Wilson says, "I believe that God planted in us the visions of liberty."[6] He taps into the imagination of his listeners in his first inaugural address, echoing this theme of America as chosen nation. Indeed he raises his earlier pronouncements to the level of poetry: "The feelings with which we face this new age of right and opportunity sweep across our heartstrings like some air out of God's own presence, where justice and mercy are reconciled and the judge and the brother are one." Wilson, like so many other democratists, believes that America is unique and ought to be exempt from the political strife and historical woes that have plagued other nations. Instead, America has been blessed by the grace of God and must therefore help to spread its blessings to the rest of the world. For Wilson, America's is "no mere task of politics" but an eschatological imperative to carry out the divine will.[7]

Wilson's conception of the state was greatly influenced by the new and progressive understanding of Christianity being proclaimed in the social gospel.[8] At the turn of the twentieth century many liberal Protestant churches professed a progressive political theology that proclaimed the imminent salvation of humanity. This variant of Christian teaching turned away from the traditional focus on the salvation of the individual soul and toward collective salvation through politics. The state, according to the social gospel, would be the vehicle through which society might be saved.

Many of the Rousseauean elements in Wilson's democratism are refracted through the social gospel movement, which to a great extent shares Rousseau's philosophical and theological assumptions. "As civilization develops, sin grows corporate," said Shailer Mathews, dean of the University of Chicago's Divinity School from 1908 until 1933 and a prominent spokesperson for the social gospel movement. "We sin socially by violating social rather than individualistic personal relations."[9] Accepting the Enlightenment conception of history and the evolutionary theory of social Darwinism, the social gospel movement rejected the traditional Augustinian distinction between the earthly city and the city of God and put forth a revised version of the Christian faith more compatible with political aspirations to transform "the city of destruction into a City of God."[10] Uniting the political and the theological was for Wilson and the social gospel not a contradiction, as it was for Augustine, but an imperative. With other social gospelers, Wilson even expected that the United States might look like the Kingdom of God on earth.[11] In this respect, he was in the theological tradition of Rousseau and Jefferson, viewing Christianity as ultimately compatible, even synonymous, with mundane political aspirations.[12] Rousseau, who does not try to rationalize Christianity, as Jefferson does, nonetheless puts forth the idea of a civil religion that is meant to serve much the same function as Jefferson's and Wilson's versions of Christianity: to unite the people in the cause of the state.

By this time, "Christian" had become a very elastic term. Wilson and other disciples of this new faith "were animated by a similar drive for innerworldly perfection as the culminating chapter in the organic evolution of human history."[13] Democracy, for Wilson, represents this final chapter in politics. According to Wilson's philosophy of history, democracy is an advanced stage of historical development, "a form of state life which is possible for a nation only in the adult age of its political development."[14] As the most "mature" form of government, democracy is suited to those of the human race who reflect this maturity.[15] Wilson mentions the people's ability to exert self-control as one precondition, but he also stresses the need for a people to be "homogeneous" in "race and community of thought and purpose." In this final stage of historical development, a democratic people will act as one body, animated by something akin to the Rousseauean general will. Americans, Wilson says, have "a common vocation" and "a common destiny—not only a 'spirit of '76,' but a sprit for all time."[16]

The Nation, at its best, is for Wilson not the product of historical development or a social contract but a living organism, having grown up and developed with the people constituting it. He believes that the state-organism has different functions but is animated by a single spirit, calling to mind the Pauline letter describing the workings of the Holy Spirit in the Church community. But Charles Darwin and Hegel are the inspirations Wilson has in mind, not St. Paul. He compares government to a living being: "No living thing can have its organs offset against each other, as checks, and live. On the contrary, its life is dependent upon their quick co-operation, their ready response to the commands of instinct or intelligence, their amicable community of purpose. Government is not a body of blind forces; it is a body of men, with highly differentiated functions, no doubt . . . with a common task and purpose."[17]

For Wilson, the democratic state personifies an actual spiritual being and it must be "prepared to *act* as an organic body," he says.[18] The unified "volition" of the people guides the organic being of the state. Its will is general. The very act of cooperation from the losing minority in democracies is "akin to actual agreement."[19] While he rejects Rousseau's social contract for being ahistorical, Wilson's political philosophy nonetheless shares many of its features, especially the fundamental idea of the general will.[20] Democracy "is not the rule of the many, but the rule of the *whole*."[21] Rousseau of course characterizes sovereignty similarly, writing, "For either the will is general or it is not. It is the will of either the people as a whole or of only a part."[22] For Wilson as for Rousseau, the state is a great being that acts upon "a universal compulsory force" moving and arranging each part in accordance with a singular vision.[23]

At the same time, Wilson, like Rousseau, seems to value the individual. Modern democracy, Wilson asserts, is based upon the establishment of "individual rights as peers of the rights of the state."[24] He condemns socialism and promotes the right of corporations to free enterprise because he believes that "individual initiative" is at the foundation of modern democracy. To understand this apparent tension between Wilson's organic conception of the state and a seeming competing belief in individualism, it is helpful to keep in mind Rousseau's philosophy. All citizens unite in the general will, Rousseau says, but each person "nevertheless obeys only himself and remains as free as before."[25] In much the same way, Wilson believes that "new" modern democracies are of a different order entirely from ancient regimes bearing the name. Modern democracy, Wilson believes, wholly unites its citizens in a common, transcendent cause and yet also preserves individualism. His understanding of democracy, like Rousseau's, goes far beyond a theory of politics in the ordinary sense.

It would be impossible to conceive of this notion of democracy apart from its transcendent or metaphysical dimension. Its presents a vision of democracy that requires "belief in things unseen." For Wilson, the sovereignty of the people is mystical rather than real. The people "do not, in any adequate sense of the word, govern," he says.[26] They play very little role in the day-to-day affairs of government, such as policymaking and legislation. It is and always has been the case that the few govern, Wilson writes in "The Modern Democratic State." Representatives are tasked with discerning and carrying out the national will, not necessarily directly translating the desires of their constituents. "Properly organized democracy is the best govt. of the few."[27] Unlike the framers of the U.S. Constitution, who believed that the art of democratic government requires compromise, negotiation, and some decisions based on political expediency, Wilson believes that the art of democratic government lies in the "persuasive power of dominant minds."[28] Compromise should be a last resort. The difference between the American framers and Wilson on this point illustrates one of the major differences between republicanism and democratism. For a republican of the American founding variety, governing is not about finding a way to elicit or manifest the "spirit" of a people or its general will, but about the practical art of compromise and keeping the peace. Wilson looked to statesmen not as persons with diplomatic skill and an ability to find common ground but as figures who can interpret the spirit of the people, whether or not the people are consciously aware of the vision or idea being attributed to them.

Wilsonian Leadership

Wilson's political theology of democracy calls for a leader of men capable of nothing less than leading democracy toward its eschatological conclusion, "the universal emancipation and brotherhood of man."[29] Implicit in the belief that a "leader of men" can articulate and guide the "inchoate and vague" Spirit of the Democratic Age is a philosophical anthropology akin to that of Rousseau.[30] Unlike many of the American framers, Wilson does not fear popular passions and factions as permanent threats to good government. "Generous emotions," he believes, can overcome "base purposes" in the modern and enlightened democratic state.[31] With the social gospel, Wilson believes that evil is largely a product of social institutions rather than individual sinfulness. A true leader will correct "the wrongs of a system . . . not wrongs which individuals intentionally do—I do not believe there are a great many of those."[32] This understanding of human nature as generally good informs Wilson's belief that the charismatic leader will not face insurmountable difficulty in guiding the people to their true, highest will. Like the hand of evolution, a leader of men can guide the people to prefer "the firm and progressive popular thought" over "the momentary and whimsical popular mood, the transitory or mistaken popular passion."[33] But this will not be done in the way that, say, Hamilton or Madison assumed, through representatives looking beyond the momentary passions of one *concrete* situation and toward a *concrete* resolution, but by looking beyond the concrete altogether and toward the universal, effectively moving beyond politics itself.

Wilson envisions a charismatic leader who, by gaining the trust of the people, can give them direction: "Let him once win the admiration and confidence of the country, and no other single force can withstand him, no combination of forces will easily overpower him." The tension between the power of the people as sovereign and the power of the politician as interpreter is a central tension within democratism. For Wilson and other democratists, the people constitute the Spirit of the Age and embody the national will, but only in a metaphysical sense. The actual wants and needs of the people are irrelevant to the task of the political leader. Wilson's belief that the leader must "rightly interpret the national thought" and then "boldly insist upon it" illustrates well the paradox.[34] The people may not understand their *true* will, and so a legislator must intuit it and demand it on their behalf.

The Role of Rhetoric

Oratory, for Wilson, provides the bridge between the people and the leader. Through rhetoric that captures the imagination, this leader can, like Rousseau's legislator, "compel without violence and persuade without convincing."[35] The orator ought to make use of "things which find easy entrance into [the people's] minds and are easily transmitted to the palms of their hands or the ends of their walking-sticks in the shape of applause."[36] Wilson no doubt had in mind the simple, abstract phrases of which so many presidents have made use: "Hope and Change," "Make America Great Again," "Build Back Better." Proclaiming simple and obvious truths, Wilson said, is like "the fierce cut of the sabre" and how "oratorical battles are won." The rhetorical work of a leader of men is like that of a skilled swordsman: he wins "by the straight and speedy thrusts of speech sent through and through the gross and obvious frame of a subject."[37] Wilson gives the example of the British statesman John Bright, who proclaims "large and obvious" moral principles and whose rhetoric is "purged of all subtlety."[38] Abstract, platitudinous rhetoric is a powerful tool for shaping minds, Wilson believes. Irving Babbitt, Wilson's contemporary, believed that such abstract rhetoric at the service of grandiose political missions was dangerous. "Words, especially abstract words, have such an important relation to reality because they control the imagination," Babbitt said, "which in turn determines action and so 'governs mankind.'"[39] Wilson senses the power of the imagination to give the substance it desires to empty abstractions. Pleasing words like "liberty" and "peace" can come to mean their opposites when concretely acted upon. Wilson's war to "make the world safe for democracy" is a salient example. It demonstrates how easy it is to overlook the costs and sometimes gruesome actions involved in pursuing a noble-sounding ideal.

Rhetorical keenness is a trait that Wilson values partly because it concentrates power in one person. "There are men to be moved. How shall he move them?" he asks of his hypothetical leader of men.[40] Wilson "loved, craved, and in a sense glorified power," McDougall says, because he felt that only with great political power could the statesman accomplish a world-historic task.[41] Wilson often treated the idea of democratic consent as an administrative hurdle, which had to be overcome by a powerful and visionary leader for the people's own good. "It is the *power* which dictates, dominates: the materials yield," Wilson says, and he believes this is a good thing.[42] In his early work *Congressional Government* (1885), Wilson regrets that the American system seems to preclude the rise of a charismatic leader. Congress is "engaged upon a campaign which has no great cause at its back," he laments.[43] Moreover, congressmen are inept at commanding the public's attention and mobilizing its will. Wilson envisions a leader unencumbered by the federal system and the need to bargain with the opposition. Instead, this person ought to focus on molding the electorate like "clay." This would open up new political vistas.[44] Something "like genius" is needed for a congressman to create "a universally recognized right to be heard and to create an ever-active desire to hear him whenever he talks."[45] The task of this person, like Rousseau's legislator, is not to channel the people's express interests but to encourage them to submit to his interpretation of their will. Wilson's vast domestic surveillance and censorship programs during the war illustrate the logical outcome of this leadership philosophy. Wilson believed that the "spirit" of the American people must support a great and noble cause such as the war, even if they did not expressly say so.

Wilson's Vision of Government

When Wilson wrote *Congressional Government* in 1885 he did not foresee that traditional barriers to the centralization of power, such as the constitutional separation of powers—"the central defect of American politics"—was about to erode under McKinley with the Spanish-American War.[46] McKinley demonstrated that a president could greatly expand war powers and consequently other powers too. It turned out not to be a member of Congress who would need to rise up as a charismatic leader. The president could now assume many of the traits that Wilson had hoped to see in a statesman. Wilson had hypothesized in 1879 in *Cabinet Government in the United States* that "extraordinary crisis or rapid transition and progress" was the way for "a man with all the genius, all the deep and strong patriotism, all the moral vigor, and all the ripeness of knowledge and variety of acquisition" to command a powerful leadership role.[47] According to Wilson, crises facilitate the rise of the type of leaders he envisions because "they are peculiarly periods of action" and, it is implied, revolutionary change.[48] Through crises such as war, the door can be opened for the expansion of presidential powers and an attendant growth of national power at the expense of the states, as McKinley demonstrated. McKinley proved that a president could indeed pursue something other than the "uninteresting everyday administration" that Wilson so despised. He could embark on a grand national mission.[49]

In 1908 Wilson observed that the president's role had changed for the better. No longer just a chief executive, now the president's "political powers more and more centre and accumulate upon him and are in their very nature personal and inalienable."[50] Given a sense of urgency generated by a real or imagined crisis, the executive can exert "transcendent influence" and move beyond constitutional constraints.[51] In *Constitutional Government*, probably Wilson's most mature political work, he says that the president now has "the initiative to enforce his views both upon the people and upon congress."[52] Wilson's desire to see the national government—either through Congress or the president—champion a great cause departs in significant ways from the intention of many of the framers of the U.S. Constitution. For them, the diffusion of power through the federalist system (embodied in the Congress) was designed to prevent ambitious individuals from centralizing power and embarking on national political adventures. Steeped in the classical republican tradition and wary of European entanglement, framers such as Washington, Adams, Madison, and in many respects Jefferson conceived of a very limited role for the national government. The notion of Congress championing a "great cause" would have frightened these men, to say the least.

For Wilson, the U.S. Constitution represents an obstacle to the "altogether modern" democracy he envisages. A well-known political scientist of the twentieth century and a president of the American Political Science Association, James MacGregor Burns, summarizes his own grievance with the American political system by quoting from Wilson's *Congressional Government*: "As at present constituted, the federal government lacks strength because its powers are divided, lacks promptness because its authorities are multiplied, lacks wieldiness because its processes are roundabout, lacks efficiency because its responsibility is indistinct and its action without competent direction."[53] Burns with Wilson desired a new sort of democracy that could look past the Constitution as written and even the actual desires of the people when necessary to take swift national action in accordance with a singular vision. This would, of course, mean a greater concentration of power in the president and Congress at the expense of the states. The framework of the Constitution is anathema to this Rousseauean and Wilsonian understanding of democracy. The Constitution's cumbersome need for bipartisan consensus and its diffusion of power across the states and different branches of government is meant precisely to prevent the type of powerful leader Wilson envisions from emerging. The desire of Rousseau and Wilson to see a legislator or "leader of men" rule for the people as a whole is sustained by the belief that the people are essentially motivated by the same hopes and desires. Such a vision would have seemed to framers such as Madison, Hamilton, and Adams and also many anti-Federalists like fantasy and a recipe for tyranny. Who is to determine the *true* will of the people? Instead, these framers believed that states and local communities ought to allow many competing and perhaps irreconcilable wills to coexist. This is not a recipe for efficiency or grand, national programs, to be sure, but that was never the intent of the framers.

Education

Wilson looks not only to a charismatic and rhetorically gifted leader to capture the imagination of the people, but also to a system of mass education that would encourage the types of civic beliefs that are compatible with his vision of a "new" democracy. For Wilson as for other democratists, a system of education is indispensable to winning the hearts and minds of the people to a particular view of democracy. For this reason, he was convinced that education must be centralized and overseen nationally. "However uniform might be the methods of instruction" locally, each group would still retain "a distinct local colour, and would be narrowed and minimized by a petty, purblind local application," Wilson warns.[54] Local control over education would permit competing voices and visions, ultimately interfering with the singular national "spirit" that Wilson believed must find expression. For Wilson, as for Rousseau, partial associations and local interests are incompatible with government by the "whole"—the only legitimate type of democratic government. One could imagine that a national leader, however charismatic, would have a difficult time marshaling the people to a national cause if "the people" in reality are a multitudinous body with a plurality of interests and local cultures. If the identities of persons inhere in their local groups, states, and interests rather than in the Nation (or the general will), they might not be inclined to partake in a national cause.[55] Uniting public sensibility through centralized, mass education will go a long way, Wilson argues, toward generating the type of national unity that he believes is the necessary vehicle to greatness and democratic liberation. This is why he believes that "higher education should be made an ally of the state."[56]

One of the central paradoxes of democratism is the belief that there is no contradiction between democracy and rule by the few. While democratists such as Wilson champion popular sovereignty, they are nonetheless eager to see a chosen few rule in the people's name, even against the people's express wishes if the democratists believe they are misguided. Wilson proclaims that the ballot box constitutes the "essence" of democracy, but that the enlightened statesman ought to play a decisive role in the actual direction of democratic government. Education, as well as other measures, will not only enlighten the people to their "true" interests; it also will help the cream rise to the top of the governing class. Even in a democracy, a natural aristocracy of some sort ought to govern, Wilson argues. He disparages the older way of politics, "an affair proper to be conducted only by the few who were instructed for the benefit of the many who were uninstructed."[57] Yet his conviction that an enlightened and able few ought to "mold" the people according to a particular vision suggests that his theory of government has more in common with that of his European forebears than he might like to believe.

Wilson's Vision of the War

For Wilson and many of the progressive Christian clergy, the Great War represented Armageddon. Good and Evil were battling for the soul of the world. While Wilson's decision to go to war may have been prompted by practical and strategic considerations, he justified it in terms of a humanitarian intervention in fulfillment of the divine plan. His imagination had long inclined him toward this type of thinking. In his 1912 campaign platform, "The New Freedom," for example, Wilson proclaims a beatific vision of earthly renewal: "We are going to climb the slow road until it reaches some upland where the air is fresher, where the whole talk of mere politicians is stilled, where men can look in each other's faces and see that there is nothing to conceal, that all they have to talk about they are willing to talk about in the open and talk about with each other; and whence, looking back over the road, we shall see at last that we have fulfilled our promise to mankind."[58] In his first inaugural address Wilson again echoes this theme: "This is the high enterprise of the new day: To lift everything that concerns our life as a Nation to the light that shines from the hearthfire of every man's conscience and vision of the right. . . . We know our task to be no mere task of politics but a task which shall search us through and through." He asks rhetorically if "we" will be up to the task of interpreting "our time and the need of our people, whether we be indeed their spokesmen and interpreters."[59] Wilson's "we" seems to implicate the American people as the spokespersons of the world. He concludes his address by exhorting the American people to "muster . . . the forces of humanity. Men's hearts wait upon us; men's lives hang in the balance; men's hopes call upon us to say what we will do. Who shall live up to the great trust? Who dares fail to try? I summon all honest men, all patriotic, all forward-looking men, to my side. God helping me, I will not fail them, if they will but counsel and sustain me!" It is possible to see American intervention in the war as an expression of Wilson's secular theology. He seems to have believed that God had in store a great mission for him and for America.

Wilson's rapturous visions, conveyed with rhetorical flourish in his campaign speeches and inaugural addresses, paradoxically paved the way for America's entrance into one of the most gruesome and destructive wars in human history. A beautiful and pristine vision wholly discordant with historical reality bids the annihilation of existing, flawed ways. Wilson expressed the well-worn democratist belief that long-term renewal and peace must sometimes be preceded by great destruction.[60] The "pacifists" who turned into some of the most vocal advocates of America going to war followed this same logic.

From Peace to War

Wilson's transition from neutrality to war was in fact a smooth one. Neutrality, at first, seemed to him the best path to the peace negotiations that he hoped would lead to a new world order of democracy. If America remained out of the war and above the fray, it would represent a disinterested party and could exert moral authority over the peace. Wilson, specifically, could dictate the terms. McDougall suggests that Wilson did not "cling to neutrality because it was American tradition, or because he was a pacifist (he was not), or because the American people were almost unanimously in favor of staying out of the war. He did it because he believed that remaining above the battle was the only way that he, Wilson, could exert the moral authority needed to end the war on terms that would make for a lasting peace."[61] To the chagrin and confusion of the European statesmen, Wilson proclaimed a new foreign policy and diplomacy of humanitarianism and abstract moralism. Americans "are trustees for what I venture to say is the greatest heritage that any nation ever had—the love of justice and righteousness and human liberty."[62] Unlike the power politics and balance-of-power foreign policy strategies of the Old World, America would inaugurate a new tradition based on a "community of power." At the outset of America's entrance into the war, this was the object Wilson hoped to accomplish in the peace.

As McDougall convincingly argues, Wilson's behavior preceding his request for a declaration of war suggests ideological rather than strategic motives. America was not, leading up to the war, neutral, as Wilson claimed. Having sold arms and lent money to the Allies totaling $2.3 billion before official entrance into the war, Wilson made the American position clear, despite his lofty request that the American people remain "impartial in thought as well as in action."[63] By 1916, Britain and France were purchasing 40 percent of their war materiel from the United States, and American banks owned millions in Allied war bonds. Wilson pretended that his foreign policy was above material interests and motivated purely by feelings of benevolence, but as McDougall notes, he "consistently served the interests of American cotton and grain exporters, manufacturers, and financiers, who made windfall profits from trade with the Allies."[64]

In addition, Wilson chose to ignore British violations of neutral shipping rights. He believed that democratic Britain, like America, stood for principles of right and justice, regardless of what its actions in the concrete might have indicated. Germany, however, was inherently illegitimate and represented not the voice of the German people but of the kaiser alone (despite the fact that, as McDougall points out, Imperial Germany was not strictly autocratic and the kaiser received greater popular support than Wilson did at the time of his election).[65] Rodney Carlisle argues that Wilson's assumptions about Britain's democratic essence is the reason he overlooked British actions, but not German actions, that harmed Americans. It is also the reason Wilson claimed that a declaration of war against Germany would not violate the principle of just war theory—that action must be proportionate to the cause. As Carlisle points out, "The actual acts of war by Germany against the United States that precipitated the decision had resulted in the deaths of forty-three seamen, of whom exactly thirteen were U.S. citizens." Only six U.S. merchant marines were killed in the submarine attacks when Wilson's cabinet recommended that he ask for a declaration of war.[66]

Concrete foreign policy aims, such as protecting American commercial interests on the high seas or ensuring the right of neutrals, were not at the forefront of Wilson's mind. McDougall says that Wilson might have sought to deter German belligerency at sea by using the navy to send Germany a message, perhaps even ending the war.[67] Germany would not have wished to see America enter the war, and neither American national security nor its national interests were in much danger, except for the financial stake that U.S. firms had in an Allied victory. "Wilson refused to embargo U.S. trade with all belligerents, refused to defend trade with all belligerents by ordering the navy across the ocean and daring either side to shoot first, and refused to instruct American citizens that they sailed on belligerent ships at their own risk," writes McDougall.[68] Instead, like many other democratists, Wilson decided that "right is more precious than peace."[69]

Wilson scarcely mentions the specifics of the incidents that precipitated his decision to request a declaration of war, and the few congressmen who did usually had the facts wrong, Carlisle points out. In several cases, members of Congress confused the losses aboard American ships with the losses of American lives aboard ships of foreign registry or with damage to American ships by German surface ships and submarines in 1915 and 1916.[70] Wilson's War Message glosses over the concrete events that would constitute the threats to American national security and instead focuses on the general humanitarian cause. He calls Germany's actions "warfare against mankind." America, on the other hand, as "one of the champions of the rights of mankind," has the unique ability to "prefer the interests of mankind to any narrow interest of [its] own." To focus on the concrete threats to American national security and national interests would have made the decision to go to war seem grossly out of proportion with the cause. Instead, Wilson focused abstractly on "the vindication of right."[71]

On the one hand, Wilson points to Germany's violation of "neutral rights" (something that is debatable given America's material involvement in the Allied effort), but on the other hand, he justifies the war in universalist and humanitarian terms. The blurring of national security with the rights of mankind is a theme that persists in democratist foreign policy thinking and foreshadows the neoconservative "hard Wilsonianism" of the twenty-first century. As the final chapter of this book shows, these modern Wilsonians find a great deal of overlap between American "national interest and global responsibility."[72] It is as if the decision to go to war did not lie with American leaders but with destiny. "The status of belligerent" has been thrust upon the United States, Wilson says. "Neutrality is no longer feasible or desirable where the peace of the world is involved and the freedom of its peoples, and the menace to that peace and freedom lies in the existence of autocratic governments backed by organized force which is controlled wholly by their will, not by the will of their people."[73] This line of thinking encourages national leaders to put the responsibility for war (and its aftermath) on an abstract duty to vindicate an imagined will of the people, whether at home or abroad. Interestingly, Wilson's message is not altogether different from that of the German chancellor's chief advisor, Kurt Riezler, three years earlier: "England's tragic error might consist of compelling us to rally all our strength, to exploit all our potentialities, to drive us into world-wide problems, to force upon us—against our will—a desire for world domination."[74] Did Wilson similarly desire a single way of life for the globe, one that he would personally oversee?

Civil Liberties and Wilson's War Propaganda Machine

Once Wilson had decided that "there are no other means of defending our rights" and that America must enter the war, he shows his own need for tremendous power that accompanies his imperative to "make the world safe for democracy." Total war called for the unflinching support of all. Wilson called for domestic surveillance programs, secret policing of citizens, and censorship of the press, print media, Hollywood, and even the private conversations of ordinary citizens, along with widespread propaganda efforts. He went to great lengths to repress dissent. "[A]uthority to exercise censorship over the press . . . is absolutely necessary to the public safety," he insisted in defense of a proposed censorship clause of the Espionage Act, which passed (without this clause) in May 1917.[75] In June 1918 Congress passed the Sedition Act, which made it illegal to publicize opposition to the war, something that had been in effect de facto since passage of the Espionage Act.[76] According to the Sedition Act, those who would "by word or act oppose the cause of the United States" or "utter, print, write, or publish any disloyal, profane, scurrilous, or abusive language about the form of government of the United States" were liable to a fine of up to $10,000 and twenty years in prison.[77] A provision of the Espionage Act gave the postmaster broad powers of censorship over news and publications, which the Wilson-appointed postmaster general Albert S. Burleson told Congress would be applied to journals that "say that this Government got in the war wrong, that it is in it for the wrong purposes, or . . . [that it] is the tool of Wall Street or the munitions-makers."[78] The Federal Bureau of Investigations put the offending organizations and the intended recipients under surveillance, then extended its surveillance over Americans through the American Protective League, a volunteer organization of citizen spies that "on the basis of hearsay, gossip, and slander" helped the FBI to arrest innocent civilians.[79] As Assistant Attorney General John Lord O'Brian said in 1919, the Justice Department had been under "immense pressure" to practice "indiscriminate prosecution" and "wholesale repression" during the war. The victims of these programs were generally ordinary citizens.[80]

In addition to legislative acts and directives to suppress dissent, Wilson created the Committee on Public Information (CPI) in order to create support for the war. According to Geoffrey Stone, "[b]ecause there had been no direct attack on the United States, and no direct threat to America's national security, the Wilson administration needed to create an 'outraged public' to arouse Americans to enlist, contribute money, and make the many other sacrifices war demands."[81] Under the direction of the progressive journalist, public relations expert, and former police commissioner George Creel, CPI produced pamphlets, posters, buttons, news releases, speeches, newspaper editorials, political cartoons, and even films. Alongside harsh legislation, these propaganda efforts created a culture of hysteria, fear, and denunciation during the war years. Wilson's demand for conformity and loyalty through such instruments as the American Protective League and CPI led to sharp divisions in the country and even violent mobs tarring and feathering, beating, and murdering fellow Americans.[82] The statement by Wilson's attorney general in November 1917 sums up the climate: "May God have mercy on them [dissenters], for they need expect none from an outraged people and an avenging government."[83]

Wilson's War, Europe's "Peace"

America's entrance was by no means a foregone conclusion, and while the so-cial gospel and progressive movements contributed to pro-war sentiment, the decision was finally Wilson's. His efforts to galvanize support and suppress dissent through legislation and a massive propaganda effort suggest that it may not have been the "people's war," as he declared it was.[84] Wilson also shows that the promise to "redeem the world and make it fit for free men like ourselves to live in," noble as it sounds, calls for violent means.[85] His desire for power is an abiding theme in his writings and actions as president. Distrustful of those outside of his immediate circle of confidants, he exhibited some of the traits of paranoia that characterized Rousseau. Even his closest friend, Colonel House, called Wilson's "second self," was unable to exert much influence over the president's decisions.[86] At the war's end, Wilson insisted on taking personal control of the armistice and the terms of the peace, producing a treaty that the U.S. Senate refused to ratify and whose legacy is the Second World War. Wilson's inability to compromise was directly connected to his idealism. With a vision in mind of right and justice, he could not allow deviation from the plan that was to bring about the world's salvation. Despite carefully choosing a peace commission composed of his closest friends and leading the American delegation to the Paris Peace Conference himself, he proved unable to control the settlement and accepted the treaty's notoriously harsh terms.[87] Wilson could not convince European leaders to sacrifice their nation's interests to an abstract notion of Right; the idea of collective security at the heart of the League of Nations was something that, Henry Kissinger says, no European state had ever seen at work or could bring itself to believe in.[88] For U.S. senators, an idea that was "tantamount to world government" in which America would act as a global police force strayed too far from the American tradition. While Wilson's intention had been for public opinion to enforce the League's covenants, many recognized the danger of such an idealistic endeavor with no counterpart in the history of geopolitics. Col. Maurice Hankey, British cabinet secretary and experienced military man, said that for Britain, the League would "create a sense of security which is wholly fictitious. . . . It will only result in failure and the longer that failure is postponed the more certain it is that this country will have been lulled to sleep. It will put a very strong lever into the hands of the well-meaning idealists who are to be found in almost every government who deprecate expenditure on armaments, and in the course of time it will almost certainly result in this country being caught at a disadvantage."[89] Others predicted that the League would prompt an arms race.

Republican Senate leader Henry Cabot Lodge, along with British and French experts, were wary of the League's sweeping clauses, the enforcement of which would mean another world war. Lodge and the "Strong Reservationists" shared the belief that the major powers would not actually go to war to enforce the League's guarantees. Vital national interest would dictate foreign policy as it always had. Yet Lodge and his constituency were still willing to ratify the treaty and "would even accept U.S. membership of the League provided Congress had a right to evaluate each crisis involving the use of American forces."[90] Wilson refused to compromise, certain that "[g]reat reformers . . . have no thought for occasion, no capacity for compromise," and he refused to accept reservations or revisions.[91] He believed that he could take the matter to the people and bypass the obstinate Senate. But his western tour of the United States to sway public opinion in favor of the League did not accomplish its mission and weakened him physically nearly to the point of death.[92] Unwilling to compromise even with senators who agreed in large part with the League but wished to see amendments, Wilson allowed the treaty to be defeated.

Yet the failure of the League of Nations in the Senate was overshadowed by the tragic and lasting failure that was the Treaty of Versailles. While the uncompromising terms of the peace greatly damaged Germany's economy and geopolitical situation, it was the insistence on German war guilt that had perhaps the most devastating long-term consequences. On June 23, the Reich government finally conceded to "the dictated peace" but issued a declaration:

> From the latest communication of the Allied and Associated Governments the government of the German Republic has learned with dismay that they are determined to compel Germany by extreme force to accept even those peace conditions that without being of material importance are aimed at depriving the German people of its honour. An act of force does not touch the honour of the German people. After the terrible sufferings of the last years the German people lack the means with which to defend its honour against the outside world. Surrendering to superior force but without retracting its opinion regarding the unheard of injustice of the peace conditions the government of the German republic therefore declares its readiness to accept and sign the peace conditions imposed by the Allied and Associated Governments.[93]

Chancellor of the Reich Philipp Scheidemann, after first learning the terms of the peace, solemnly said that the Germans were now witnessing "the nadir of Germany's fate. . . . [W]e stand at the graveside of the German people if all the things described here as peace conditions become contractual facts."[94] The German Foreign Ministry predicted that from the maltreatment of the German people would one day arise a great nationalist movement.[95]

Wilson's Romantic Idealism and Democratism

Paul Johnson, reflecting on the words of Winston Churchill, observes, "It is commonplace that men are excessively ruthless and cruel not as a rule out of avowed malice but from outraged righteousness. How much more is this true of legally constituted states, invested with all the seeming moral authority of parliaments and congresses and courts of justice! The destructive capacity of the individual, however vicious, is small; of the state, however well-intentioned, almost limitless."[96] In 1917 Wilson proclaimed, "Woe be to the man or group of men that seeks to stand in our way in this day of high resolution when every principle we hold dearest is to be vindicated and made secure for the salvation of the nations."[97] Did Wilson's outraged righteousness help to lead America into a war it might have avoided? And did it contribute to a "peace" that preceded another bloody and brutal world war? The limitless, abstract end calls for limitless means. It demands total war.

Wilson's statement at the conclusion of the war, that "America had the infinite privilege of fulfilling her destiny and saving the world," could hardly have contrasted more sharply with the grim reality.[98] Over 17 million had died and some 20 million were wounded. Large areas of Europe lay in ruins. Those who came of age during the war in France were referred to as the *Génération au Feu*, "Generation in Flames," and in the Anglophone world, the Lost Generation. Wilson's dream of the imminent peace and salvation of the world held such powerful sway over his imagination that it seems to have distorted his interpretation of reality. His imaginative vision did not grant the possibility that peace and democracy might not emerge at the war's conclusion or that the victory over Germany had been a pyrrhic victory. The romantic lens through which he interpreted these events gave rise to his belief that humanity's redemption was all but a fait accompli. It did not seem to enter Wilson's mind that a covenant for world peace drafted by the very actors who had helped stage the carnage might be gruesomely paradoxical.

Wilson's romantic idealism, evident in both his political writings and actions as president, is a poignant and human illustration of the democratist mindset. Not unlike Rousseau, he claimed to be the mantle-bearer of democracy for the world, but in practice he severely restricted the civil liberties of his own people and did little to contribute to democracy in other nations. Wilson believed that he had been anointed to bring democracy to the world, which manifested as a crusading idealism, a practical outcome of the type of imagination that his contemporary Babbitt calls romantic. This imagination inclines one toward "metaphysical politics," Babbitt says.[99] That is, instead of concrete political goals, it desires a type of heavenly renewal. Often uncompromising, the idyllic imagination clings to a vision of a felicitous future that is supposed "to super-vene upon the destruction of the existing order."[100] When given the opportunity, those who are motivated by what Babbitt calls a "sham vision"—a political vision that glorifies abstractions and is untethered from historical possibility—will embark, like Wilson, on political crusades. Dissatisfied with the way things are, the romantic escapes into a "land of chimeras." "[S]eeing nothing that existed worthy of my exalted feelings," Rousseau writes in his *Confessions*, "I fostered them in an ideal world which my creative imagination soon peopled with beings after my own heart."[101] The description of Wilson by one biographer could well have been written of Rousseau:

> Wilson was poetic in the romantic, exalted fashion of his time, with all its distinctive marks, its quirks, if you will. He was a man of imagination and creativity, oversensitive, passionate, and lonely in spite of all his so-cial contacts. Above all he was a man who clung ever more tightly to the phantasm of his dreams and even identified himself with it. He found his deepest peace not in reality but in his ideal, which he sought out more and more by going from poem to poem, that is, from speech to speech, approaching the perfect truth of his dream as a poet.[102]

The romantic desire to escape to a place in which people are, as Rousseau says, "celestial in their virtue and their beauty, and of reliable, tender, and faithful friends such as [are] never found here below," comforts the dreamer and at the same time makes the dreamer feel noble. This perfect idyllic vision is assumed to be moral and good even if impractical. A look at its results, however, casts doubt on its moral value. Holding out the prospect that humanity can "live in happy freedom, look each other in the eyes as equals, see that no man was put upon, that no people were forced to accept authority which was not of their own choice" is dangerous because it sets up an ideal that is unattainable in reality.[103] The farther the dream from really existing conditions, the greater the perceived need to overturn the current order, by any means necessary.

Babbitt identifies two distinct types of imagination: the "moral" or historical imagination and the "romantic" or idyllic imagination. The former values mod-eration and readily incorporates the facts of history into its imaginings about future possibilities. The latter is often uncompromising, clinging to a vision of a fantastic future. For Babbitt, politics motivated by a "sham vision" inclines toward violent imperialism when given the opportunity. It was no surprise to Babbitt that a romantic visionary like Wilson embarked on a bloody crusade in the name of democracy. Having gone from the president who declared the na-tion "too proud to fight" to the one who exhorted the nation to "Force, Force to the utmost," Wilson revealed the bitter truth of the oracle famously attributed to him: "Once lead this people into war and they'll forget there ever was such a thing as tolerance.... The spirit of ruthless brutality will enter into every fibre of our national life."[104]

Wilson believed that he was tasked with nothing less than completing Christ's work at Calvary. If the world would but heed his counsel, he could help to bestow on humanity "the full right to live and realize the purposes that God had meant them to realize."[105] His secularized theology led him finally to conclude that tremendous violence in the name of noble-sounding ideals is justified. One year after his request for a declaration of war, Wilson proclaims, "Force, Force to the utmost, Force without stint or limit, the righteous and triumphant Force which shall make Right the law of the world, and cast every selfish dominion down in the dust.... [T]he majesty and might of our concerted power shall fill the thought and utterly defeat the force of those who flout and misprize what we honor and hold dear."[106] The human and material destruction that results from policies motivated by righteous idealism ought to raise serious questions about the real worth of the ideal. Is an abstract ideal such as "making the world safe for democracy" or "ending tyranny," for example, useful even as a heuristic if it invariably necessitates the use of violence? As it becomes clear that nothing less than revolutionary change can bring about the Promised Land, the idealist feels the need to take increasingly drastic measures. This seems to have been the path that led Wilson to enter the war. His dream of global democracy did not end as he had hoped but instead resulted in death and destruction of enormous proportions in Europe and the loss of over 100,000 Americans. Power in the hands of the political idealist is rarely idle. The trajectory of Wilson's idealism should not surprise. It follows closely the logic of democratism. Thomas Carlyle said of Jacobin idealism, "Beneath this rose-colored veil of Universal Benevolence [there very often lies] a dreary void, or a dark contentious Hell-on-Earth."[107] It would seem paradoxical to argue that idealism creates an imaginative framework that leads to violence, but many historical examples, including Wilson's, suggest that a logic of coercion is inherent.

Jacques Maritain

Catholicism under the Influence of Democratism

Introduction

After the Second World War, the social gospel and other forms of progressivism that shaped Wilsonian thinking about the war and the future found new expression in America, usually in more obviously secular forms, and in Europe. This was the case, paradoxically perhaps, even in Catholic thought. A prominent example of this tendency is the writings of Jacques Maritain, one of the most respected Catholic philosophers of the modern age. Rousseau and various progressives who have contributed to the evolution of democratism have been deeply suspicious of, even hostile to the Catholic Church and its intellectual traditions. That a person who is widely seen as a leading Catholic intellectual might be attracted to the same kind of thinking about democracy and human nature is a telling sign of its pervasiveness in the Western world and perhaps even indicative of the Catholic faith being transformed under its influence. Despite Maritain's apparent resistance to messianic ideology as well as his sustained criticism of Rousseau's *Social Contract* and of contemporary totalitarian regimes, he nonetheless entertains visions of an earthly paradise of the brotherhood of man under the aegis of democracy—an idea that is central to democratism.

Given the prolificacy of Maritain's writings, one cannot undertake an exhaustive analysis of this complex thinker in a single chapter. Maritain's thought as a whole is not easily classified. It contains disparate elements, some of which appear contradictory. The main purpose here is not to sort out the different lines of thought in his work or to offer a rounded estimate of his contribution. As in previous chapters, the emphasis will be on dimensions of thought of most interest to this study. Without ignoring other aspects of Maritain's philosophy, attention will be concentrated on the prominent ingredient of democratic enchantment in his work. This chapter carefully examines Maritain's hope for a revived Christian

The Ideology of Democratism. Emily B. Finley, Oxford University Press. © Oxford University Press 2022.
DOI: 10.1093/oso/9780197642290.003.0005

civilization in the postwar period and focuses attention on his mature political work *Man and the State* (1951). In particular, it analyzes Maritain's vision of global democracy, one that is sustained by a philosophy of history that imagines as a culminating moment the transformation of political life on a global scale. Maritain anticipates the development of a democratic order in which people live in peace and justice and through which they will ultimately construct an ideal civilization distinguished from all others by its social, political, and spiritual harmony. For Maritain, the experience of the totalitarian regimes of the twentieth century was central to the development of this idea. Witnessing the evils that the grand ideological systems wrought, Maritain was convinced that the time had come when the world would at last recognize Christian democracy as the one form of government most in keeping with human nature and the transcendent moral order.

Democracy, for Maritain, is not only most desirable in the abstract but historically necessary. Given that Maritain is, perhaps in other ways, within the neo-Scholastic Catholic tradition, it is certainly tempting to view his political thought as a species of conservatism geared toward checking the moral and spiritual degeneracy of modernity. Indeed, his argument in *The Person and the Common Good* (1947) may be profitably viewed in this light. However, a careful reading of *Man and the State*, in conjunction with a comparative look at other figures in the democratist tradition, necessitates a reevaluation. Some of Maritain's underlying assumptions about human nature and the possibilities and limits of Christianity as a civilizing force in history raise suspicion. Some of the guiding assumptions about human nature behind Maritain's philosophy of democracy are remarkably similar to those of Rousseau.

Maritain breathed new life, especially for Catholics, into many of the democratist ideas disseminated in America and Europe in earlier generations. He worked to revise the Catholic and Christian aversion to political idealism, specifically democratic idealism. His political philosophy may in fact be the first systematic attempt to reconcile Catholicism and Christianity more broadly with democracy. His political works were so influential that they inspired the formation of many of the Christian Democratic parties in Europe and Latin America in the twentieth century, and his involvement in the drafting and advancement of the Universal Declaration of Human Rights demonstrates just how significant was his international political influence.

Maritain's vision of global peace and democracy is, like Wilson's, imbued with Christian language and symbolism. There are obvious differences between Wilson and Maritain, such as the latter's willingness to acknowledge man's sinfulness, but their similarities betray an underlying commitment to a shared political theology, a variant of democratism. Perhaps more as a result of the developing zeitgeist than because of deep philosophical or religious kinship, the two nonetheless exhibit largely compatible political theories expressed in a common language. For both of these men, as for other democratists, democracy represents the fulfillment of history and even Christian revelation.

For Maritain, as for many others, liberal democracy is by definition something other than ideology.[1] Examining his conception of democracy, however, raises the distinct possibility that even so-called liberal democracy, if it is understood in a particular way, can have the characteristics of a thoroughgoing ideology. For obvious reasons, the term "ideology" acquired a pejorative connotation in the twentieth century, partly through the contributions of figures such as Maritain who recognized the dangerous, totalizing aspects of political movements such as Bolshevism and Nazism. But ideology can exist in a variety of forms and may have the appearance of being *non*ideological despite being systematic and doctrinally elaborate. Maritain's philosophy of democracy would seem to qualify as this type of ideology and fits well within the democratist framework that this book outlines and identifies. There need not be a single manifesto or political treatise detailing its tenets for a political worldview to qualify as an ideology. Indeed Marx's *Communist Manifesto* is the exception rather than the rule.

Maritain's Christian Genealogy of Democracy

Although approaching it from different perspectives, Jefferson, Wilson, and Maritain arrive at a similar philosophy of history, in which liberal democracy represents the apex of political as well as social and moral achievement. As one would expect, the Enlightenment naturally influenced Jefferson, and the role of Progressivism influenced Wilson, but Maritain employs an ostensibly Christian genealogy to explain and justify the rise of modern democracy. Democracy is the result of the evolution of Christianity from the sacral to the temporal realm, he argues. The Middle Ages represented a sacral age, in which Church and politics were undifferentiated. The modern age is a secular age in which the sacral and temporal realms have split. For Maritain, the modern democratic age is superior to the Middle Ages insofar as that spiritual differentiation has inspired a widespread recognition of human dignity and freedom.[2] While Maritain laments the fact of modern religious division, he accepts this misfortune as necessary to democratic progress.

Maritain's position on the historical development of democracy may be called religiously deterministic. He attributes the unfolding of democracy to providential design and the work of the gospel in history. "Democracy," writes Maritain, "is the only way through which the progressive energies in human history do pass."[3] It is only through gospel inspiration, however, "that democracy can progressively carry out its momentous task of the moral rationalization of political life."[4] By this Maritain means that there will be widespread "recognition of the essentially human ends of political life, and of its deepest springs: justice, law, and mutual friendship" and "a ceaseless effort to make the living, moving structures and organs of the body politic serve the common good, the dignity of the person, and the sense of fraternal love."[5] Because democracy is the only system of government that legally and rationally recognizes freedom, Maritain says that "we may appreciate . . . the crucial importance of the survival and improvement of democracy for the evolution and earthly destiny of mankind."[6]

Like Wilson and Rousseau, and to a lesser extent Jefferson, Maritain places great hope in the ability of the democratic political system to solve, once and for all, social and political challenges. In this sense, all of these thinkers are deeply antipolitical. Politics for Maritain and other democratists is not an ongoing challenge, a series of compromises, negotiations, and problem-solving. The Rousseauean, democratist vision of democracy expects essentially an end to the ceaseless struggle for the common good that has challenged humanity since the dawn of social existence and been the subject of study for philosophers through the ages. Plato was perhaps the first thinker to imagine an end to politics with his *Republic*, but Maritain at times puts himself in the same tradition. Partly for this reason, democratism nearly always takes on a religious dimension. It is to be found in the civil religion that grounds Rousseau's democratic theory, in Jefferson's religious reading of historical events, in Wilson's Christian interpretation of the war, and here in an ostensibly Catholic philosophy of democracy. Politics is an art, but religion proclaims eternal truths and calls its believers to look beyond an apparent reality and toward a transformed existence in the transcendent. The democratist understanding of democracy is of much the same character. Maritain represents particularly well this dimension of democratism, as he tries to unite the transcendent aspect of Christianity with mundane political existence.

"Personalist Democracy"

Maritain is careful to distinguish between different types of democracy, identifying false democracy or bourgeois and individualist democracy; totalitarian democracy, which rejects liberal ideas and treats citizens as slaves; and "personalist democracy." The former two do not promote the common good or treat citizens with dignity. True democracy, on the other hand, is not based on "childish greed, jealousy, selfishness, pride and guile . . . but instead on a grown-up awareness of the innermost needs of mankind's life, of the real requirements of peace and love, and of the moral and spiritual energies of man."[7] Maritain's various characterizations of "personalist democracy"—the "democratic charter," the "democratic secular faith," and more generally the democratic "state of mind"—tend to be rather diffuse, but at the heart of this normative concept of democracy is the requirement of universal "brotherly love." Maritain shares the romantic belief that the gospel command to "love thy neighbor" is a general exhortation to "love mankind." Brotherly love, Maritain says, must "overflow the bounds of the social group to extend to the entire human race." Sensitive to history's examples of state-sanctioned "brotherly love" quickly becoming "brotherhood or death," he is careful to explain that the gospel or transcendent understanding of brotherhood must take precedence.[8]

A fraternal sentiment for our fellow human beings is written on our hearts, Maritain believes, and spontaneously emerges from shared human experience, especially emotionally charged experience. Together in "great catastrophes, in humiliation and distress," as well as in "the sweetness of a great joy," human beings realize their brotherhood and equality.[9] In this respect, Maritain shares the moral-spiritual sensibility of Rousseau, who believes that "pity" or compassion is the bonding agent of social and civil life. In general, democratism is oriented by this romantic ethic; compassion and a sense of fraternal love dramatically overshadow original sin, if such a thing even exists, and when allowed to flow freely, translate politically into democracy. This view might be contrasted with that of earlier Christian thinkers in the traditions of Christian realism and Thomism who believe that the sinfulness of human beings is formidable and is an obstacle to lasting peace and the common good. Good government depends on the quality of character of those in power and the constitutional makeup of the people. Democracy is not necessarily a better form of government if its leaders and people are rotten, they would say. Maritain's contemporary and fellow Catholic Heinrich Rommen, while supposedly operating from within the same tradition as Maritain, arrives at a conclusion more in line with the thought of earlier Christian philosophers as well as the classical thinker Aristotle that the best type of government cannot be determined in the abstract. Discussion about the best form of government must appreciate fully a nation's "geographic location, its economic basis of life, its national traditions, its particular cultural development, and all other such elements that establish the nation's individuality," Rommen says.[10]

A New Christian Equality

The concept of brotherhood for Maritain is informed by his understanding of equality, which represents a similar departure from the orthodox Christian understanding. Maritain defines equality as "the natural love of the human being for his own kind which reveals and makes real the unity of species among men."[11]

Just as we have an instinct for brotherhood, human beings also have a natural or "primary" instinct for feelings of equality. Asserting that other, competing instincts such as pride and envy are secondary to feelings of benevolence and fraternity, Maritain distances himself from the older Augustinian and Thomist beliefs about the centrality of original sin and the perpetual need to overcome selfish behaviors.[12] For Augustine especially, sins such as pride and envy constantly threaten the social order.

On the one hand, Maritain disavows "idealist egalitarianism" that "wish[es] that all inequality among [human beings] should disappear." Instead, equality in the true sense, as understood by "Christian realism," should include "those fruitful inequalities, whereby the multitude of individuals participates in the common treasure of humanity, should develop themselves."[13] On the other hand, however, Maritain concludes, "The community of essence is of greater importance than individual differences; the root is more important than the branches."[14] Without a careful reading of his philosophy, it is easy to gloss over some of Maritain's conclusions and assume that he is a traditionalist. While giving a nod to the older idea of the inescapability of innate differences in human beings, Maritain nonetheless concludes that a "community of essence" ultimately eclipses individuality. Is a "community of essence" something akin to Rousseau's general will? It seems to convey the same idea of a moral will that is shared by all citizens. This is an idea much more in line with the social gospel than with traditional Catholic thought, and it easily fits within the democratist paradigm. The difference between Maritain's understanding of equality and that of thinkers such as Augustine and Aquinas becomes even more pronounced in Maritain's belief that equality requires that "natural inequalities be compensated for by a process of organic redistribution."[15] It is "just or equitable," Maritain says, "that individuals should receive in proportion not to their needs or desires, which tend to become infinite, but to the necessities of their life and development, the means for putting to use their natural gifts."[16] Again, it is possible to read such a statement in a conservative light, which would hold that attempting to fulfill the infinite desires of its citizens is certainly impossible and also that some basic human needs ought to be met. But Maritain is calling on the *state* to ensure a certain *material* equality among citizens that would in addition promote their spiritual well-being. The older Christian idea of the state did not envision it acting as a vehicle to salvation or spiritual betterment. Material conditions should be irrelevant to salvation, the Church taught. According to a more traditional Christian perspective, for the state to be tasked with providing for the "necessities" of "life and development" would be to give it broad, practically unlimited power to determine what constitutes social welfare. Maritain's preoccupation with the role of the state in promoting material prosperity and equality is a radical departure from earlier Catholic political thought, which focused on the state only as it applied to the Church's mission of saving souls. In this respect, Maritain is in the same tradition as many secular, liberal thinkers and progressives, from Wilson to John Rawls.

Liberalism and Catholicism

Maritain injects a material understanding of equality into an earlier, more spiritual Christian notion. For Maritain, the redistribution of wealth is actually required to create or maintain equality even in the Christian sense. This is a decided reorientation of the Christian mission and its traditional philosophy of equality. Equality can be understood only in a spiritual sense, according to the older Christian view. Erik Von Kuehnelt-Leddihn represents the earlier Catholic position. He was alarmed by the tide of the progressive social gospel sweeping America in the twentieth century and transforming Christianity under its influence. In particular, he cautioned against misusing the term "equality" in connection with Christian doctrine:

> Christianity was by no means egalitarian, but merely established new values and new (physical as well as metaphysical) hierarchies. Human equality, theologically analyzed, is restricted to the equality of souls in the very beginning of their existence; but this equality is not continuous throughout a person's lifetime. Potentiality and actuality should not be confused. The spiritual equality of two new-born babes in the sight of God is merely a 'start.' Judas Iscariot expiring in the noose and St. John the Evangelist closing his eyes on Patmos are spiritually not equals.[17]

Maritain, on the other hand, writes that the state owes the Church the "material task" of the "promotion of prosperity, the equitable distribution of the material things that are the support of human dignity." He goes so far as to say that in so doing, the state contributes to "the spiritual interest of the Church."[18]

Maritain's attempts to blend Catholicism with the "democratic secular faith" often involve argumentation that is not only incompatible with traditional Catholic beliefs but also at times internally inconsistent. On the one hand, Maritain recognizes the inevitability of inequalities among persons and even says that those inequalities ought to be channeled in fruitful ways, but on the other hand he calls for leveling of the material sort. He says that universal brotherhood ought not devolve into coercion, but he believes that the state can promote feelings of equality, even the Church's mission to save souls, through material redistribution.

The Papacy and the Democratic Welfare State

There is a great deal of overlap between Maritain's thinking and that of secular liberal thinkers. Like Rawls, Maritain's philosophy pretends that something like the modern welfare state is natural and inevitable. With other secular democratists, Maritain believes that a spiritual-intellectual awakening of the population can bring about a "new age of civilization," with democracy at its foundation and in which broad "rights of the human being in his social, economic, and cultural functions" will be recognized. This includes everything from the right to employment and to unionize to having a share in "economic life," a just wage sufficient for a family, unemployment relief, sick benefits, social security, and "the elementary goods, both material and spiritual, of civilization . . . free of charge."[19] In this respect Maritain represents a decisive break with the older Catholic tradition, which stressed spiritual over material goods. Aquinas, to be sure, considered the duty of the better-off to be charitable to the needs of the poor. He even said that whatever the rich have in superabundance is due to the poor, according to natural law. In defending the rights of the destitute, Aquinas quotes St. Ambrose: "It is the hungry man's bread that you withhold, the naked man's cloak that you store away, the money that you bury in the earth is the price of the poor man's ransom and freedom."[20] But it would not have occurred to Aquinas, Ambrose, or others in the older Christian tradition to look to the state or secular authorities to compel charity.

In the twentieth century, the idea of the democratic welfare state as a Christian imperative percolated all the way to the top. Pope Paul VI's encyclical *Gaudium et Spes*, promulgated in 1965, reveals a strong continuity with Maritain's understanding of personalist democracy, the need for material equality, and a distinctly secular understanding of human rights. The encyclical makes use throughout of the Rousseauean ideas of a "brotherhood of men," "the whole human family," "the destiny of the human community," and the "universal community." Despite Paul's use of such ethereal, abstract descriptors, he considered this whole community to be real and growing more enlightened by the day, although faced with new threats: "Never before has man had so keen an understanding of freedom yet at the same time new forms of social and psychological slavery make their appearance."[21] What Paul has in mind are certain preoccupations with the historical particularities of existence that tend to distinguish one person from another rather than forge bonds of sameness and equality. These parochial concerns, he says, are ultimately grounded in human sinfulness. It is therefore imperative that the human race work to advance universal rights and democracy and to do so without undo attachments to outmoded national distinctions. Like Maritain, Paul imagines that there is one destiny for the entire human race, and the irresistible force of providential history moves all nations, albeit at different paces, in the same direction. Paul shared Maritain's response to the historical predicament of the postwar period by calling for the broad implementation of political rights that overlap with those of the modern welfare state: "There must be made available to all men everything necessary for leading a life truly human, such as food, clothing, and shelter; the right to choose a state of life freely and to found a family, the right to education, to employment, to a good reputation, to respect, to appropriate information, to activity in accord with the upright norm of one's own conscience, to protection of privacy and rightful freedom even in matters religious."[22]

Paul's predecessor Pope John XXIII expressed similar views in the encyclical *Pacem in Terris* (1963). John wrote that the "rights of man" ought to include "security in cases of sickness, inability to work, widowhood, old age, unemployment, or in any other case in which he is deprived of the means of subsistence through no fault of his own." Each has the right to "respect for his person, to his good reputation; the right to freedom in searching for truth and in expressing and communicating his opinions. . . . The natural law also gives man the right to share in the benefits of culture, and therefore the right to a basic education and to technical and professional training," to "higher studies," to "choose freely the state of life which [human beings] prefer," to healthy working conditions, to a "standard of living in keeping with the dignity of the human person," to private property, to assembly and association, to freedom of movement within one's own country and to "emigrate to other countries and take up residence there" when justice requires it.[23] Human beings are becoming increasingly enlightened and ever "conscious of their human dignity": "There will soon no longer exist a world divided into nations that rule others and nations that are subject to others." Even concepts like borders and national distinctions will become fluid, as men across the globe "will soon have . . . [the] rank of citizens in independent nations."[24] This is due as much to rational progress as to the "progress of moral conscience."[25] Although different in other ways, Maritain, John XXIII, and Paul VI share with Karl Marx the broad assumption that through politics, the historical dialectic is moving societies inexorably toward spiritual and material fulfillment.[26]

Maritain, John XXIII, and Paul VI stand in contrast in important ways with John Paul II, whose response to modern social and political problems emphasizes another side of Catholic social teaching. At first glance, Maritain appears to have much in common with John Paul, who was similarly a staunch opponent of totalitarianism and saw the need to ground political order in the transcendent, but John Paul was no political universalist and did not believe that it was the Church's place to offer "technical solutions" to what are ultimately political problems. "The Church does not propose economic and political systems or programs," he says, "nor does she show preference for one or the other, provided that human dignity is properly respected and promoted, and provided she herself is allowed the room she needs to exercise her ministry in the world."[27] John Paul was in the Augustinian tradition in this respect. He believed strongly in economic and political rights and hoped that the human condition on earth could be ameliorated by beneficial public policies, but he never advocated for one single form of government, and he seemed to sense in such a desire the presence of ideological thinking about democracy: "Democracy cannot be idolized to the point of making it a substitute for morality or a panacea for immorality. Fundamentally, democracy is a 'system' and as such is a means and not an end. . . . Even in participatory systems of government, the regulation of interests often occurs to the advantage of the most powerful, since they are the ones most capable of manoeuvering not only the levers of power but also of shaping the formation of consensus. In such a situation, democracy easily becomes an empty word."[28]

Maritain's Idea of Innerworldly Redemption

For Maritain, as for many others who share his democratist disposition, true democracy is just around the corner, following the widespread observance of new political practices and ways of thinking, possibly accompanied by a major destructive event, such as war. Maritain expresses a quintessential democratist belief when he says, "The tragedy of the modern democracies is that they have not yet succeeded in realizing democracy."[29] According to democratism, historical democracies have always fallen short of "real" democracy. Like Wilson, Maritain was convinced that a more genuine form of democracy was about to replace the old, broken democracies of the West. Both Wilson and Maritain interpreted global war as portending an apocalyptic, world-historic moment that would fundamentally alter the conditions of human life. According to Maritain:

> [If] the struggle of those who are fighting Nazism and its satellites is not truly animated by an heroic ideal of the liberation of human life, and if victory is not to bring about the foundations of a world reorganization which enlists men's efforts in a common task dominated by such an ideal, civilization will have escaped from the imminent threat of destruction only to embark on a period of chaos, when, after having militarily wiped out Fascism and Nazism, it will run the risk of being morally conquered by their substitutes. . . . It is from this work that we may expect a transforming power. The creation of a new world will not be the work of the war but the force of vision and will and of the

energies of intellectual and moral reform which will have developed in the collective conscience and in the responsible leaders.[30]

Like Wilson, Maritain seems not to appreciate the paradox of imagining that the leaders responsible for generating a new world order could be the same ones who orchestrated the war in the first place. But for whatever role such leaders might play, the direction and character of the new age to come would be forged literally on the battlefield. "The war will not be truly won," writes Maritain, "unless during the war itself a new world takes shape which will emerge in victory—and in which the classes, races and nations today oppressed will be liberated."[31] Through a process of destruction and regeneration, a general purification of thought and action will occur, and the new democratic order will emerge on a global scale.[32]

Such views place Maritain, and by extension a line of papal thought that thrusts in the same direction, in the company of other democratists as well as political millenarians dating back to the Protestant Reformation. Apparently influenced by the utopianism of the Book of Revelation, these figures were captured by the prospect of a new earth, "the holy city, a new Jerusalem," which will appear in the wake of great and terrible destruction.[33] Unlike many in this tradition, however, Maritain does not envision the disappearance of political life altogether. While a purified democracy will rise from widespread recognition of its moral superiority, it will still require guidance by political leaders who are committed to the "democratic creed," as he calls it. As with religious creeds, the democratic creed would require protection from "political heretics" who would threaten "freedom and the practical secular faith expressed in the democratic charter."[34] One of the general characteristics of democratism is the indispensable role of a cadre of enlightened experts who are charged with, among other tasks, the development of a system of public education whose curriculum will act as a social and political preservative for the regime.

In the final section of *Man and the State* Maritain presents a vision of world government and describes the types of leaders who will craft it. Not unlike Wilson, he believes that the peace settlement would be the opportunity for an intellectual and moral vanguard to engineer a new democratic world order. The "ultimate solution" to man's historical and political predicament heretofore fraught with conflict, suffering, inequality, and oppression is a system of global governance composed of a universally respected leadership class.[35] Like the American system, it would comprise legislative, executive, and judicial branches. Maritain refers to the governing body as a "world council" and "senate of wise men."[36] He stipulates that the senators would be stripped of national citizenship to ensure loyalty to no particular people or place. A comparison might be made with the section in Rousseau's *Social Contract* in which he says that local attachments must be sundered to facilitate the general will. Like Rousseau's legislator, Maritain's senate would "give a voice to the conscience of the peoples" and provide "organized international opinion."[37] It would enact the general will of the world—a will, says Maritain, that is for freedom.

The Material Dialectic of Democracy

Human beings will come together to live in a global community because they will recognize the common goal of humanity, which is to live in freedom and brotherhood. While this realization is already coming to pass, it will not endure without a global desire "strong enough to entail a will to share in certain common sufferings made inevitable by the task, and by the common good of world-wide society."[38] Maritain's thought here bears an uncanny resemblance to the materialist philosophy of Marxism-Leninism that emphasizes the role of struggle in the historical dialectic. Maritain believes that realizing a world-historic ideal of Democracy requires great sacrifice. Through "moral heroism," he says, human beings can work to equalize material conditions. For example, Westerners can assent to the lowering of their standard of living in order to raise that of those living in the Soviet Union. And after global government is established, material conditions will naturally equalize: "The very existence of a world-wide society will also inevitably imply a certain—relative no doubt, yet quite serious and appreciable—equalization of the standards of life of all individuals."[39] These economic changes will be accompanied by tectonic shifts in political life. This global reorganization—a "new creation of human reason"[40]—will "inevitably imply deep changes in the social and economic structures of the national and international life of people," especially those "attached to profit-making."[41]

This brings to mind an image that Marx presents in the *Communist Manifesto*, that the forces of capitalism disrupt the very economic system from which it sprang. The bourgeoisie will become obsolete under the crushing weight of the social, economic, and cultural changes that their class wrought. Marx predicts that the natural result of these changes and corresponding displacement will be a trend toward centralization and globalization, a conclusion Maritain reaches.[42] Pope Paul VI also writes of the "evolution" of modern material conditions and attendant social disruptions. Globalism will bring about "more thorough changes every day" for "traditional local communities such as families, clans, tribes, villages, [and] various groups and associations," but these changes are necessary, he says, for fulfilling "the destiny of the human community."[43]

In *Integral Humanism*, Maritain acknowledges Marx's "profound intuition" about the alienating and dehumanizing tendencies of the modern capitalist system. He hopes, however, that Christianity can take Marx's intuition, which is "pregnant with Judeo-Christian values," and save it from the atheist philosophy that underlies it.[44] Maritain criticizes Marx's philosophy for its professed atheism and for espousing a "radical realist immanentism."[45] For Marx, according to Maritain, the solution to man's experience of alienation in the capitalist system is to accomplish the Promethean task of replacing God with Man and transforming existence for ourselves. Maritain says that liberation for Marx "is in the name of collective man, in order that in his collective life and in the free discharge of his collective work he may find an absolute deliverance ... and in a word deify within himself the titanism of human nature."[46] Its atheism is the source of communism's evils, but its idea of communion, Maritain says, is at the heart of Christianity. While communion inspires communism, communism alienates the Christian virtues that would sustain genuine communion: "[I]t is the spirit of faith and of sacrifice, it is the religious energies of the soul which Communism endeavors to drain off for its own uses, and these it needs in order to subsist."[47] The political ideology of communism is ultimately incompatible with religious faith, for that faith must be channeled into politics and into the earthly task of building utopia.

Maritain argues that Marx's atheism ultimately undermines the pursuit of meaningful community in his theory, but is it enough for Maritain to profess the need for Christianity to "ground" politics when he shares Marx's philosophy of history and even, to an extent, philosophy of materialism? Maritain's vision of earthly renewal founded in a new brotherhood of humanity resembles Marx's broad outline of the same idea. Are the differences between the two visions on these major points substantive or merely rhetorical? Maritain articulates a vision of international brotherhood, freedom, and equality that is to be accomplished through major socioeconomic reorganization at the hands of a knowing vanguard, aided by what is nothing other than a secular political faith—the "democratic creed." Because Maritain's language and sentiment are peppered with references to Christianity, it is tempting to interpret his political philosophy as being in keeping with traditional Christianity. But his fixation on the material, and especially the desire to level material conditions, suggests that Maritain has diverged sharply from the older, orthodox version of Christianity that he purports to be representing. Such a focus on the material and political must come at the expense of the spiritual and, worse, at times spiritualizes the political—a charge Maritain laid on Marxism. Under the auspices of Christian "democracy," Maritain seems to be a major contributor to a new political ideology not so different from the one he repudiates.

Democratic Vanguardism

Nothing can force the dialectic of Christian democracy. The final stage of history will simply unfold—an assertion that Marx makes about socialism. On the other hand, Maritain believes that a revolution and central planning can speed the historical process.[48] One of the paradoxes of democratism is that while it professes the will of the people sovereign, its theory requires an elite to alert the people to their true will.[49] Experts must stimulate an "awakening [of] common consciousness," Maritain says, to the value of the democratic creed as he envisions it. The element of vanguardism within his philosophy presents a problem of authority that reflects that same problem for democratism in general. This is a paradox that Maritain never quite resolves. True authority rests only with God, he contends, and so even the people are not sovereign in the final sense. Practically and politically, though, only the people and their designated agents have the political authority to rule.[50] Yet neither God nor the people appear to be sovereign according to Maritain's theory. A global senate is tasked with encouraging the historical "process of maturation." Maritain, like Jefferson, admires "the stock and resource of humanity in those who toil close to nature," but he believes that the simple folk are in need of guidance.[51] "Large portions of humanity," Maritain says, "remain in a state of immaturity or suffer from morbid complexes accumulated in the course of time and are still no more than the rough draft or the preparation of that fruit of civilization which we call a people."[52] Certain "prophets of the people" have a duty to wake the people, who "as a rule prefer to sleep."[53] Maritain's examples of these types of prophets are revealing. The fathers of the French Revolution and of the American Constitution—specifically "men like Tom Paine or Thomas Jefferson"—are the first two in a short list (that also includes John Brown, the originators of the Italian Risorgimento and the liberation of Ireland, and Gandhi).[54] Maritain seems not to consider that the violent persecution of Christians and attempts to eradicate traditional religion during the French Revolution suggest not just theoretical but real incompatibility between the "democratic mentality" he sees in the Revolution and lauds in Christianity. It may be no coincidence that Paine was an atheist and Jefferson a suspected one. These political leaders often tried to "awaken" the people to a new mode of political existence that they hoped would replace traditional religion.

In the end, Maritain, like so many other democratists, is uncomfortable with the people as they are. He often proclaims the sovereignty of the people, but he has a clear normative vision in mind that sees the need to overturn existing practices and beliefs. His language of the "immaturity" of the people and their being a "rough draft" of a real body politic indicates that, in the end, Maritain lacks faith in.

The Secular Faith of Democratism and Modern Gnosticism

Maritain argues that the "democratic impulse" is the "temporal manifestation of the inspiration of the Gospel." The "democratic faith" cannot be "justified, nurtured, strengthened, and enriched without philosophical or religious convictions," but those convictions may be of the secular variety.[55] In this respect, Rawls's secular philosophy of liberal democracy has received unexpected help from Maritain's thought. In the introduction to UNESCO's *Human Rights* publication, Maritain writes, "Agreement between minds can be reached spontaneously, not on the basis of common speculative ideas, but on common practical ideas, not on the affirmation of one and the same conception of the world, of man and of knowledge, but upon the affirmation of a single body of beliefs for guidance in action."[56] This is an idea that would inform the work of Rawls, one of the twentieth century's most influential political philosophers.

One author points out, "Like Rawls, Maritain acknowledges the fact of religious pluralism and the right of individual conscience. Thus, the only just consensus in a pluralistic democracy is one based upon practical, not philosophical, adherence to strictly temporal values."[57] The difference, this author points out, is that "Maritain insists that these temporal values are in essence the embodiment of the transcendent spirit of the Gospel into the immanent affairs of men."[58] Maritain says that "the Christian political society which we are discussing would be aware of the fact that Christian truths and incentives and the inspiration of the Gospel, awakening common consciousness and passing into the sphere of temporal existence, are the very soul, inner strength, and spiritual stronghold of democracy."[59] A Catholic and an atheist, Maritain contends, while disagreeing on philosophical and religious beliefs, can still agree on the fundamentals of a liberal political order. Rawls would agree.

This idea raises some important questions about the real role of Christianity or religion in politics. Is it necessary to democracy, as Maritain maintains? Democratic consensus can be reached on purely secular grounds through reason alone. "In other words," one scholar and contemporary of Maritain, Aurel Kolnai, acerbically points out, "our most important beliefs and thoughts are quite irrelevant to our most important task in earthly life; each of us may quietly worship his own preferred Allah or Christ or Idea or Matter or History in his own private tin chapel, while all of us jointly build, in cheerful harmony, the huge world-wide Temple of Civilization—the one thing that really matters."[60] Kolnai argues that a Thomist should be especially sensitive to the fact that "men's 'practical' preferences and schemes are closely conditioned and intimately molded by their 'speculative' views. . . . [A] 'practical' agreement without a 'speculative' one is a wooden iron, though the 'speculative' presuppositions held in common may be merely implicit and unformulated."[61] In other words, ideas matter, especially deeply held religious and philosophical views. According to Kolnai, a working consensus that is not based on shared convictions is ultimately untenable. Maritain's discussion of the political "leavening" effect of the gospel notwithstanding, Christianity is superfluous if a democratic consensus can be reached without it, and, moreover, Maritain unwittingly suggests that traditional Christianity may actually be a hindrance to the competing secular religion of the state. For Maritain, Kolnai says, "the 'practical' aim of 'creating' a manmade paradise on earth, is all-important. For this higher realization of the real core of Christianity, Catholic 'motives' are worth just as much as any other 'motives' so long as they subserve the one true and operative religion of humanism."[62]

Is Kolnai being too harsh on Maritain, or is Maritain's attempt to reconcile Christianity with a secular philosophy of democracy ultimately contributing to the rise of Christianity's substitute? Democratism often resembles a religion in its profession of an orthodox democratic creed, its censure of heretics, theology of the general will, and millenarian beliefs about a golden age of freedom and equality that will follow a mass awakening. Maritain's political philosophy, although ostensibly Christian, often exhibits the traits of this ersatz religion. He believes that Christians can "transform the world temporally," thereby altering human existence. Indeed it is a Christian duty, Maritain asserts.[63] The Christian's temporal mission is "to *intervene* in the destiny of the world, winning at great pains and at the risk of a thousand dangers—through science and through social and political action—a power over nature and a power over history, but remaining, whatever he does, more than ever a *subordinate* agent: servant of divine providence and activator or 'free associate' of an evolution he does not direct as a master, and which he also serves insofar as it develops according to the laws of nature and the laws of history."[64]

Does the final emphasis, for Maritain, lie on God's authorship of the world or on the human effort to win "a power over nature and a power over history"? It is possible to view such an exhortation as a modern expression of the ancient gnostic (from "knowledge") heresy, which Eric Voegelin says animates liberal progressivism and romantic conservatism alike. Dissatisfaction with social and political reality and the belief that human beings can fundamentally change existence through social reorganization is at the core of modern gnostic thinking for Voegelin. The gnostic acts as the prophet who unveils the ideological formula "to alter the structure of the world, which is perceived as inadequate." The gnostic quest is to bring about worldly salvation—"the immanentization of the Christian idea of perfection."[65] Maritain attempts to distance himself from modern gnostics like Marx, pointing out the permanent existence of good and evil in history and the fact that perfection is possible only in the Kingdom of God, but his belief in the culmination of history in global democracy closely resembles Marx's belief in the historical inevitability of global communism. History, according to Maritain, progresses and tends "unknowingly toward the kingdom of God, but [is] incapable in itself of reaching this final term"—not because the Kingdom of God is not of this world but because human beings must intervene.[66] Marx similarly contends that history progresses through stages toward communism, but revolution is ultimately required to bring about the final phase. For Maritain, the Christian must similarly revolutionize the world:

> to make the earthly city more just and less inhuman, to assure to every one the goods basically needed for the life of the body and the spirit, as well as the respect, in each one, of the rights of the human person; to lead peoples to a supra-national political organization capable of guaranteeing peace in the world—in short, to cooperate with the evolution of the world in such a way that the earthly hope of men in the Gospel should not be frustrated, and the spirit of Christ and of his kingdom would in some fashion vivify worldly things themselves.[67]

Although he sometimes says that Christ and the gospel are ultimately responsible for bringing about a new political existence, Maritain nonetheless believes that human beings are capable of creating a world that very much resembles the kingdom of God. This is a core belief of gnosticism as well as democratism. The idea that human beings can have power over nature and history and can fundamentally transform reality is, according to Voegelin, partly inspired by a desire to dominate, partly inspired by Christianity itself, which places a heavy burden of faith and uncertainty on the believer. Voegelin writes, "The reality of being as it is known in its truth by Christianity is difficult to bear, and the flight from clearly seen reality to gnostic constructs will probably always be a phenomenon of wide extent in civilizations that Christianity has permeated."[68] To determine the extent to which Maritain conforms to Voegelin's definition of gnosticism is beyond the scope of this study. What does seem beyond question is that his proclivity for democratist thinking pulls him strongly in the direction of gnosticism, which like democratism follows an ideological structure. At least in this respect, Maritain emphatically rejects St. Augustine's distinction between the Earthly City and the City of God. For Maritain, the two may be brought together through human will.

A Competing View of Christianity and Democracy

Maritain's attempt to merge Christianity with democracy sometimes gives the impression that the two are nearly identical in their basic beliefs and that to be a good Christian, one must also be a good democrat. But Orestes Brownson, an American Catholic political thinker writing a century before Maritain, demonstrates that admiration of democracy on the part of Catholics need not entail the embrace of democracy as a law of history, culminating in a world socialist state. Brownson defended liberal democracy at a time when the official Church teaching rejected the separation of church and state and called for an establishment state (although the Church was willing to tolerate religious liberty for reasons of stability and expediency). Brownson esteemed the American republic, with its pluralist and democratic traditions, yet this admiration never extended to a call for democracy for the rest of the globe. Such a move, in fact, would have been "as unstatesmanlike as unjust," Brownson declared.[69] The national will of a country may establish any number of legitimate political orders: "The nation, as sovereign, is free to constitute government according to its own judgment, under any form it please—monarchical, aristocratic, democratic, or mixed. . . . Any of these forms and systems, and many others besides, are or may be legitimate, if established and maintained by the national will. There is nothing in the law of God or of nature, antecedently to the national will, that gives any one of them a right to the exclusion of any one of the others."[70]

It can be argued that Brownson is much closer than Maritain to Thomistic political philosophy. Aquinas, following Aristotle, believed that when a tyranny at least produces stability, there is something to commend in it, and it ought to be tolerated for the time. "The only form or system [of government] that is necessarily illegal is the despotic," and even that, Brownson says, must sometimes be peaceably tolerated as "a matter of prudence."[71] Aquinas believed that the best regime is one that balances the elements of monarchy, aristocracy, and democracy—a virtue that Brownson sees in the American system. Yet Aquinas did not advocate a universal system for all times and all places. Brownson would agree with Aquinas that the best regime must be one that is practicable, which means that it must work for a particular people and place, not simply appear to be the best in the abstract. Rommen similarly believes that the value of all regimes "is functionally dependent on the actual service they afford in the actual circumstances to the realization of the common good." Therefore, "neither hereditary monarchy, 'sanctified through its old traditional continuity through centuries,' nor representative democracy can claim an exclusive legitimacy on the basis of natural or divine law and in its name."[72] Brownson holds a similar view: the American system is the "best and only practicable government for the United States, but it is impracticable everywhere else, and all attempts by any European or other American state to introduce it can end only in disaster."[73] Rommen condemns the American priest Isaac Hecker, founder of the Paulist Fathers, for this reason. Hecker argued that "the specific form of democracy as represented in the American Constitution is everywhere and always an unsurpassable ideal for all nations and all times," and he was censured by Leo XIII for this assertion.[74] Rather, "the constitution of the government," according to Brownson, "must grow out of the constitution of the state, and accord with the genius, the character, the habits, customs, and wants of the people, or it will not work well, or tend to secure the legitimate ends of government."[75] It is interesting that Brownson wrote these words in 1865, perhaps seeing in the Civil War an incipient crusader mentality.

Superficially, Brownson and Rommen agree with Maritain that democracy has certain merits that, under the right circumstances, make it compatible with Christianity, but it is clear that Maritain's understanding of the possibilities and limits of politics differs greatly from that of the other two thinkers. Indeed, the question might be asked whether calling their two respective philosophies "Catholic" robs the term of meaning. Where Maritain saw world government as the solution to man's earthly predicament, Brownson saw decentralization and subsidiarity as the answer. For example, he commends the locally governed polities in the New England states as conducive to freedom and the popular will: "Each town is a corporation, having important powers and the charge of all purely local matters, chooses its own officers, manages its own finances, takes charge of its own poor, of its own roads and bridges, and of the education of its own children."[76] Individual rights are protected not by the federal government but by the state government and are in turn protected from the state government by the municipal government. At the most local, decentralized level, the needs and concerns of persons are best addressed, Brownson believes. "Democracy," or universal suffrage, is simply an abstract term that does not actually protect individual rights and dignity in the concrete: "Experience proves that the ballot is far less effective in securing the freedom and independence of the individual citizen than is commonly pretended. The ballot of an isolated individual counts for nothing. The individual, though armed with the ballot, is as powerless, if he stands alone, as if he had it not. To render it of any avail he must associate himself with a party, and look for his success in the success of his party; and to secure the success of his party, he must give up to it his own private convictions and free will."[77] Because the raison d'être of parties is to acquire and hold power, they are beholden to the majority's will in order to keep power. "Government becomes practically the will of an ever-shifting and irresponsible majority," Brownson says. The result is democratic centralism, the enemy of liberty. Better than the ballot or parchment barriers is the division of power. Permitting those closest to the problem to take care of the solution is the best way to promote individual liberty and protect human dignity, according to Brownson. The principle of decentralization and division of power is compatible with Brownson's belief that "no one form of government is catholic in its nature, or of universal obligation."[78] Political solutions must be devised in the concrete. Democratism believes that political solutions should be devised abstractly, and power ought to be concentrated and administered centrally, so that all peoples can uniformly benefit from the democratist way of life.

Maritain and a Global Democratic Order

Maritain mentions subsidiarity and the need for pluralism, but his advocacy for world government betrays a different priority. He stresses throughout *Man and the State* that "the basic political reality is not the State, but the body politic with its multifarious institutions, the multiple communities which it involves, and the moral community which grows out of it."[79] The state cannot replace the social, cultural, and religious institutions that compose civil society, Maritain maintains. However, his vision of a global state competes with his belief that civil society must determine the social reality. If politics must be administered globally, then local initiatives and ways of life must give way to the dictates of the central authority, the entity that finally determines what is in the interest of the "common good." Maritain assumes that a global government can be a beneficent entity—that it would simply set local democratic machines in motion according to a singular vision, yet it would somehow preserve local self-determination. But government and bureaucracy generate their own raison d'être. And a political system such as Maritain imagines must be "run" by someone. What is to guarantee that those individuals entrusted with such enormous power will use it for good? The American framers were convinced that power is checked only by countervailing powers, not by feelings of goodwill. They imagined that institutions such as federalism and intermediary associations, of the kind that so impressed Alexis de Tocqueville, could help to check the ambitions of those in power, preventing its abuse.

Maritain assumed that the global government he envisioned would, through the historical dialectic—the "leaven" of the gospel working in history—inevitably embrace democratic pluralism: "Once the perfect society required by our historical age, that is the world political society, has been brought into being, it will be bound in justice to respect to the greatest possible extent the freedoms—essential to the common good of the world—of those invaluable vessels of political, moral, and cultural life which will be its parts."[80] But how to reconcile this expectation with the darker side of humanity that was taken so seriously by earlier Christian and classical political thinkers and that was such a prominent consideration within traditional American political thought? What of the original sin that has been central to the Christian understanding of politics, human nature, and society? That human beings are fallen in some sense is not ignored by Maritain. Yet expecting human reason to institute a benevolent, hands-off global government implies that human sinfulness is not sufficiently significant to stand in the way of solving the intractable problems of politics that have frustrated societies and philosophers since time immemorial. It also accords with Rousseau's belief that poorly designed institutions, not human sinfulness, are the primary cause of worldly evils.

Maritain's vision of global governance overlooks the historical reality of the *libido dominandi* and of local resistance to dictates from faraway places. What Maritain fails to realize, his critic Kolnai argues, is that "a wholesale dethronement of power by a stroke of a pen . . . directly invites the despotic rule of *one* massive totalitarian power claiming to determine the lives of men, without stopping short at individual rights or Church autonomy, on behalf of their general and identical 'liberty,' so as to make the concerted unity of their 'wills' fully manifest and valid."[81] In other words, seeking to eliminate power for the sake of liberty only creates a situation ripe for totalitarian "liberty" of the Rousseauean variety. People will be "forced to be free" under the democratist general will. Kolnai's criticism of Maritain calls to mind the observations of Robert Nisbet, who argues in *Quest for Community* precisely this point: secondary associations are the main bulwark against unchecked state power. Uniform, global government would do away with these little centers of power that respond to the particular needs of local citizens and diffuse the power of the state. Pluralism, Kolnai says, is by nature "incompatible with utopian concepts of 'perfection' and once-for-all 'planning'; it relies precisely on *given realities* in their manifoldness, contingency and limitation—capable indeed of local reforms, aptly devised corrections, revisions and enrichments, but essentially refractory, so long as they remain alive, to all attempts at a stream-lined 'creation' of social reality by human consciousness bent on enforcing a self-contained and fully 'satisfying' world order."[82]

Maritain was uncomfortable with the inherent diversity and hence uncertainty of pluralistic society. Without a central planner, these little platoons are able to go in many different directions, depending on what suits their needs. They may or may not choose the democratic way of life as Maritain envisions it. But he seems closed to the possibility that the common good may be achieved through a variety of ways.

The Legacy of Maritain's Democratism

There appear to be two competing and very different understandings of politics and society within Catholicism. One, derived from the thought of Christian realists such as Augustine and even qualified supporters of democracy such as Rommen and Brownson, is hard to reconcile with democratism. The other, in many ways compatible with Rousseau's philosophical anthropology, is a natural companion of democratism. Maritain, alongside Michael Novak, John Courtney Murray, George Weigel, and others who are beyond the scope of this study, is a leading representative of the latter strain of Catholic thought. This modern way of thinking about Catholicism and democracy that Maritain helped generate continues to exert great influence. In 2011, under Pope Benedict XVI, a pope who otherwise rejects democratist beliefs, the Pontifical Council for Justice and Peace issued a letter calling for a "global public authority" with worldwide scope and "universal jurisdiction" to govern financial institutions and facilitate the global common good. After an opening lamentation about the injustice of inequality, degenerate financial institutions, and corporate greed, the letter asks, "What has driven the world in such a problematic direction for its economy and also for peace?" The answer: "First and foremost, an economic liberalism that spurns rules and controls"—the capitalist economic system. Although the letter disavows technocratic solutions, it proposes a "supranational Authority" and exhorts the people of the globe to "adopt an ethic of solidarity to fuel their action. This implies abandoning all forms of petty selfishness and embracing the logic of the global common good which transcends merely passing and limited interests. In a word, [the people] ought to have a keen sense of belonging to the human family." Drawing on the works of John XXIII and Paul VI, the document discusses the need for "moral communion on the part of the world community." The Council hopes that the consciousness of the peoples of the world might be raised so that history can progress toward freedom and equality: "It is a matter of an Authority with a global reach that cannot be imposed by force, coercion or violence, but should be the outcome of a free and shared agreement and a reflection of the permanent and historic needs of the world common good. It ought to arise from a process of progressive maturation of consciences and advances in freedoms as well as awareness of growing responsibilities." Focusing on the need for experts with international jurisdiction to devise structural solutions, the letter does not address the role of personal sin in perpetuating social and political ills. Instead it abstractly states that "the economy needs ethics." In a spirit of optimism characteristic of the democratist mindset, the document expresses sincere belief that through the proposed technical solutions accompanied by a general sense of "solidarity" on the part of the human family, the world's economic woes can be ameliorated: "Thanks to the principle of solidarity, a lasting and fruitful relationship would build up between global civil society and a world public Authority as States, intermediate bodies, various institutions—including economic and financial ones—and citizens make their decisions with a view to the global common good, which transcends national goods."

Pope Francis, who canonized Pope John XXIII and beatified Paul VI, issued the encyclical *Laudato si'*, which has within it a prominent strain of the type of democratist thinking that characterizes the thought of Maritain. *Laudato si'* primarily takes up the cause of environmental issues and calls for humanity's "ecological conversion." The "self-improvement on the part of individuals" and "the sum of individual good deeds," Francis says, are not enough to "remedy the extremely complex situation facing our world today."[83] Lasting change for the environment will come rather through "community conversion." In its focus on the role of "community networks" and a "culture of care," *Laudato si'* resembles the same message of the progressive social gospel. Drawing on Paul VI's *Message for the 1977 World Day of Peace* Francis writes, "[T]he Church set before the world the ideal of a 'civilizational love.' Social love is the key to authentic development."[84] In this letter Francis stresses the need for a universal awakening or "discovery" and for strongly held "conviction." In this respect, he resembles Maritain, who also has a tendency to emphasize feelings of communion over concrete individual action. Francis says that the requirements of "gratitude," "recognition," "loving awareness," and human feeling "joined in a splendid universal communion" are foremost in a global ecological conversion.[85]

This way of thinking fits into the romantic tradition that dwells on emotion and feelings of togetherness over individual responsibility and personal action. The romantic ethic, which heavily informs democratism, tends to focus in an abstract and dreamy way on the way that things *could be* rather than the way they are. At bottom is the desire for a dramatic transformation of reality, whether into a communist utopia, a democratic state of perfect equality, or anything else. Generalizations about infusing the Christian spirit into the practice of democracy pepper the thought of thinkers such as Maritain, Francis, and others who tend toward romantic and democratist thinking, but to what extent is Christianity really necessary to the new world order?

As the social gospel movement earlier in the century made clear, Christianity can be transformed into many, often opposing things. Using words like "God" and "faith" can mask what is ultimately secular progressivism. It is in the concrete instantiations of the theory that the actual nature of the theory is revealed.

Conclusion

Within Catholicism there appears to be two competing ideologies. One is represented by thinkers such as Maritain, Pope John XXIII, Pope Paul VI, John Courtney Murray, Michael Novak (who credits Maritain as one of his major influences), George Weigel, and Pope Francis.[86] The other is represented by strains of thought found within the writings of Orestes Brownson, Heinrich Rommen, Erik Von Kuehnelt-Leddihn, Aurel Kolnai, Pope Benedict XVI, and Pope John Paul II. All are Catholic, devoutly so, and yet they disagree fundamentally about what is politically possible and desirable. The latter thinkers tend to focus on historical givens, offering political philosophies that elucidate the human condition more than they offer solutions to it. They tend to avoid proposing grand systems that promise to ameliorate what have heretofore been intractable political problems, their assumption being that there can be no systematic and final solution to challenges endemic to human nature and ultimately rooted in the permanent fact of human sinfulness. Given the cleft nature of the human soul, conflict, poverty, suffering, and other social ills will always remain an unfortunate part of our earthly existence. The best that we can do is try to mitigate their effects through salutary social practices and encouraging personal responsibility and virtue. No political system, even democracy, can permanently fix pathologies that originate from human beings themselves.

Maritain's attempt to reconcile Christianity with an ideal concept of democracy, coinciding in many ways with liberal progressivism, ends up looking something like a political religion of democracy, or what this book identifies as democratism. Nor do Maritain's appeals to natural law and rational distinctions between the administrative state and the organic body politic save his philosophy from the implications which it bears. Maritain's rational delineation between "the state" and society ignores the fundamental reality that human beings make up the state. Those human beings have passions and motivations of their own that will require the checks and balances of other powers. Power cannot simply be eliminated with the "stroke of a pen," as Kolnai points out. Maritain's generalizations about the leaven of the gospel working in history downplays the significance of individual human action and assumes that an immanent historical dialectic is at work, a belief that has more in common with progressivism, gnosticism, and even Marxism than traditional Catholic teaching. Maritain's philosophy, although claiming dependence on Aquinas and Aristotle, is thoroughly modern and possibly secular. Unlike Aquinas and Aristotle, who leave room for the contingent and complex nature of political life, Maritain takes a highly rationalistic and abstract approach that logically culminates in the uniform application of one type of rule for the globe. That he believes he is in possession of the knowledge to devise such a government is all the more telling of his distance from the traditional Christian ethic which emphasizes, above all, humility.

Brownson's wise observation in 1865 might have been useful for the twentieth century: "The constitutions imagined by philosophers are for Utopia, not for any actual, living, breathing people. You must take the state as it is, and develop your governmental constitution from it, and harmonize it with it. Where there is a discrepancy between the two constitutions, the government has no support in the state, in the organic people, or nation, and can sustain itself only by corruption or physical force."[87] What comes to mind immediately are the totalitarian regimes which Maritain abhorred, but the democratic ideology appears increasingly to resemble this description as well.

At the end of *Man and the State*, Maritain hints that rational plans for society may be futile and wonders if he too has "perhaps yielded to the old temptation of philosophers, who would have reason, through the instrumentality of certain wise men, be accepted as an authority in human affairs."[88] The reader is left to wonder where that leaves Maritain's treatise, the focal point of which is the rational conception of a new political program. Ultimately he seems to fall back on the authority of reason in human affairs, pointing the way to thinkers like Rawls, who hope to demonstrate the irrelevance of "comprehensive doctrines" such as Christianity to finding working consensus in liberal democracy. That Maritain's political thought is largely compatible with Rawls's suggests that Maritain belongs in the political tradition of Rawls and other secular democratic theorists more so than he does in the Thomist or orthodox Christian tradition.

Deliberative Democratism

Introduction

Democratism does not conform to a single set of rules. Sometimes it manifests as a foreign policy of idealism abroad and sometimes it is more subtle. Deliberative democracy is one example of a powerful yet understated expression of democratism. Deliberative democracy has been described as an "ideal in which people come together, on the basis of equal status and mutual respect," to discuss and decide political issues.[1] It would seem to be a much-needed democratic corrective to democratism's typical reliance on an enlightened leadership class to "represent" the people. This approach to democracy, however, tends to incline toward the same paradoxical embrace of "the people's" will as democratism, and it overlaps considerably with Rousseau's philosophy of democracy.[2] Indeed, many deliberative democracy theorists self-consciously draw on Rousseau's political ideals.[3] The editors of the recent *Oxford Handbook of Deliberative Democracy* (2018) bemoan the global ascendancy of "post-truth" politics and the rise of populist leaders. These deliberative democrats and others assume that if the people were better educated and more informed, they would naturally reject the populist leaders whom they had once supported. The corrective for this failure of democracy, according to deliberative democracy, is deliberation "to help the citizens to understand better the issues, their own interests, and the interests and perceptions of others." Where agreement is not possible, the deliberative democracy framework is supposed to help "structure and clarify the questions behind the conflict" before the issues are finally put to a vote.[4]

But what if an electoral majority nonetheless opts for the "populist" candidate that deliberative democracy repudiates as "undemocratic" and a proponent of "post-truth"? Is such an outcome precluded from possibility according to the procedures of deliberative democracy? If so, is deliberative democracy actually democratic? Given that some version of deliberative democracy appears to be hegemonic within modern democratic theory, it needs to be asked whether deliberative democracy

The Ideology of Democratism. Emily B. Finley, Oxford University Press. © Oxford University Press 2022.
DOI: 10.1093/oso/9780197642290.003.0006

helps to promote democracy in the classic sense of the word ("rule by the people") or whether it conforms to the democratist version of democracy in which knowing elites rule on behalf of the people, disregarding the people's intentions and desires.

President Bill Clinton credited the deliberative democracy theorist John Rawls with helping "a whole generation of learned Americans revive their faith in democracy itself."[5] Clinton's praise demonstrates that the influence of Rawls and of deliberative democracy extends well beyond the ivory tower. The news media often announce the need for "national conversations" about the controversies or incidents making headlines. In 2016, the anchor of *World News Tonight*, David Muir, moderated a "town hall" with President Barack Obama called "The President and the People: A National Conversation." The Woodrow Wilson Center and National Public Radio coproduce "The National Conversation," a "forum for deep dialogue and informed discussion . . . of the most significant problems facing the nation and the world."[6] Lofty appeals to the need for a national conversation are so frequent and so abstract that they hardly mean anything, yet testify to the core idea of deliberation that is at the heart of deliberative democracy, as if the nation's "deliberating" would clarify issues and render political decisions more legitimate. This language and way of thinking reflects the same belief of deliberative democracy that public discourse ought to be normative, even central, in political decision-making. Unreflectively, many would likely agree with this notion. However, it must be asked *how* such deliberation would clarify issues. If a bunch of uninformed people get together in a forum, what is to say that their discussing issues will improve their thinking? Implicit in deliberative democracy's assumption (as well as that of Muir and other hosts of "national conversations") is that the discussion will be carefully moderated by enlightened experts of some sort.

Approach

Rawls and Habermas are different in many respects. While this chapter examines some of their commonalities it does not claim that they are identical thinkers or that their thought necessarily broadly overlaps. It analyzes them together be-cause, while they express different versions of deliberative democracy, their re-spective philosophies both harken to the same idea of democratism. To examine deliberative democracy through the thought of one but not the other would be to assess one particular thinker rather than the idea of deliberative democracy more generally. This analysis seeks breadth over depth in this instance, hoping to show that some of the basic assumptions of deliberative democracy in general, rather than merely one of its exponents, align in important ways with democratism. It is possible to accept that Rawls and Habermas are different in significant ways while also agreeing that they share some normative assumptions about democracy. This chapter examines some of those shared overarching assumptions, including those of other deliberative democracy theorists, to broaden the picture even more. Thus, its intention is not to explore any single figure in great detail or to sort out the many nuances and competing perspectives within deliberative democratic theory. The purpose of this chapter is to demonstrate the connection between fundamental epistemological and philosophical assumptions of deliberative democracy and democratism.

Introduction to the Core Ideas of Deliberative Democracy

Habermas and Rawls generated tremendous interest in the deliberative democratic approach to democratic theory and political theory more broadly, and there has since evolved a "second generation" of deliberative democratic scholarship. Deliberative democrats are largely in agreement that democracy practiced through the ballot box alone is inadequate, substituting the mere aggregation of separate interests for a genuine notion of the common good. They hold that democracy ought to approximate a more transcendent notion of justice and a more holistic idea of Good. This thought squares with Rousseau's bifurcation of a general will and a mere "will of all." Citizen deliberation, deliberative democracy believes, is the way in which an "overlapping consensus" may be profitably discovered. Habermas's theory of discourse ethics seeks to ground social and legal norms in "communicative action." Rawls's incredibly influential 1971 work, *A Theory of Justice*, is also broadly within this tradition, although it elaborates different norms. Together, these thinkers and other deliberative democrats argue that political norms in pluralistic societies stand in need of some kind of rational legitimation that goes beyond merely discerning the preferences of a numerical majority.[7] Without a common religious, philosophical, or metaphysical system of belief, tradition can no longer be the leading source of political legitimacy in the West.[8] Reason and discourse must to a great extent replace the normative role of inherited systems of beliefs.

Rawls develops the concept of "public reason," which is a method for discerning and expressing the general will in a pluralist society. While Habermas believes that the actual act of public reasoning—the illocutionary exchange among "free and equal" citizens—is essential, Rawls believes that the individual need only consider the reasons that he or she *would* offer in public dialogue. In general, deliberative democracy seeks to institutionalize the ideal of "free public reasoning among equals."[9] In the introduction to the massive *Oxford Handbook of Deliberative Democracy*, the editors say that its more than one hundred contributors all agree that deliberative democracy is about "mutual communication that involves weighing and reflecting on preferences, values and interests regarding matters of common concern" and that "deliberative interactions have normatively valuable qualities that should be protected, supported, and institutionalized."[10]

Joshua Cohen, a student of Rawls, defines deliberative democracy as "a framework of social and institutional conditions that facilitates free discussion among equal citizens—by providing favorable conditions for participation, association, and expression—and [it] ties the authorization to exercise public power (and the exercise itself) to such discussion by establishing a framework ensuring the responsiveness and accountability of political power to it through regular competitive elections, conditions of publicity, legislative oversight, and so on."[11] Dennis F. Thompson's "Deliberative Democratic Theory and Empirical Political Science" provides a brief but extensive survey of both theoretical and empirical work in the field. He says, "At the core of all theories of deliberative democracy is what may be called a reason-giving requirement. Citizens and their representatives are expected to justify the laws they would impose on one another by giving reasons for their political claims and responding to others' reasons in return."[12] Seyla Benhabib, who closely follows Habermas, adds, "Power is a social resource and a social relation in need of legitimation. Legitimacy means that there are good and justifiable reasons why one set of power relations and institutional arrangements are better than and to be preferred to others. I maintain that the legitimation of power should be thought of as a public dialogue."[13] As citizens, we have "dialogic obligations," Bruce Ackerman asserts. "If you and I disagree about the moral truth, the only way we stand half a chance of solving our problems in coexistence in a way both of us find reasonable is by talking to one another about them."[14]

Habermas, following fellow discourse theorist Robert Alexy (who was influenced by Habermas), outlines an "ideal speech situation" for public dialogue:

> (3.1) "Every subject with the competence to speak and act is allowed to take part in the discourse.
> (3.2) a. Everyone is allowed to question any assertion whatever.
>   b. Everyone is allowed to introduce any assertion whatever into the discourse.
>   c. Everyone is allowed to express his attitudes, desires, and needs."
> (3.3) No speaker may be prevented, by internal or external coercion, from exercising his rights as laid down in (3.1) and (3.2)."[15]

Habermas admits that real discourse will stray from the ideal. However, the closer historical dialogue is to the "ideal speech situation," the more legitimate its outcome. According to Benhabib, "each participant must have an equal chance to make assertions, recommendation, and explanation. All must have equal chances to express their wishes, desires, and feelings."[16] Rawls stresses the principle of "reciprocity": "citizens are to think of themselves as if they were legislators and ask themselves what statutes, supported by what reasons satisfying the criterion of reciprocity, they would think it most reasonable to enact."[17]

This turn in democratic theory, "a paradigm that is now perhaps the dominant—if not the hegemonic—orientation within democratic theory," has arisen as an alternative to the notion that democracy functions as an aggregation of preferences expressed through voting.[18] Deliberative democracy theorists believe that the majoritarian model of government sets the bar too low and that a more legitimate—because based on better consensus—democracy is possible. Andre Bächtiger et al. admit that deliberative democracy is based on aspirational ideals, which, although impossible to achieve perfectly, are no less valuable as standards toward which to strive. It is even worth incurring "significant costs" to come closer to the ideal, these authors say. Depending on circumstances, different ideals ought to be prioritized: "[A]ttending to the greater or lesser importance and the greater and lesser costs of different ideals in different contexts, applies to all aspirational democratic ideals, including deliberative ones."[19] This book in general tries to examine the value of democratic idealism and to demonstrate the relationship between idealism and ideology. To that end, this chapter assesses the extent to which the idealism that motivates deliberative democracy contributes to a more or less democratic outcome.

Jürgen Habermas

Habermas's major work on deliberation, *Theory of Communicative Action*, argues that communities must determine political norms through a process of rational legitimation, what he terms "communicative action."[20] For Habermas, the liberal model of government is inadequate because "[it] hinges, not on the democratic self-determination of deliberating citizens, but on the legal institutionalization of an economic society that is supposed to guarantee an essentially nonpolitical common good by the satisfaction of private preferences."[21] Communicative action, on the other hand, fosters citizen dialogue that ultimately justifies the political order with reasons that all can accept. Agreement is "evaluated in terms of the intersubjective recognition of validity claims."[22] That is, majority assent to a certain political norm or course of action must be based on reasons that the majority finds acceptable. If consensus proves unattainable, consent is at least possible with this method, according to Habermas.

Public consensus along the lines that Habermas outlines reveals the people's "common will." Habermas emphasizes the "intersubjective process of reaching understanding," and in that way differs from Rawls, whose theory of democratic justice is monological rather than dialogical.[23] Speakers reach understanding and consensus by "rationally motivating" one another to accept their claims: "The fact that a speaker can rationally motivate a hearer to accept such an offer is due not to the validity of what he says but to the speaker's guarantee that he will, if necessary, make efforts to redeem the claim that the hearer has accepted."[24] That is, claims need not be backed by truth in any objective sense but by the speaker's confidence that his or her normative statement could be accepted as reasonable (and therefore legitimate) by the majority of the listeners. "The moral principle is so conceived as to exclude as invalid any norm that could not meet with the qualified assent of all who are or might be affected by it," Habermas says. "This bridging principle, which makes consensus possible, ensures that only those norms are accepted as valid that express a general will."[25] In order for a norm to be valid, according to Habermas, "[a]ll affected can accept the consequences and the side effects its *general* observance can be anticipated to have for the satisfaction of *everyone's* interests (and these consequences are preferred to those of known alternative possibilities for regulation)."[26]

Habermas tries to avoid the ahistoricism of which some have accused Rawls and considers the historical dimension of life in his theory of deliberative democracy. Dialogue, for Habermas, helps persons to clarify identities and commitments. It gives them "a clear understanding of themselves as members of a specific nation, as members of a locale or a state, as inhabitants of a region, etc."[27] However, Habermas is not historical in the sense of, say, Edmund Burke. Reason, not tradition or generational and experiential knowledge, ought ultimately determine what is politically normative.[28] For Habermas, it is not lived experience *as members* of a nation, locale, region, etc. that shapes ideas about political norms, as it is for Burke, but the rational understanding and articulation of that experience. Habermas believes that citizens "*determine* which traditions they will continue," "*determine* how they will treat each other, and how they will treat minorities and marginal groups," and "*get clear* about the kind of society they want to live in."[29] The political process for a historical thinker like Burke, on the other hand, is grounded in generational knowledge; practical experience often guides political norms in unreflective and unspoken ways. This inherited wisdom, as Burke would call it, foregrounds actions, beliefs, and customs in a way that, in a certain sense, defies rational explanation. Citizens cannot determine which traditions are valuable by rationally dissecting them, Burke would argue. Although Habermas takes the Aristotelian position that human beings are naturally social and shaped by social networks and relations, he believes that a universal "abstract core" guides moral intuitions.[30] Thomas McCarthy says that for Habermas, our natural, universal sociability implies "the inviolability of the person and the solidarity of the community," two ideas "at the heart of traditional moralities."[31] But this obfuscates a major difference between Habermas's political theory and that of the Aristotelian and Burkean varieties. According to the traditional or historical perspective, "reasoned agreement" alone cannot justify political norms, and indeed the solidarity of the community depends on the continuity of traditional norms. Experience, rather than reason, is foremost in shaping habits and customs and in determining the course of civic life, according to Aristotle and Burke. Norms that come about through the fires of trial and error might not follow rational logic or be easily justified through reasoning. Only in dispensing with them does their inherent value really become clear.

John Rawls

Rawls's understanding of deliberative democracy relies on a similar belief in the universality and objectivity of reason. Rawls invites us to reimagine political possibilities through his famous hypothetical, the "veil of ignorance." Ignoring personal, social, and historical circumstances, we are to imagine what should constitute the norms of political existence in general. Within these constraints and others (and working with givens, such as basic knowledge of biology, psychology, the natural sciences, etc.), Rawls believes that we can reason or internally deliberate our way to a political (and social and economic) system acceptable to all "reasonable" persons. He calls this thought experiment the "original position," the most famous aspect of which is the veil of ignorance. The original position mimics the imaginative function of the state of nature in the philosophies of the social contract thinkers. Stripped of historical, religious, cultural, social, ethnic, national, and any other particular self-knowledge, persons are assumed to be free to act on the basis of objective reason. Given that there are competing conceptions of the good and differing philosophical, religious, and moral convictions, the best way to determine principles of justice is to rationally determine them, according to this theory. Following Rousseau, Rawls believes that disinterested reasoning can guide our thinking and that when applied to politics can result in something like the general will. For Rawls, liberal democracy is the only rationally plausible form of government given his first principles, although there may be different legitimate variants of liberal democracy.

Public reason, Rawls believes, is one of the essential elements of deliberative democracy and relates to citizens' *reasoning* concerning constitutional questions and matters of justice.[32] Unlike Habermas's theory, in which citizens must actually deliberate, Rawls's theory has citizens reason only theoretically, imagining what sorts of justifications they would offer in public. "A citizen engages in public reason," Rawls explains, "when he or she deliberates within a framework of what he or she sincerely regards as the most reasonable political conception of justice, a conception that expresses political values that others, as free and equal citizens, might reasonably be expected reasonably to endorse."[33] A crucial component of public reason is the criterion of "reciprocity": legitimate reasons are only those that other citizens *could* accept, even if they ultimately disagree on other reasonable grounds. Guided by the principle of reciprocity, the goal of public reason is to find overlapping conceptions of justice. Mirroring the original position, the "dialogue" in public reasoning is similarly hypothetical and imaginary.[34] For both Rawls and Habermas, the goal is to discern a general will through some sort of dialogue.

By assenting at minimum to the legitimacy of the reasons given, citizens theoretically are united in a certain sense. In this respect, deliberative democracy aims at the Rousseauean ideal of universal acceptance of the political order (even if all do not necessarily agree with each specific policy). What is significant is the underlying belief that reason is an objective and disinterested force, and that citizens coming together and engaging in reasoned debate can ultimately change their minds or at least accept the reasoning of others and therefore the final outcome as legitimate. This understanding of democracy sharply contrasts with the older view of, say, Plato, who believed that democratic interests compete in such a way that democracy must eventually give way not to consensus but to such disorder than a strongman must finally put an end to the chaos. So many discordant preferences and voices, which stem from antithetical beliefs about life and politics, cannot coalesce around shared ideas about what is "reasonable" in the Platonic perspective. Instead, according to Plato, Aristotle, and other skeptics such as the framers of the U.S. Constitution, these competing interests form factions and thwart the emergence of anything like a general will. Compromise, negotiation, and a federated system of some kind holds the political order together, according to the classical republican tradition of Aristotle or Hamilton.

At bottom, these two perspectives ultimately differ in their conceptions of human nature. One inclines toward the Rousseauean view that human nature is naturally good and the other toward the Augustinian view that human beings are fallen. For the deliberative democrats, procedures and norms help to guide thinking away from selfish or myopic views and toward the common good. This idea shares with Rousseau the belief that if people organize and reason in a particular way, the political outcome can be very different from what it has been historically.

The Autonomy of Reason?

"Political reason," Cohen says, following Rawls, is "autonomous" and does not need to rely on "an encompassing philosophy of life" in order to articulate a conception of democracy.[35] Deliberative democracy believes that citizen deliberation, properly ordered, would have a general purifying effect when reason is permitted to "float freely."[36] Parochial beliefs would tend to give way to the common good, which is assumed to be in line with reason. Deliberative democracy agrees with John Stuart Mill that reason and free inquiry ought to be promoted so that the truth can emerge through public filtration of ideas.[37] Jefferson also held this belief about the epistemological role of reason; it is why he was so committed to the idea that the people, when permitted to debate freely, would come to the right opinions. The belief that rational inquiry and dialogue can act as disinterested forces in the search for truth and justice is quintessential of Enlightenment thinking and informed its progressive philosophy of history. As citizens become more educated in scientific and rational principles, they will naturally discern what is right and moral. These ideas helped to give life to a new sensibility and ethic that held that morality is not a result of habit and struggle with self, as the older classical and Christian traditions held, but a function of right reasoning. Deliberative democracy follows this Enlightenment tradition, believing that the major obstacle to a thriving democracy is not moral-spiritual but rational and educational.

Deliberative democracy's first principle is the belief that reason *is* autonomous and that, through it, we can arrive at shared conceptions of the good, regardless of our personal beliefs. "Citizens must judge, from within [their] separate philosophies," Cohen says, "that autonomous political argument is appropriate, and accept, as a public matter, that the diversity of such philosophies recommends an autonomous political reason."[38] Historical circumstance and personal experience, identity, and worldview are not only unnecessary in determining what is politically just but cloud that determination. The procedures and methods of proper deliberation are to guide citizens toward the type of thinking that deliberative democracy believes is "objectively reasonable." That such thinking must be cultivated suggests that it is not as natural as deliberative democracy would initially have us believe.

Deliberative democracy's belief that abstract reason ought to guide discussion places quite a burden on citizens. They must practice "conversational restraint," listening to and engaging with other speakers on equal terms. A citizen is not permitted to "respond by appealing to (his understanding of) the moral truth; he must instead be prepared, in principle, to engage in a restrained dialogic effort to locate normative premises that both sides find reasonable," Ackerman says.[39] Using one's own experience or philosophical views as justifications for an argument is not acceptable. Amy Gutmann and Dennis Thompson expect "citizens and officials to espouse their moral positions independently of the circumstances in which they speak. This is consistency in speech and is a sign of political sincerity: it indicates that a person holds the position because it is a moral position, not for reasons of political advantage."[40] While deliberative democracy poses this as an ideal, it might be argued that such an ideal is incompatible with human psychology. Are we able to radically divorce our reasoning from the circumstances and experiences that have formed us and arguably informed that very reasoning? This raises certain epistemological questions about how we form opinions in the first place. But deliberative democracy has little to say about that.

Democratism in general holds the view of deliberative democracy that reason is an impartial force capable of discerning general political truth. It contends that a majority of the people, when brought together, can give form to their general will. Rousseau, like Rawls, believes this is accomplished through inner reflection, while deliberative democracy generally believes that an exchange of ideas must take place. But the end result is to be the same: the general will is somehow to be elicited from this process. However, with Rousseau, deliberative democracy is not confident that actual popular desires will result in the general will. This lack of confidence is betrayed by Rousseau's dependence on the legislator and deliberative democracy's reliance on correct procedures for discussion. That the general will must be coaxed in such a way suggests that democratists such as Rousseau and the deliberative democracy theorists either do not believe that reason is an impartial arbiter of truth or believe that some other force holds greater epistemological sway than reason; thus the people must be cajoled into the "right" beliefs.

Equality in Deliberation

Another requirement of deliberative democracy is that all citizens be considered equal. Thompson says that equality "refers to the resources, including talents, status, and power, that participants bring to the deliberation."[41] Equality also refers to the dynamic of the dialogue. The "random selection" of speakers, "proportional representation," and equal time to speak, for example, are supposed to lead to better discussion.[42] Citizens ought to have equal opportunity to advance persuasive arguments and ought to give equal weight to all "good" arguments, regardless of the background of the speaker. Most deliberative democrats agree that the more the "deliberation is influenced by unequal economic resources and social status, the more deficient it is."[43] While some have observed that this would require "'equality of resources,' including 'material wealth and educational treatment,'" deliberative democracy nonetheless sees it as an ideal that can serve as a useful heuristic.[44] The idea of entirely equal citizens pursuing the general will is an essential aspect of Rousseau's version of democracy. For the same reason that Rousseau wishes to prevent communication among citizens, deliberative democracy hopes to add the requirement of equality as a corrective to the potential for thought leaders to emerge and sway citizens unduly.[45] Rousseau would likely disagree with Cohen that each citizen may be equally "recognized as having the capacities required for participating in discussion aimed at authorizing the exercise of power."[46] It is therefore somewhat paradoxical that Rousseau should be one of the guiding lights of deliberative democracy, given his belief that deliberation would only perpetuate existing social hierarchies. For Rousseau, the only way to prevent thought leaders from emerging and swaying public opinion is to prevent all citizen communication prior to debate. He would acknowledge the inevitability of some people being inherently more eloquent, more tenacious, more opinionated, while others are happy to follow their more outspoken or intelligent counterparts.

Deliberative democracy is with Rousseau in its fear of social hierarchy, even what democratic societies might traditionally consider leadership or statesmanship, believing that differentiation among citizens will interfere with the emergence of the general will. Deliberative democracy, like Rousseauean democracy, believes that partial societies prioritize their own interests and generate cleavages in society. These divisions, according to this perspective, are adverse to democracy properly conceived, which is not composed of a plurality of interests but is reconcilable in some form of the general will. At bottom, this is what distinguishes the deliberative democracy understanding of democracy from the republican vision of the framers of the U.S. Constitution. James MacGregor Burns, although not a deliberative democrat, was frustrated with the American federated system precisely because it aims to balance rather than reconcile so many competing interests.[47]

How Democratic Is Deliberative Democracy?

Deliberative democracy's reliance on procedures at times amounts to the type of coercion it seeks to avoid in deliberation. To demand citizens suppress the expression of thoughts and ideas which arise from particular considerations does not encourage the "frank and free flow of ideas" that it purports to seek.[48] Is it fair to say that citizens whose moral positions derive from their particular circumstances are acting with a view to "political advantage"? It is not clear that citizens attempting to suppress "whatever moral principles they hold privately" in favor of the common good is possible or desirable.[49] Personal moral convictions may be as conducive to the common good as not; it is not possible to determine in the abstract. The demand that citizens act, or more importantly *think* in this way inclines dangerously toward a type of thought-policing that deliberative democracy would no doubt wish to avoid.

One of the major sources of tension within deliberative democracy and also a source of its kinship with democratism is its assumptions about human psychology and what ultimately motivates human beings. Prescribing rules to change the nature of civic debate does not, on its own, bring about the desired changes. Power to restrain must be exercised internally or externally on the part of citizens. Benjamin Barber, whose participatory democracy dovetails with deliberative democracy, "suggests that man is a 'mutable' creature whose capacity for 'self-transformation' stems from deliberation and interaction with his fellow men. Democratic participation, [Barber] claims, changes both 'the community' and 'the participating member.' "[50] According to this author, Barber's interpretation "is not atypical" of those who look to some version of "participatory democracy" as normative.[51] It is implied within deliberative democracy that experts must guide the discussion and the outcome. Gutmann and Thompson's assertion that citizens "can *learn* how to take each other seriously as moral agents" implies that citizens are not, on their own, up to the task of deliberation. Ideals such as mutual respect and equality may need to be enforced.[52] In this respect, deliberative democracy seems to veer in the direction of other democratist schemes that rely on an elite to institutionalize "the people's" will. The devices of the democratist require philosophically elaborate treatises detailing the types of practices that must become normalized, suggesting how far these ideas are from the minds of ordinary people—the people who are supposed to be the beneficiaries of these ideas. Deliberative democracy generally does not expound upon the fact that the political philosopher or intellectual is to play a major role in the creation of the new "democratic" system.

In a controlled study of deliberation in Switzerland, Bächtiger et al found that citizens who were presented with "carefully balanced materials" changed their minds prior to voting on a contentious issue.[53] The authors concluded that "preference transformations via deliberation occurred in more complex ways than previous studies have found." Indeed, they "happened before the discussion, as a result of information as well as internal reflection." This, the authors say, supports the claim that "the discussion component may be less important for opinion change than the information phase and the internal-reflective process in participants' heads prior to discussion."[54] This report does not give details about the information given to participants, but the effect of the information was to sway participants in the direction of the policy that the authors of the study believed was "less simplistic and more balanced." Finding that "deliberating citizens change their opinions quite dramatically, frequently in the direction of more common good–oriented policies," the authors are optimistic that deliberative democracy might even prove "a cure against populism, making citizens aware of the dangers related to simplistic populist initiatives."[55] Interestingly, it was not deliberation or rational exchange among participants that changed their minds, but the *information* presented, as the authors themselves say.

The authors imply that their view, which is the opposite of "simplistic populist initiatives," is the correct one, even self-evidently so, without specifying the content of either view. But what is to say that right is on the side of the deliberative democracy theorists? Could the opposing viewpoint have equal claim to democratic legitimacy? What is to determine the legitimacy of either? For deliberative democracy's framework to determine which is legitimate is to have deliberative democracy as the jury in its own trial. As another example, Paul Quirk et al. contend that the British referendum to leave the European Union ("Brexit") illustrates that referenda without the "institutional support" of deliberative democracy is downright harmful.[56] The implication is that the information leaflets or seminars that deliberative democracy could provide would have prevented Brexit. What is to sort out the superior, legitimate version of the people's will? Bächtiger et al.'s study indicates that dialogue not only is not necessary for changing minds but is actually less effective than simply a presentation of materials that goes in one direction. But that is not an exchange and exhibits the power dynamic of inequality that deliberative democracy claims to wish to overturn. Or does deliberative democracy simply wish to replace one ruling elite with another? Deliberative democracy theoretically provides a framework for the free exchange of ideas among equals, but it nonetheless condones a certain hierarchy in which more informed and knowledgeable experts are to guide the preferences of citizens toward particular outcomes.

"Epistemic Elitism"

For deliberative democracy, politics is not an ethical and historical challenge but an institutional and procedural problem, to be solved through expert knowledge, "education" of citizens, and a rearrangement of social institutions and norms. While procedural politics makes possible reasoning among equals, the reasoning of experts is required to makes possible a procedural politics. The intellectual must first determine the criteria for the procedure, which itself encompasses a normative framework, presumably precluding the possibility of "simplistic populist narratives." If all persons are equal by virtue of their ability to weigh and consider arguments as well as to put forth arguments, what is to justify deliberative democracy's parameters for "proper" discussion? This is a paradox that

Gutmann and Thompson acknowledge but do not resolve. Deliberation among citizens along the lines that deliberative democracy theorizes is "not a purely natural process," they concede. Artificial social constructs that "may be quite complex" are necessary to facilitate it.[57] But how can citizens be made to participate? They can't, Gutmann and Thompson respond, and so "civic education" that would teach citizens to appreciate this new framework must be a component of the overall project of deliberative democracy. In this way, deliberative democracy exemplifies the democratist paradox: the need to find a way for the people willingly to adopt the new system. Once again, education (understood in a particular way) provides the key. As soon as the people see that the new plan is in their interest, they will happily adopt it, democratism and deliberative democracy alike assume.

This would seem to suggest "epistemic elitism," a charge leveled at deliberative democracy's forefather John Stuart Mill. Gutmann and Thompson are "unequivocal about the influence of John Stuart Mill" on deliberative democracy and that he is "rightly considered one of the sources of deliberative democracy."[58] But as Simone Chambers points out, Mill's endorsement of institutional arrangements that would facilitate discussion but not actually affect legislation suggests that at least this aspect of his philosophy is "at odds with the ideals of deliberative democracy." Yet deliberative democracy seems unknowingly to trend in the same direction as Mill's thought, relying on the force of intellectuals and experts to ensure that deliberation is conducted properly and ignorance is not, in the words of Mill, "entitled to as much political power as knowledge."[59] When Gutmann and Thompson say that citizens "*can learn how* to take each other seriously as moral agents," they seem to mean that they might teach us.[60] "[C]lasses that teach deliberative techniques" are needed, these authors say.[61] And similarly, when Bächtiger et al. emphasize the role of "carefully balanced information" in changing citizens' minds, they imply that deliberative democrats such as Bächtiger will determine what is "balanced" and what is "simplistic" and "populist."[62]

Moral Geometry Leads to a Predetermined Outcome

The philosopher Michael Saward argues that Rawls's theory of deliberative democracy leaves no room for actual deliberation or conclusions that might differ from Rawls's own. The rational framework that Rawls provides via public reason mirrors that of the original position and preordains the outcome of a theoretical "dialogue." Both public reason and the original position lead necessarily to Rawls's own conception of justice, says Saward.[63] The citizen engaged in "public reason" and the citizen in the original position are both constrained by a theoretical framework in which only "certain sorts of arguments about courses of action are appropriate or acceptable."[64] However, as Saward points out, even internal "dialogue" is not necessary in Rawls's conception of deliberative democracy. Given the provisions of the ideal dialogue, which mirrors the original position, Rawls's conception of justice—"justice as fairness"—is a foregone conclusion. In *Political Liberalism*, Rawls writes, "[T]he guidelines of inquiry of public reason, as well as its principle of legitimacy, have the same basis as the substantive principles of justice. This means in justice as fairness that the parties in the original position, in adopting principles of justice for the basic structure, must also adopt guidelines and criteria of public reason for applying those norms."[65] The original position sets the terms of public reason. The " 'overlapping consensus of reasonable comprehensive doctrines' is itself the conception of 'justice as fairness,' " Saward says.[66] Rawls claims that "many liberalisms" are possible under the terms of public reason, but given its limiting criteria, the differences among the "liberalisms" must be inconsequential. Rawls provides at the outset only a "family of reasonable political conceptions" from which citizens may hypothetically choose. In *A Theory of Justice*, a person in the original position is limited to the choice of "traditional conceptions of justice" listed by Rawls; in "The Idea of Public Reason Revisited" Rawls constrains discussion with the reciprocity criterion that citizens must put forth reasons on grounds that others could accept through appeal to rationality.[67] More subtly, however, Rawls's modern, Enlightenment understanding of persons as free, equal, and rational itself constitutes a comprehensive doctrine about human nature, epistemology, and political society. Contrast, for instance, Rawls's interpretation of these concepts with that of Islam or orthodox Christianity, both of which have a rather different understanding of what constitutes freedom and equality and believe that human beings are motivated primarily by something other than abstract reason. What is to say that Rawls's post-Enlightenment understanding of these concepts is objectively true or final?

Rawls's ostensibly objective conception of justice takes on a definitive form politically. In "The Idea of Public Reason," he states that "three main features" necessarily arise from public reason:

> First, a list of certain basic rights, liberties, and opportunities (such as those familiar from constitutional regimes);
>
> Second, an assignment of special priority to those rights, liberties, and opportunities, especially with respect to the claims of the general good and perfectionist values; and
>
> Third, measures ensuring for all citizens adequate all-purpose means to make effective use of their freedoms.[68]

What emerges is a picture of the modern liberal, democratic state in the West. Specifically, Rawls's conception of justice inclines toward the modern welfare state.[69] In *A Theory of Justice* he makes even more explicit his assumption that "social justice in the modern state" entails government assurance of competitive markets, full employment, redistribution of property and wealth, and education for all.[70] Given that Rawls believes that discerning political justice is a matter of "moral geometry," there can be little doubt that, like a geometrical proof, there is but one correct result. Rawls claims that there are many different possible conceptions of justice, but in practice there could be few substantive differences among them. "The content of public reason," he avers, "is given by a family of political conceptions of justice, and not by a single one. There are many liberalisms and related views, and therefore many forms of public reason specified by a family of reasonable political conceptions."[71] However, the methodology of Rawls and of deliberative democracy in general does not allow for much diversity of opinion or differences in worldview. That deliberative democracy in general equates justice with the democratic norms of advanced Western nations suggests that "deliberation" is less about an honest discovering of what might be "overlapping consensus" than a pretense to democratic legitimacy.

While those who follow Habermas's variant of deliberative democracy over Rawls's stress the importance of *actual* discussion and even historical circumstance, the result is much the same. For Habermas, the give and take that characterizes speech and communication indicates the naturalness of freedom and equality, understood to mean egalitarianism and lack of constraint. Habermas's first principle, that human nature is discursive and that this implies ahistorical liberty and equality, draws from the same epistemological paradigm of rationalism as does Rawls. Upon examination, deliberative democracy as Rawls and Habermas express it assumes that something like an a priori general will will become evident through rational dialogue. Even accounting for "affective appeals, informal arguments, rhetorical speeches, personal testimony and the like as important ingredients in the deliberative process," deliberative democracy's proceduralism betrays normative commitments that are not necessarily aligned with the beliefs and preferences of ordinary citizens. Its "proceduralist" methodology reveals a latent proclivity for social engineering. Citizens are expected to discern, through the proper type of dialoguing, what has already been determined as just, evident in the very rules and procedures used as guides. Habermas confirms this assertion. "The normative content," he says, "arises from the very structure of communicative actions."[72] Despite the claims of Habermas disciples such as Benhabib that "proceduralism does not imply formalism and ahistoricism," the assumption that a formal structure for communication can produce a certain outcome implies formalism and ahistoricism.[73]

Although Habermas especially hopes to avoid metaphysical claims, the assumption that human beings can discern a general will through dialogue reveals the centrality of metaphysics even to his version of deliberative democracy. One of the major normative assumptions of deliberative democracy is that something like a general will exists and can be rationally articulated and legislated. This is not to say that a common good does not exist, but that deliberative democracy puts forth the radical claim that discerning and legislating the common good based upon expediency, contingency, and compromise among inherently competing interests is illegitimate as a form of democratic government. It bases this claim on the empirically suspect notion that deliberation, carefully controlled by guidelines that deliberative democracy theorists set forth, will result in a common consensus, or at least acceptance on the part of dissenting participants. It also assumes that the common consensus will be just. The historical record would seem to refute this hypothesis, as nothing like it has ever occurred. Even townhall meetings can become riotous events.

Deliberative Democracy in the Concrete

The editors of *The Oxford Handbook of Deliberative Democracy* say in their introduction that although they believe that populists and authoritarians are often to blame for a lack of political deliberation, even when deliberation is not suppressed, "we too often see levels of political polarization that signal inabilities to listen to the other side and reflect upon what they may have to say."[74] Despite this observation, the focus of the *Handbook*, with a few exceptions, is on the *ideal* the editors assert. Two of the contributors express concern over the "disparity" between deliberative democratic theory and practice but conclude that "to deny the relevance of the theory to practice is exactly the wrong response to this challenge."[75] For most deliberative democracy theorists, the divide between the real and the ideal suggests not the need to recalibrate expectations but to find more robust theories and to push policies to engineer the conditions in which proper deliberation might take place.

Deliberative democracy claims to be democratic in the sense that citizens discover for themselves the norms that ought to guide politics, but its bias in favor of a certain type of reasoning and the direction that reasoning ought to go calls into question its claim to be democratic. To allow local and partial considerations to guide decision-making, deliberative democrats describe as "self-interested bargaining" that which "advance[s] only [citizens'] own interests."[76] However, if human psychology is such that we are epistemically incapable of envisioning a "general" good abstracted from any particulars, then deliberative democracy's notion of an "overlapping consensus" discerned through abstract reasoning of one sort or another (including affective or emotional appeals, narrative, etc.) cannot result in such a consensus. This includes the Habermasian idea that citizens, although perhaps motivated by partial concerns, are nonetheless able to come together to "jointly determine how the different needs, interests, and values of all the participants should be reconciled in an impartial manner."[77] Who might decide which version of justice is "impartial"? Alternatively, how might different viewpoints finally be reconciled into one "general" position on justice for any particular matter? It seems easier to envision this in the abstract than in an actual civic debate.

There are, to be sure, deliberative democrats sensitive to the difficulty of reaching consensus in certain contexts and open to traditional democratic practices of compromise, negotiation, and "even bargaining." Although, one author points out, these are practices of the "adversary tradition" of democracy and are "controversial" among deliberative democrats.[78] Monique Deveaux highlights that for some deliberative democrats, cultural or identity-based disagreements ought not preclude dialogue and eventual compromise of some sort, even if that means pluralism rather than unity. Sometimes compromise is the best that can be hoped for when deep cleavages separate citizens. However, most deliberative democrats willing to consider the need for compromise and pluralism do so out of sensitivity to "the justice claims of indigenous, racialized, and cultural minority groups" rather than the belief that deep political cleavages may exist because of fundamental differences in worldview and first principles.[79] Moreover, those deliberative democrats willing to make theoretical accommodations for the "requirements" of deliberation do so to ensure that "cultural minority citizens" do not need to "bracket their identity-related interests in order to make normative claims consistent with public reason and impartiality"—something these theorists acknowledge would be problematic or unjust. However, it may be that deliberative democracy overestimates the possibility of a rationally articulated "overlapping consensus" among the dominant cultural group. It may indeed be problematic or unjust to require *anyone* to bracket his or her particular interests in an attempt to engage in abstract reasoning of the Rawlsian or Habermasian sort. While it certainly can be argued that marginalized voices are disadvantaged in many ways and often excluded from the public sphere, deliberative democracy seems not to consider the *epistemological* possibility that *all* perspectives are "diverse and situated," regardless of identity, and that these will inherently influence one's conception of what is normative.[80] That is not to say that consensus is impossible and that all viewpoints are radically individualistic and opposed but that the methodology of deliberative democracy may be based in a faulty epistemology, a possibility that is suggested in the willingness to make room for "multicultural" voices in dialogue. It may also suggest that tradition is not necessarily antithetical to genuine democracy, if it reflects the accumulated preferences and experience of a particular people.

If deliberative democracy's new version of democracy based on the general will of particular communities (or nations or the globe) is possible only theoretically and not in actuality, then what might the "procedural constraints" of deliberative democracy accomplish in practice?[81] A cynic might suggest that these constraints are a means of control and a way of forcing certain outcomes. The arbiters of "legitimate" discussion are the deliberative democracy theorists who, rather than creating freedom and equality, may be embarking on a project of social engineering. Two authors seem unwittingly to reveal the importance of control within Rawls's deliberative democratic theory. In a review of Rawls's religious reasoning proviso, these authors says that in updating his earlier position, "Rawls allowed that such defections from the normal requirements of public reason could be justified provided that 'in due course proper political reasons'" are given.[82] That Rawls would "allow" what these sympathetic authors characterize as "defections" suggests that deliberative democracy may be less democratic than the name would imply and might instead be another form of dogmatism, inseparable from the elaborate and abstract vision of its theorist. Deliberative democracy is prima facie supremely democratic, but implied in its normative assumptions might be the very elitism that it hopes to overturn.

Focusing on the ideal of a general will and the hopeful prospect that it can emerge given the right conditions, deliberative democracy glosses over the practical need to silence or ignore the voices that do not offer reasons that conform to deliberative democracy's criteria of "reasonableness" and "reciprocity." Implicit is that the benefit from "constraints on public discussion" is worth the cost of restricting the liberties of insubordinate citizens. Deliberative democracy does not make explicit that there is such a price to pay. If the general will can emerge, then the good that would be accomplished would outweigh any seeming drawback of the program. Power always "in principle rests with the citizenry as a whole," deliberative democracy asserts, but coupled with this belief is the assumption that experts must coax the *right* general will out of the people.[83]

Under the guise of using reason and impartial logic, thinkers such as Rawls argue that our common human nature as free, equal, and rational beings naturally implies a version of "procedural justice" like the one he elaborates. Yet an entire philosophy of human nature and politics is behind his and deliberative democracy's understanding of these concepts. It is not always spelled out, but at the heart of deliberative democracy is the epistemological belief that reason is an objective investigation into truth and that its proper use leads to indisputable revelations about justice and the common good. Idealized conceptions of persons as "free" and "equal" form the basis of deliberative democracy's prescriptions, but other conceptions surely are possible.[84] Pre-Enlightenment understandings of freedom, equality, and rationality, following Plato, Aristotle, Aquinas, and classical and Christian traditions, for example, hold that persons are not autonomous individuals, and, for good or ill, hierarchy and leadership are natural. Reason, according to this older tradition, is often weaker than other forces that motivate and move human beings, such as the appetites and imagination. "I do not understand my own actions," St. Paul says in the epistle to the Romans. "I can will what is right, but I cannot do it. For I do not do the good I want, but the evil I do not want is what I do."[85] Plato, although prone to a certain philosophical rationalism that is in many ways compatible with deliberative democracy, nonetheless was sensitive to the weakness of reason in the face of appetitive desires and also to the power of imagination. The careful control of myth and imaginative content in the *Republic* was central to Plato's own procedural and institutional designs that were to bring about justice in the city.[86]

For Rawls, "procedural justice" simplifies political justice and the difficulty of taking into account an "endless variety of circumstances."[87] The "relative positions of particular persons" are unimportant, he specifies, in meeting the demands of justice. "It is the arrangement of the basic structure which is to be judged, and judged from a general point of view. Unless we are prepared to criticize it from the standpoint of a relevant representative man in some particular position, we have no complaint against it."[88] That is precisely one of the central tensions that this chapter has highlighted, namely that judging the basic structure from the standpoint of the "general" instead of the particular is deeply problematic for actual, pluralistic democracy. Has Rawls's basic structure been determined just by the relevant parties, the "relevant representative man" that Rawls seems to think has little relevance? It would seem that the actual people to be affected by the system should have greater relevance and importance, not in spite of their limited, particular viewpoints but *because* of them. These are the people whose lives will be affected by the changes and by the new system. Surely they should have a say, even if their reasons for desiring this or that policy are motivated by something other than "objective reasoning."

Rawls's "just basic structure" in society and deliberative democracy's procedures and constraints are similar to the rules of a game, as he says. All players are expected to abide by the rules and accept the results. Justice relates to the whole, not to individual outcomes. A closer look at Rawls's understanding of what constitutes the "intuitive idea" of basic justice reveals that he is closely aligned with modern progressives on the Left. He expects a heavy-handed government to redistribute wealth, provide free education, and guarantee "a reasonable social minimum." But these concepts are all vague abstractions, requiring concrete interpretation and application. Unlike the rules of a poker game, there is a wide range of beliefs about what constitutes "basic justice," from the libertarian belief in privatization to the socialist belief in nationalization. Yet Rawls suggests that the modern welfare state is written on the heart.

That Rawls calls on us to avoid assessing his theory from the standpoint of individual persons should give pause. His and deliberative democracy's reliance on abstract ideals invites us to assess the theory not from the standpoint of real human practices and concerns but from purely theoretical, even wishful thinking. Lofty ideals and abstractions might easily appear to be self-evident and the tenets of "basic justice" obvious until concretized in real life. Such specifics are "the complications of everyday life" that Rawls believes we ought "to discard as irrelevant."[89] But even small, controlled studies of so-called democratic deliberation attest to the chimeric nature of deliberative democracy's ideals.[90] Thompson admits, "The conditions under which deliberative democracy thrives may be quite rare and difficult to achieve."[91] One study of juries found that the social and economic status and level of education of the jurors significantly impacted discussion and levels of participation.[92] Jury members with higher-status jobs, more education, and higher income speak more and are perceived to be more credible. Studies also demonstrate that sex and race play a role in levels of participation and influence. These types of empirical findings suggest to many deliberative democracy theorists the need for institutionalized procedures to "provide a more level playing field for the disadvantaged" and that such findings justify officials taking special measures to equalize conditions.[93] But again, who is to be in charge of the system? Clearly not the people themselves if they are considered the perpetrators of the old, unequal status quo.

Deliberative Democracy's Imaginative Orientation

Deliberative democracy's abstract and procedural understanding of justice and democracy lend themselves to governance by bureaucracy, in which the particularities and experiences of individual persons and communities are unimportant, even hindrances to the system. Administered and overseen by experts, deliberative democracy is "democratic" in the sense that other democratist theories are. Hiding behind an apparent rationalism and objectivity and orienting it is a comprehensive and imaginative vision. Engaging in extensive and elaborate reasoning, deliberative democracy fundamentally *reimagines* political possibilities. It wishes for us to drain our consciousness of experiential reality and known cause and effect. Its use of logic confirms something that has already happened at an imaginative level. Rawls's "veil of ignorance" relies primarily on the power of imagination. He does not try to demonstrate that humans are epistemically disposed to the type of abstract rationalizing to which he enjoins us. Whether or not we are capable of divorcing our identities and experiences from our beliefs about what is normative is not a question on which Rawls and other deliberative democrats dwell. They take for granted that not only are we capable of this, but also that it is the moral thing to do. But it may be that human psychology is not foremost rational in the sense that deliberative democracy believes. Considering the evidence of historical experience, a question that needs to be asked is whether the average citizen, in the end, will be moved by the better argument or by some other force or impulse. It needs to be considered whether the types of arguments that deliberative democracy considers "good" are indeed normative and also have the kind of epistemic sway that deliberative democracy takes for granted. History suggests that reason is not an impartial faculty but is closely bound with other, sometimes competing motivations and instincts.

The extent to which deliberative democracy itself relies on an unreal vision—"ideals"—to support its reasoning suggests that some other, imaginative capacity holds sway over our beliefs and ultimately worldview. Is it reasonable to envision a new way of conducting politics that has never happened before? If the imagination, perceptions, and emotional longing influence opinion-formation and, more important, action, then to what extent will citizens behave according to what is "rational" or "reasonable"? And to what extent will citizens agree and conform to deliberative democracy's rules for deliberation? If, in general, citizens cannot be expected to follow deliberative democracy's regulations, then should only the few, "true" democrats govern? Do those who defect from the deliberative democracy framework, as Patrick Deneen observes, "forfeit the right to be considered full-blown members of the democracy"?[94]

Deliberative democracy places great faith in its procedures to bring about justice and believes that translating the general will into law involves the technical task of programing "the regulation of conflicts and the pursuit of collective goals."[95] According to deliberative democracy, politics is largely a matter of reprogramming the citizenry according to rational rules. While deliberative democracy assumes that the proper exchange of reasons will elicit the general will, as in Rousseau's *Social Contract*, the way in which the general will actually emerges and finds concrete expression is shrouded in some mystery. Like other democratist theories, deliberative democracy requires us first to believe. Thompson has admitted as much: "The general conclusion of surveys of the empirical research so far is . . . mixed or inconclusive." While trying to identify the conditions under which deliberative democracy might be possible is a worthwhile endeavor for deliberative theory, "[t]here would be no guarantee that deliberative democracy would be vindicated."[96] We might ask how a political theory that largely contradicts relevant empirical findings in the field could have such traction in the academy and the broader culture. It is perhaps because it compels belief at a nonrational or imaginative level, which this book argues holds tremendous epistemic power.

The degree to which the ideal orients deliberative theories suggests that the type of imagination informing them inclines toward the romantic. Favoring the ideal over the historical and empirical as a heuristic is one of the central features of democratism and animates many of its beliefs. Rousseau, too, believes his conception of democracy exists only in the abstract. "Taking the term in the strict sense," he writes, "a true democracy has never existed and never will. . . . Besides, how many things that are difficult to unite are presupposed by this government!"[97] Democratism constitutes an ideology in part because of its preference for the abstract and the ideal, which do not constrain felicitous visions of freedom and equality. It does not focus on historical possibility and patterns of human psychology and behavior to determine what is possible and normative. "When confronted with findings that seem to confute his theory, Habermas is unfazed," Thompson says. "He reads the 'contradicting data as indicators of *contingent* constraints that deserve serious inquiry and . . . as detectors for the discovery of specific causes for existing lacks of legitimacy.' "[98] Evidence, even ample empirical evidence that refutes the hypothesis, to the committed democratist, does not indicate weakness or possible falsehood in the theory. Instead, the gap between theory and reality suggests to democratists in general and deliberative democracy theorists in particular that a great deal of work needs to be done to bring historical political societies closer to the ideal. The findings of this book suggest that such political idealism is dangerous. Insofar as the ideal sets our gaze on beautiful abstractions at the expense of real human beings, it does violence to reality. Rawls implies the irrelevance of the individual in his definition of procedural justice: "It is a mistake to focus attention on the varying relative positions of individuals and to require that every change, considered as a single transaction viewed in isolation, be in itself just."[99] Rawls's liberalism here resembles Plato's republic. "How would you defend yourself, Socrates, [Adeimantus] said, if someone told you that you aren't making these men very happy and that it's their own fault?" Socrates replies, "We aren't aiming to make any one group outstandingly happy but to make the whole city so."[100] It would sound like a noble ideal until it justifies the use of force against the noncompliant, in the name of an abstract ideal.

Even today we are witnessing the dangers of "general" theories of justice. Those on both sides of the political spectrum criticize the alienating and dehumanizing effects of abstract theories that promise an "overall rise" in the standard of living or the "trickle-down" effects of the free market, for example.[101] Similar abstract hypotheticals orient deliberative democracy. It promises that we will all be better off if everyone will just follow the procedures. But we have heard these promises before, and the burden of proof ought to be on those proposing to overturn and disrupt established ways. Without hard evidence that its vision of democracy is an actual possibility, there is little chance of its success and of people willingly participating. Deliberative theory claims that "heuristics, such as tradition," represent oppressive practices because citizens have not rationally consented to them. The question may be asked whether deliberative democracy's "procedural constraints" represent legitimate heuristics.[102] They might or might not, but they reveal that deliberative democracy, like other democratist ideologies, is not democratic in the classical sense.

Does justice demand the sacrifice of individuals? Rousseau is emphatic that it does. He famously asserts that those who would contradict the general will need to be forced to be free, but he also says that violators of the social compact may be put to death: "For such an enemy is not a moral person, but a man, and in this situation the right of war is to kill the vanquished."[103] It is hard to imagine deliberative democracy going this far, but implied in its theories of "good deliberation" is the need to silence those who do not follow the rules. If deliberative theorists were given the type of power they imagine they should have—recall the belief of Paul Quirk that a referendum on Brexit is dangerous without the institutional support of deliberative democracy—how would they deal with those whom they view as noncompliant? They would probably feel morally righteous in excluding people with views they have previously labeled "simple" or "populist," for example. How far would that exclusion go? If deliberative theorists were at the very heights of political power, would they go so far as to exclude these insubordinate people from the market, the financial system, healthcare— all aspects of social life that could be painted as constituting the real "national conversation"? If certain people or groups of people are not willing to behave as the deliberative democracy theorists believe they should, can they legitimately be excluded from society? China is attempting just this with a "social credit" system. If given the power, would deliberative democracy theorists attempt to "improve" democracy along these same lines?

In a 2020 Senate Judiciary Committee hearing, chief executive Mark Zuckerberg of Facebook and Jack Dorsey of Twitter defended their companies' rights to "moderate" conversations on their social media platforms, citing the preservation of democracy as a reason. "We are required to help increase the health of the public conversation while at the same time ensuring that as many people as possible can participate," Dorsey said. Zuckerberg stressed the importance of "the role internet platforms play in supporting democracy, keeping people safe and upholding fundamental values like free expression."[104] Yet their "moderation" amounted to plain censorship of ideas. Their justifications for this censorship in the name of democracy mirror the type of logic that deliberative democracy uses to justify its "parameters" for discussion. Public conversation, proponents of such thinking believe, must be moderated in such a way that "extreme" or "misinformed" views are excluded. The assumption is that the "moderators" are rational and enlightened, and it is appropriate for them to be the arbiters of truth. Ordinary citizens, on the other hand, may need to be "deplatformed" or have their public postings removed, paradoxically, to protect "the health of our democracy." It is not that Zuckerberg or Dorsey has studied deliberative democracy, but their horizon for thinking about norms of democracy is the same as that of deliberative democracy. That horizon is the ideology of democratism. They share the Rousseauean-democratist belief that a democratic *ideal* is normative, and undemocratic methods may be legitimate to achieve that ideal.

War Democratism

Introduction

This chapter examines military-backed democratism from the perspective of the Bush Doctrine and the George W. Bush administration's involvement in the wars in Iraq and Afghanistan. The neoconservative influence on U.S. foreign policy in the early 2000s represents a continuation in many respects of Jefferson's notion of an "empire of liberty" and also of Wilson's desire to "make the world safe for democracy." It is but a chapter in a longer story of democratic imperialism, which has been touched upon in this book. This foreign policy is one of the hallmarks of democratism.

Over the past twenty years, armed intervention in the name of democracy and humanitarian ideals has become second nature as a response to threats to freedom around the world. Guided by the belief that "the survival of liberty in our land increasingly depends on the success of liberty in other lands," U.S. foreign policy is not restrained by actual threats to national security or national interests. Considerations of territorial integrity, national sovereignty, and maintaining a balance of power—concrete goals which historically guided questions of foreign policy prior to the turn of the twentieth century—are second (or third) to grandiose aspirations such as "ending tyranny in our world."[1] The wars of the Bush administration are very much a part of Wilson's legacy. The neoconservatives, who served a prominent role in the Bush administration, acquired the epithet "Hard Wilsonians," but they probably are not any "tougher" than Wilson, if by that it is meant that they are less idealistic or less inclined to use force. Wilson's paradoxical "pacifism" is reflected in the liberal militarism of yesterday's neoconservatives and today's liberal internationalists alike.[2]

Few would venture to argue that Bush was familiar with the history of political thought, thinkers such as Rousseau or Leo Strauss, and many would even concede that he knew little about neoconservatism when he entered office. There is no evidence that Bush read the *Social Contract* or *Natural Right and History* or

The Ideology of Democratism. Emily B. Finley, Oxford University Press. © Oxford University Press 2022.
DOI: 10.1093/oso/9780197642290.003.0007

that he sat around philosophizing with Strauss's academic disciples. Still, these philosophical ideas penetrated to the very top of American society and specifically into the foreign policy establishment that proved so influential during the Bush years and continues to exert influence today, albeit under other guises. The influence of Strauss specifically on many of the decision-makers in the Bush administration has been well-documented and is discussed in this chapter. But Rousseau's influence can also be detected in Bush's thought and actions insofar as he was inclined toward the same type of thinking about a general will toward democracy written on the heart, a disinclination to take seriously the effects of a society's historical evolution on its present constitution, and the belief that, upon the ruin of the old society, a new egalitarian society can be legislated into existence. Bush need not have been familiar with the specific arguments or even general philosophy behind the strategy that he found himself pursuing, ad hoc or ill informed as it may have been. He likely stumbled into Afghanistan and Iraq with precious little understanding of what he was doing, and it is probable that he entered office without any strong ideological commitments. In fact, he ran for president in 2000 as an opponent of U.S.-backed nation-building. Yet the path of foreign intervention and nation-building that he embarked on has distinct parallels in American history.

It was no coincidence that he continued a legacy that began in full with Wilson but could be traced back even to Jefferson. The thesis of this book is that a profoundly influential ideology has permeated the thought of many of the decision-makers in the West. It acts as a background for understanding and interpreting political events. Bush was acting on ideas that have been pronounced in Western political thinking, especially the idea that democracy has been foreordained as the system of life and government that is destined to cover the globe. Moreover, Bush was surrounded by advisors who *did* have strong ideological commitments, some of whom were well versed in a progressive democratic philosophy of history, of which Bush may have been only vaguely aware. Like others who have been examined in this book, Bush was acting on ideas, the paternity of which he had little or no knowledge. Nonetheless, his words and actions demonstrate the effect on his thinking of the democratist interpretation of democracy. How conscious Bush or some of his advisors were that they were acting on these ideas is impossible to say, nor is it the purpose of this chapter to undertake such a task. This chapter aims to contextualize the Bush administration's actions and to demonstrate that the major impetus behind the wars in Iraq and Afghanistan fits well within the democratist paradigm.

Many have become alert to the possible ideological underpinnings of the liberal internationalist grand strategy of "benevolent global hegemony" that has prevailed in the United States since at least the mid-twentieth century. Recently John Mearsheimer and Stephen Walt have drawn attention to the deleterious effects of this foreign policy strategy.[3] These scholars have examined the nature of and motive behind this grand strategy, articulating their arguments in the language of international relations theory. Although Mearsheimer and Walt are sensitive to the role of ideology in driving U.S. foreign policy, they do not attempt a wide assessment of its influence or a comprehensive definition of the ideology behind it. Like many, they are more interested in the contemporary practical implications of the ideology than its philosophical roots and a thoroughgoing understanding of it. This book as a whole attempts to contribute to a deeper understanding of international relations theory by demonstrating the comprehensive nature of an ideology of democracy that many scholars of foreign policy implicitly or explicitly assume. This chapter in particular tries to illustrate the ways in which the pursuit of global hegemony follows the general pattern of the democratist ideology. By showing the connection between a grand strategy of liberal internationalism and an imaginative and idealistic interpretation of democracy, this chapter finds that jettisoning grand ambitions of liberal hegemony may depend upon a great deal more than "the future structure of the international system . . . and the degree of agency or freedom liberal states have in choosing a foreign policy," as Mearsheimer argues.[4] The more daunting variable might be whether the West can overcome the even more profound "delusion" that is a particular and powerful understanding of democracy itself, before we might hope to shake the grand strategy that reflects it.

To do this, however, it is necessary first to recognize the presence of this mighty force in American and Western politics. This chapter deals primarily with the Bush Doctrine, a variant of liberal internationalism, and the neoconservative grand strategy of the Bush administration. Like other chapters, this one expressly aims to elucidate the nature of democratism and to investigate its inner logic and practical implications. To accomplish this, it focuses on the foreign policy thinking of the Bush administration as it relates to various themes of democratism, many of which have been covered in other chapters, including its expansive imagination, totalizing tendency, proclivity for millenarian thinking, militarism and violence, and its dependence on supporting institutions to compel and reinforce its beliefs. There is overlap between Rousseau's ahistorical and idealistic understanding of democracy and that of the neoconservatives. The thinking of Strauss, too, has much in common with neoconservatism and democratism. As will be shown, neoconservative foreign policies stem from the type of natural rights thinking that guides Strauss's philosophy. Demonstrating the connection between Strauss's thought, which openly disdains democracy, and neoconservatism helps to illuminate a profoundly undemocratic dimension of neoconservatism and democratism. In order to deepen the discussion of neoconservatism as it relates to democratism, this chapter examines its interpretation of American history and its concept of the American exceptionalism myth.

It concludes with an assessment of the extent to which neoconservatism relies on democratic vanguardism that pursues the ever elusive and paradoxical idea of peace through war. By examining the philosophy behind neoconservatism through concrete examples, this chapter illustrates some of the foreign policy outcomes of this powerful expression of the democratist ideology.

The Term "Neoconservative"

"Neoconservative" may be an outdated term if by it we mean someone from the coterie of academics and elites who came to power in the 1990s and were influential in the Bush administration. However, neoconservatism as an ideology is far from needing an "obituary."[5] Its beliefs about human nature, society, history, and foreign policy are not limited to one particular political party or intellectual sphere but are shared by a wide contingent of American politicians, elites, academics, and media and public figures. The line between neoconservative and left-of-center liberal, at least on the issue of foreign policy and many domestic social policies, has blurred in recent years to the point of nearly disappearing altogether. The well-known neoconservative Max Boot openly declared that he has voted exclusively for Democrats since 2016 ("to save our democracy"), for example, and fellow neoconservative Robert Kagan is one of the leading proponents of liberal interventionism, the foreign policy that has enjoyed bipartisan consensus since at least 2001.[6] American Republicans, Democrats, and neoconservatives overlap in their shared faith in the ideology of democratism.[7]

Democratism extends from the thought of Jefferson and Wilson to Maritain and Catholic circles to Rawls and other secular liberal thinkers and finally to the Bush presidency, which would be followed by one Republican and two Democratic presidents who largely continue his legacy. Donald Trump tried to buck the trend of foreign intervention and succeeded in bringing some troops home, as he had promised to do, but even Trump, who campaigned for a more restrained foreign policy, faced an uphill battle extricating America from its various entanglements around the globe, demonstrating the grip of "liberal hegemony" on the Washington foreign policy establishment. Joe Biden's pullout from Afghanistan, fraught as it was, may signal a turn in U.S. foreign policy, at least for now, away from armed intervention in the name of democracy. But his vow to defend Taiwan in the event of a Chinese attack illustrates that the United States has not abandoned its commitment to "protect democracy" around the globe. Afghanistan may soon be replaced by other interventions that we will be told are crucial to making the world safe for democracy or saving a particular nation from "authoritarianism" or "tyranny."

While the so-called neoconservatives are the primary focus of this chapter, they can be considered something of a stand-in for many twenty-first-century liberal internationalists, who run the political gamut, are represented in non-governmental organizations, and are even represented in religious groups; the former editor of the Catholic publication *Crisis Magazine* Deal W. Hudson (who calls Maritain his "intellectual mentor") says that neoconservatism is merely an extension of Catholic social teaching.[8] It is more manageable to examine the beliefs of neoconservatism than the more sprawling "liberal internationalism" because of the decisive foreign policy actions of the former during the Bush administration and because its actions are backed by a clearly articulated philosophy, leaving little doubt about its system of beliefs and the real-world implications of those beliefs. Yet this chapter reveals as much about U.S. foreign policy and its architects in the past three decades as it does about neoconservatism, which is only one pointed expression of what so many politicians, leading intellectuals, and public figures have supported, especially since 2008, when a genuine bipartisan consensus formed around Barack Obama's continuation of the strategy of liberal internationalism. Interestingly, the election of Trump forged a tight friendship between many neoconservatives and Democrats, who united in opposition to Trump's foreign policy strategy of limited engagement and restraint. While many Democrats openly opposed Bush's intervention in Iraq and Afghanistan, beginning in 2016 they resembled neoconservatives in their pleas for U.S. troops to remain in those nations. This chapter, then, although examining the major figures of a particular movement whose day in the sun seems to have passed, is as relevant as ever as presidents continue to pursue those same foreign policies that neoconservatives long prescribed.

Leo Strauss and Natural Right

One of the most influential political philosophers of the twentieth century, Leo Strauss has been identified as the intellectual forefather of neoconservatism.[9] His teachings impacted many of those who were to become leading neoconservatives, especially Paul Wolfowitz, deputy defense secretary under Bush; Abram Shulsky, director of the Office of Special Plans (a government agency created, among other reasons, to look for evidence of weapons of mass destruction in Iraq) under Bush; and Irving Kristol, Richard Perle, and John Podhoretz.[10] Strauss is a famous critic of modernity and the Enlightenment and, to a lesser extent, of Rousseau, but his political philosophy represents a fundamental ahistoricism and corresponding conception of abstract right that is fundamentally in keeping with Enlightenment modes of thought and also with Rousseau's philosophy. It is perhaps not as paradoxical as it might seem that Strauss's skepticism of democracy, even disdain for it, represents a quintessential tenet of democratism. Strauss contends that the proper ordering of politics depends on knowledge of the ahistorical truths of natural right. This itself presupposes a "legislator" or lawgiver figure who establishes a polis (as opposed to a historical understanding of the organic development of a polis). Existing customs and institutions that do not reflect universal truth are inherently unjust and illegitimate, according to the philosophy of natural right. Modernity is in crisis, Strauss argues, because it has turned away from the insights of classical thinkers like Plato, whose doctrine of the Forms exemplifies the notion of right by nature. According to Strauss, modernity's descent into moral relativism and nihilism can be traced to the philosophy of historicism—the belief that human existence is historical—supplanting natural right. Not unlike Rousseau, Strauss claims to have the insight needed to restore what he takes to be the natural order.

Strauss admires classical antiquity's separation of *nomos* and *physis*, convention and nature, and draws on this distinction for his own understanding of what is normative. Philosophy itself, Strauss says, implies the distinction between right and history.[11] "[T]he only solid basis of all efforts to transcend the actual" are universal norms.[12] The actual—cultural practices, traditions, religious beliefs, manners, and mores—constitutes artifices that are perversions of nature, although Strauss acknowledges their use in creating social stability. In this sense, he is in agreement with Rousseau. For Strauss, however, following the classical thinkers, the highest existence is the life of contemplation, the life of the philosopher. With Plato, Strauss believes that only the few are able "to ascend from the cave to the light of the sun, that is, to the truth."[13] Those able to escape the darkness of the cave and to discern Justice in the abstract are in the best position to act as lawgivers.

Plato's *Republic*, which is Strauss's own political guide, well illustrates the implications of the theory of natural right. In the *Republic* Plato conceives of a perfectly just city, governed by the best (*aristoi*). Those who are able to contemplate justice in the abstract, the philosophers, Plato designates the city's guardians. The masses, incapable of understanding pure justice, are not disposed to ceding sovereignty willingly to the philosophers, so Plato devises a "noble lie" to explain the social stratification using divine mythology.[14] According to the myth, some are fit to rule and others to be ruled. Within the ruling class are two types of rulers: Philosopher Kings who legislate and a military class of "Auxiliaries" who protect the city. The rest are the producers, artisans, and all others unfit for leadership. Individuals can rise above the station of their parents through merit, but all are more or less naturally disposed to one of the three character types. Education plays an important role in the *Republic*, but it seems to be as much about weeding out those unworthy of the life of a Philosopher King as it is about cultivating that life. Central to Plato's project is identifying the traits that he believes make a qualified leader. The system of education he develops in the *Republic* is one designed to bring out these traits, primarily the ability to contemplate justice.

Strauss largely adopts Plato's normative understanding of the Philosopher King, who is able to penetrate the true nature of reality and to understand justice in general. He or she is concerned with the perfection of the whole community and not merely the individual, Strauss says. This extraordinary person represents "the full actualization of humanity."[15] Able to see beyond mere partisan attachments to the Good in the abstract, the "wise legislator" frames laws that reflect absolute justice, Strauss says, and if necessary can "complete" the law using his or her discretion.[16] Those who are wise legislators or "good men" are known generally by their willingness "to prefer the common interest to their private interest" and to do the right thing in each situation because "it is noble and right and for no ulterior reason."[17] Because of their superior vantage, power, and benevolence, "the judge and ruler has larger and nobler opportunities to act justly than the ordinary man."[18] The vast majority of people are not capable of this nobility of spirit and require the direction of the leadership class. Quoting Jefferson, Strauss asserts, "That form of government is the best, which provides the most effectually for a pure selection of [the] natural *aristoi* into offices of the government."[19]

It is clear that Strauss's philosophy is not compatible with democracy in the ordinary sense. His reading of the classics and his belief that the classical natural right doctrine "is identical with the doctrine of the best regime" assumes an inherent conflict between right and the popular will.[20] Although Strauss states that "the fundamentals of justice are, in principle, accessible to man as man," he agrees with Plato and Rousseau that only a few possess the virtue necessary to prefer the general over the particular. The political philosopher, who is concerned with the question of "the best political order as such," must act as "umpire" in all questions of political controversy, according to Strauss.[21] But this poses an obvious problem for democracy. For Strauss, "[t]he political problem consists in reconciling the requirement for wisdom with the requirement for consent." He says that "wisdom takes precedence over consent," but he understands the importance of gaining consent in modern democracies. Thus, citizens must be "duly persuaded" that it is in their interest to be ruled by a wise elite.[22]

On this point, Strauss's philosophy is compatible with Rousseau's. A wise legislator is expected to "found" the just city (or nation). Although not all people will be able to recognize the wisdom of the legislator and the superiority of his vision, the common good demands that they accept his rule. From this perspective, Strauss's political philosophy as well as Plato's *Republic* are democratic in the same sense that Rousseau's *Social Contract* is democratic: in the democratist sense. That is, all three profess a view of popular sovereignty in which the popular will is carefully curated to reflect the philosopher's own vision of democracy. Rousseau's legislator, Plato's Philosopher King, and Strauss's wise statesman all ostensibly rule in the name of the people but are expected to control and give direction to the people's desires. Strauss's thought is guided by his belief in "natural right," yet all of the democratists examined in this book share to an extent his conviction that what is normative is not integrally related to historical norms. This ahistorical epistemology necessarily requires political translation—an enlightened elite of some kind to mediate "democracy." One of the touchstones of neoconservatism is the belief that the United States is based on natural rights and universal, abstract principles. Neoconservative foreign policy essentially extends Strauss's natural right philosophy into a grand strategy of liberal hegemony. In practice, the neoconservatives themselves determine through policy prescriptions the ways in which so-called universal principles find concrete expression.

While there is certainly a connection between Strauss and many neoconservatives, and indeed some openly acknowledge his influence, it is possible to overstate the connection.[23] The genealogy of the neoconservative worldview is complex and can be traced back to many others, including Ronald Reagan, Franklin Delano Roosevelt, Theodore Roosevelt (men who might have merited inclusion in this book), even Marx in certain respects, but finally to the seminal thinker Rousseau. Neoconservatism represents one expression of what is ultimately a deeper ideological phenomenon affecting the wider Western world. Nonetheless, it is profitable to examine the political philosophy of neoconservatism's most immediate philosophical forebear to shed light on those aspects that clearly illustrate the wider phenomenon of democratism.

This book advances the view that an eighteenth-century French philosopher has had an enormous impact, directly and indirectly, on Western political thinking, specifically its understanding of democracy. Whether or not Jefferson or Wilson or Maritain read Rousseau does not impact the thesis that the major tenets of Rousseau's political philosophy, often channeled through others who were influenced by him, can be discerned in the works and imagination of thinkers of various partisan affiliations across time and space. Wilson, in fact, outwardly repudiated Rousseau's *Social Contract*, but his writings and actions nevertheless suggest a deep kinship between the two. Strauss, too, was critical of certain aspects of Rousseau's philosophy, but many of his underlying assumptions about human nature and epistemology suggest meaningful similarity between the two.

The Neoconservative Reading
of American History

Examining the neoconservative understanding of American history reveals a great deal about its underlying philosophy and points toward its foreign policy prescriptions. Following the interpretation of the American founding by Thomas Jefferson, Thomas Paine, Louis Hartz, and their own main intellectual figures, neoconservatives hold that the United States originated as a compact based on the universal principles of freedom and equality.[24] This reading of American history supports the belief that America is based on an "idea" and did not form organically and historically as did other nations. According to this narrative, America is unique and has a special role in the world. "Most nationalisms are rooted in blood and soil, in the culture and history of a particular territory. But in the case of the United States, the Declaration of Independence and the Revolution produced a different kind of nationalism, different from that of other nations," Kagan asserts.[25] Americans freely came together in Philadelphia and rationally decided the course of their government. The Constitutional Convention was not, according to this interpretation, the result of historical process and the colonists' attempt to recover their historical English rights from the tyrannical King George III. Rather, the American founders transcended their heritage and broke radically, even metaphysically with the past. The American represents a "new man."[26] Quoting Hans Kohn's 1957 essay, "American Nationalism," Kagan contends that Americans escaped the "confines of historical-territorial limitation."[27] Citing Jefferson and Paine, neoconservatives argue that the American founders were the first to assert their natural rights and to found a nation based on universal principles. In the words of Charles Krauthammer, America is "uniquely built not on blood, race or consanguinity, but on a proposition."[28]

Presenting their philosophy and specifically foreign policy as having deep roots in American thought and the Western tradition more generally, neoconservatives initially gave the appearance of embracing a brand of American conservatism. Many American conservatives were in fact attracted to the ideas of neoconservatism, assuming that because some of their beliefs were based on ideas of founders such as Jefferson, their philosophy must be an antidote to progressivism, which tends not to glamorize the American founders. Traditional conservatives, drawing on such sources as the *Federalist Papers*, have interpreted the American founding in light of the framers' fear of large government and their desire to check and decentralize power.[29] This older brand of conservatism has found in Washington's Farewell Address a message similar to the major point of John Quincy Adams's Fourth of July address, that America ought not go "abroad in search of monsters to destroy."[30] The neoconservative interpretation of American history, by contrast, suits its foreign policy aims, which eschew limited government, fiscal conservatism, and a restrained foreign policy. Much of neoconservatism's historical argument for American interventionism rests on an Enlightenment strain of thought that they trace to Jefferson and Benjamin Franklin and some of the other founders. They have even looked to Rousseau as a thinker largely compatible with the American political tradition. Strauss's disciple Allan Bloom, for example, concludes from Rousseau's famous dictum "Man was born free. Everywhere he is in chains" that "it should be evident that Rousseau begins from an overall agreement with the [American] Framers and their teachers about man's nature and the origins and ends of civil society."[31] Rereading American history as a sort of rational social contract, such as Rousseau and Jefferson envisioned, neoconservatives imagine that the Constitutional Convention was a "moment" that gave birth to America.[32] This country is not the result of an organic and historical process, like other nations.

America, the Exceptional Nation

This retelling of American history as a social contract has helped to inform the neoconservative logic of regime change. America is a testament, according to this interpretation, to the idea that a political order can be rationally decided upon and codified. Replacing or reeducating the ruling class with one versed in "universal principles" can bring a state closer to the democratic ideal, at home or abroad. Neoconservatism does not dwell on the historical and cultural conditions of a society because, it assumes, inherited practices are largely arbitrary and irrelevant to the new order. Consideration of a people's ancestral practices, rooted in the "meaningless process" of history, in the words of Strauss, should not be a major factor in questions of politics.[33] Political order has its source in "nature" and "universal principles," which are taken to be identical with the American regime.

Kagan argues that the American founders "unwittingly" invented a new and revolutionary missionary foreign policy based on the myth of American exceptionalism.[34] To deploy the military on behalf of oppressed peoples in foreign lands is thought to be a natural expression of America's "universalist ideology."[35] Bush's secretary of state Condoleezza Rice interprets the American mission to mean "extending the benefits of liberty and prosperity as broadly as possible."[36] Proponents of this grand strategy reject what they take to be outmoded notions of national interest and are motivated instead by abstract goals such as "the success of liberty" around the globe. America's foreign policy is rooted in "values," the neoconservative Krauthammer says, quoting the words of John F. Kennedy.[37] Disparaging "classic" definitions of national interest as Old World and selfish, neoconservatives redefine national interest to include the freedom and prosperity of other nations and argue that it is in America's self-interest to pursue these goals. Transforming other nations into democracies would mean fewer enemies for America, they claim. Additionally, the economic system that is an integral part of liberal democracy, the "free market," ostensibly promotes peace as it increases prosperity.

With pronounced moralistic overtones, neoconservatives present the motives behind their policy of "benevolent global hegemony" as unquestionably noble.[38] America may incorporate intervention and preemption as justifiable dimensions of its foreign policy because it is, in the words of Krauthammer, "Beyond Power. Beyond Interest."[39] According to Kristol and Kagan, "It is precisely because American foreign policy is infused with an unusually high degree of morality that other nations find that they have less to fear from its otherwise daunting power."[40] And if America may be considered imperial for its global ambitions, says the (former) neoconservative Boot, there is "no need to run away from the label," for America is acting in the name of justice. Drawing on the words of Jefferson, Boot declares that the American empire is "an empire for liberty."[41] Even if American imperialism is "at gunpoint," he insists that it is for the good of oppressed peoples.[42] America's humanitarian motives separate its foreign intervention from the meddling, self-interested monarchs of the past. The United States is "less self-interested than any other great power in history."[43] Bush similarly described the U.S. mission in the world as "beyond the balance of power or the simple pursuit of interest."[44] American foreign policy is and always has been, say neoconservatives, of a different order than that of other nations in history.

The neoconservative philosophy of history reflects the democratist dialectic of history in general. The world is moving inexorably toward democracy, and enlightened nations such as the United States can help in the unfolding dialectic of freedom. Providence or fate vouchsafed to America the ideals of liberty and equality, and America therefore has a moral duty to "lead freedom's advance."[45] A new, global democratic order is just over the horizon, but America must act as the vanguard. In 1991, George H. W. Bush declared in his State of the Union address that America was on the precipice of a "new world order," and America's decision to take decisive action against the perpetrators of evil can forever alter the course of liberty in history.[46] Later, the George W. Bush administration spoke of America's "historic opportunity" to permanently alter the course of world events. America can, said Rice, "break the destructive pattern of great power rivalry that has bedeviled the world since the rise of the nation-state."[47] In his second inaugural address, George W. Bush asserted that "the force of human freedom" is the "only one force of history that can break the reign of hatred and resentment, and expose the pretensions of tyrants, and reward the hopes of the decent and tolerant."[48] The spread of democracy "can be hastened," Kagan declares, through military intervention.[49] America has already helped to usher in this "post-history" phase of the democratic dialectic in Europe, according to Kagan, and it is America's moral duty to bring the European "paradise" to other nations, by force if necessary.[50]

"The Public Interest"

The universal principles guiding all nations, which neoconservatism maintains coincide with American "values," parallels the Rousseauean idea of the general will. Under the heading "What is the public interest?" Daniel Bell and Irving Kristol, in the first pages of the first issue of the neoconservative public policy journal *The Public Interest*, quote Walter Lippmann: "The public interest may be presumed to be what men would choose if they saw clearly, thought rationally, acted disinterestedly and benevolently."[51] Bell and Kristol admit that the public interest as defined by Lippmann has never existed in any society; the people have never really known or realized the will that is attributed to them. It is an ideal, but one that we must strive for nonetheless. Implicit in this understanding is the belief that someone must midwife the general will, or what is in "the public interest," into existence. In foreign policy thinking, this translates to the idea that the U.S. military and other American institutions ought to help foreign peoples express their will, which neoconservatives assume is democratic and in opposition to their leaders. The will of the good people of Iraq, for example, is for American-style democracy.

From the Ashes, Democracy

Democracy does not come without a price, though. Many neoconservatives follow the belief of Jefferson and Wilson, that social and political upheaval must precede democratic peace. The Bush administration actively pursued destabilizing policies in states it considered illegitimate in the Middle East in an effort to disrupt and replace traditional ways of life. In 2004 in a speech to the United Nations, Bush said that the United States had mistakenly excused oppression in the name of stability, but now "we must take a different approach."[52] The neoconservative Ralph Peters mentioned the ways in which policies of destabilization would at once aid in the process of democratization and directly benefit America. In the essay "Stability, America's Enemy," Peters observes that "wars, revolutions, and decade after decade of instability opened markets to American goods, investors, and ideas."[53] In the Middle East America should try, in a sense, to re-create these conditions or at least not actively avoid them for fear of the consequences. Disrupting the ways of life within states considered to be backward or illegitimate will, according to neoconservatism in particular and democratism in general, open the door to a more rational, better political order. This philosophy holds that revolutionary upheaval, spontaneous or instigated by a foreign power, makes way for democracy and capitalism—the natural desires of all peoples. It will even potentially benefit the United States. Michael Ledeen's description of "creative destruction" illustrates this mentality:

> Creative destruction is our middle name, both within our own society and abroad. We tear down the old order every day, from business to science, literature, art, architecture, and cinema to politics and the law. Our enemies have always hated this whirlwind of energy and creativity, which menaces their traditions (whatever they may be) and shames them for their inability to keep pace. Seeing America undo traditional societies, they fear us, for they do not wish to be undone. They cannot feel secure so long as we are there, for our very existence—our existence, not our politics—threatens their legitimacy. They must attack us in order to survive, just as we must destroy them to advance our historic mission.[54]

Dismantling the old ways of life is not an end in itself, but a means toward building a better, more democratic world. Cultural and educational programs help at once to dismantle the old ways and to institute new norms. The U.S. Agency for International Development (USAID) spends a considerable amount on education services that, according to its website, fit into its larger mission to "further America's foreign policy interests on issues ranging from expanding free markets, combating extremism, ensuring stable democracies, and addressing the root causes of poverty, while simultaneously fostering global goodwill." Reflecting Kristol and Kagan's argument for nation-building, the USAID mission statement says that foreign aid "investments" constitute a "strategic, economic, and moral imperative for the United States and [are] vital to U.S. national security."[55] In Afghanistan specifically, the United States spent billions of dollars on what the USAID categorizes as "basic education." Its stated mission of education to support the "full and productive participation in society" of impoverished and disaster-struck peoples of the world suggests an underlying philosophical commitment to the Lockean and Anglo-American understanding of the political role of productive labor.[56] For neoconservatives and many others, non-Western peoples engaging in the free market through capitalist trade will simultaneously produce a political transformation toward liberal democracy.

The education programs that the U.S. State Department undertakes are invariably guided by "our values," and specifically democratist values.[57] After the invasion of Afghanistan and Iraq, many of the USAID programs targeted women, hoping that by transforming their traditional role in society, they might lead the way toward a new form of social and political existence.[58] In 2004 Secretary of State Colin Powell announced the creation of the Iraqi Women's Democracy Initiative, a $10 million project to help "women become full and vibrant partners in Iraq's developing democracy."[59] One of the recipients of a grant from the Initiative, the Independent Women's Forum, hosted a Women Leaders Conference in 2005 meant to give women "a better understanding of the universal principles of democracy."[60] Many have pointed to ideological motives behind the Bush administration's focus on women's programs and argued that such efforts to promote women's rights in Iraq and Afghanistan were to galvanize support for the wars and for the administration.[61] However, the desire to liberate women fits within the general logic of "creative destruction" and parallels, in many ways, the same efforts at women's emancipation of the Soviets in Central Asia in the twentieth century.[62] The Soviets also recognized that in order to "build" a new system of government and way of life, the linchpin holding together traditional society, women, must be removed. Removing women from their traditional domestic and social roles would cause major disruption to the existing order. Neoconservatives insisted that bringing women into the national and global economy through "entrepreneurship" would help generate a democratic ethos more broadly. One scholar observed that for the Bush administration, "[e]ntrepreneurial women . . . are the sign of a free market economy, which is itself taken as a stand-in for a democratic government."[63] Microfinance and loan programs were designed specifically in order to "enhance women's ability to achieve economic independence."[64] One of the consequences of this would be the loss of men's exclusive hold over financial resources. Even the looming threat that women could survive apart from their male family members would have a tremendously disruptive impact socially, Americans and Soviets believed, and would drive these traditional societies toward the anticipated political end. Women would be in positions of greater social and political independence; whether for good or ill, it was supposed that in Asia this would result in an erosion of the Islamic patriarchy and a corresponding strengthening of the replacement regime. Liberating women is a revolutionary tactic expected to set in motion the historical dialectic, whether toward democracy or communism. "The advance of women's rights and the advance of liberty are ultimately inseparable," said Bush.[65] Releasing women from their historic role in Islamic society would permit "nature" to take its course and the desired political regime to unfold.

Using the Military to Help Win the Culture War

While creative destruction generally refers to the cultural-economic forces of democratic capitalism, it is impossible to overlook the military operations that almost invariably accompany these "softer" tactics to dismantle existing norms. However, the military objectives are not always made clear, largely because they are means that are incommensurate with the desired end. "Benevolent global hegemony," as an abstraction in the imagination, suggests a sort of friendly leadership role for the United States, but in practice it demands force to back its desire to establish global norms. The policies behind benevolent global hegemony are as nebulous and sprawling as the concept itself. Military victory, neoconservatives admit, is neither possible nor the objective. Richard Holbrooke, U.S. special representative for Pakistan and Afghanistan from 2009 to 2010 under Obama, said in 2010, "[W]e can't win [the war in Afghanistan and Pakistan] militarily, and we don't seek to win it militarily because a pure military victory is not possible."[66] Holbrooke and many others have looked to the words of retired general David Petraeus, former commander of multinational forces in Iraq and a proponent of the war, that "military victory is not possible."[67] Indeed the ideological objective of spreading democracy alongside the "progress of our values in the world" means that victory on the battlefield does not mean an end to the war. The real battle must be a protracted cultural battle, as America's two decades in Afghanistan revealed.[68]

Chuck Hagel, a longtime critic of the war in Iraq, said in 2006 while a senator from Nebraska that "militaries are built to fight and win wars. . . . America cannot impose a democracy on any nation — regardless of our noble purpose."[69] Henry Kissinger, the famous theorist of the international relations realist tradition, said in 2006 that "a clear military victory" along the lines that the United States sought was not possible.[70] Yet many neoconservatives have concluded that the failure to democratize the Middle East is not due to an inherent contradiction between means and ends but to the means being insufficient to accomplish the end. Expressing a sentiment common to neoconservatives, retired army general Stanley McChrystal, who preceded Petraeus, in 2017 said of his 2009 surge, "While flawed due to ambitious timelines and the failure to execute a truly whole-of-government approach, [it] could have succeeded had Washington demonstrated the necessary patience and commitment."[71] At that time, the war in Afghanistan was in its ninth year. If democracy is not taking root, it is believed, it is because the United States is not doing enough to eliminate the forces standing in the way of a people's natural desire for liberalism and democratic capitalism. Neoconservatives called for more spending, additional "surges," and greater power for U.S. civilian agencies not only to collect intelligence but also to directly issue orders to kill.[72] Such an attitude informed the Lyndon Johnson administration, which had been convinced that additional troops in Vietnam would finally produce victory.[73] Neoconservatives seemed to believe, as Undersecretary of State George Ball presciently predicted of the escalating war in Vietnam, that "our involvement will be so great that we cannot—without national humiliation—stop short of achieving our complete objectives."[74]

As additional measures failed to produce the intended results, many of the Iraq and Afghanistan wars' neoconservative proponents became even more zealous in their calls for justice. Peters, for example, exasperated at the deteriorating situation in the Middle East in 2009, called for a redoubling of efforts: "Win. In warfare, nothing else matters. If you cannot win clean, win dirty. But win. Our victories are ultimately in humanity's interests, while our failures nourish monsters."[75] Peters attributed America's inability to win a decisive victory in Iraq and Afghanistan to effeteness and an unwillingness to spend money and manpower. "Had we been ruthless in the use of our overwhelming power," Peters asserted, we could have lessened the death toll and had victory in both countries.[76] Conservative commentator and New York Times columnist David Brooks noted the "irony" of liberation by force and conceded that attempting to establish democracy in Iraq "in retrospect, seems like a childish fantasy." Incredibly, Brooks's solution was not to reconsider the mission but to give "the good Iraqis, the ones who support democracy," a "forum in which they can defy us."[77] Democracy ought to be pursued yet. In his article "Better a Stalemate Than Defeat in Afghanistan," Boot blamed the failed surge of 2009 on inadequate numbers of troops and insufficient time. After analyzing various reasons for recurring U.S. failures in Afghanistan, situations that continued to produce "déjà vu" experiences for the casual observer, Boot asked, "Is it worth maintaining and even expanding the U.S. commitment to what is already the longest war in American history?" Yes, he responded. He called on Trump to eschew his predecessor's timidity and to send in many thousands of additional troops, at least 100,000, "without an attached timeline" or "rigid numerical caps." There cannot be a limit to the blood and treasure that the United States is willing to spend on democratizing despotic nations.

A "Democratic" Strategy After War Communism

In 2017, at the end of the sixteenth year of the war in Afghanistan, McChrystal argues for "staying the course" and expanding the war in Pakistan. In a piece in *Foreign Affairs*, he and his co-author Kosh Sadat look to none other than the Russian revolutionary Vladimir Lenin for guidance in Afghanistan: "In 1902,

Vladimir Lenin published a now famous pamphlet titled *What Is to Be Done?*, in which he prescribed a strategy for what later became the Bolsheviks' successful takeover of Russia's 1917 revolution. Lenin argued that Russia's working classes required the leadership of dedicated cadres before they would become sufficiently politicized to demand change in tsarist Russia."[78] McChrystal and Sadat laud Lenin's "clear-eyed assessment of reality" and conclude, "[T]he same is needed for Afghanistan now."[79] It is certainly curious that McChrystal would look to Lenin, of all world leaders, for insight. Could it be that an underlying philosophical kinship exists between neoconservative and communist vanguardism and revolutionary tactics? McChrystal, like Lenin, believed that he was helping to bring noble ideals—freedom and equality—to the oppressed. The general ideology of democratism calls for dedicated cadres disciplined to its ideological principles. For neoconservatives and many other advocates of military intervention on behalf of democracy, it is no contradiction to bring about democratic peace and prosperity through war.

The parallels between the communist plans to replace bourgeois and Islamic societies with socialism and the U.S. plan to replace "terror" with democracy should not be dismissed. The concerted military, social, economic, and educational U.S. efforts to overthrow and replace existing regimes resemble the revolutionary "whole-of-government" tactic of Lenin and later Stalin to "build socialism." "War communism" was the official name for what was to be an emergency measure to build socialism in Russia.[80] It was premised on the belief that the old society had to be forcibly and completely dismantled. Although it was meant to be an extreme, temporary measure to "leap" into socialism, it proved the modus operandi throughout Soviet rule in Russia and its satellites. It may be appropriate to title the neoconservative strategy to build democracy internationally "war democratism." Removing the old elite by military force and consolidating military gains with cultural and institutional programs are, like its communist antecedent, at the heart of its program. War democratism is similarly premised on the belief that the military can provide a jump-start for democracy in countries under the rule of dictators. Clearing away the old and backward norms, neoconservatives and many other liberal internationalists assume, will open the way for the people's natural desire for liberal democracy to come to fruition: "[T]he force of American ideals and the influence of the international economic system, both of which are upheld by American power and influence," will inevitably erode the inherited ways of undemocratic nations.[81] Through regime change, America can accelerate the historical process of modernization and democratization (which are held to be synonymous). This should happen, according to Kristol and Kagan, across the globe, "in Baghdad and Belgrade, in Pyongyang and Beijing," and "wherever tyrannical governments acquire the military power to threaten their neighbors, our allies and the United States itself."[82]

Grandiose Vision as Moral Heroism

The neoconservative vision of democracy is greatly informed by its imaginative, sometimes Manichaean, understanding of good and evil. Kagan draws on romantic images of sheriffs in the old west when he describes the American mission; like Gary Cooper's character in High Noon, America needs to stop the bad guys.[83] His metaphor, however, breaks down. In saying that international outlaws must be stopped "through the muzzle of a gun," Kagan obscures the real nature of American interventionism, which is often conducted from afar with military technology. Unmanned aircraft or drone warfare is now the order of the day.[84] This image, however, does not elicit the same sentiment as Cooper facing the gunmen in the classic western. Yet creating an imaginative link to the heroic is an important aspect of neoconservative grand strategy as well as democratism. Democratism, as this book argues, depends a great deal on the imagination and relies on it for grand visions of the world transformed. Neoconservatives make use of abstract rhetoric and dreamy sentiment in order to marshal support for its international cause. America ought to "relish the opportunity for national engagement, embrace the possibility of national greatness, and restore a sense of the heroic, which has been sorely lacking in [its] policy," Kristol and Kagan triumphantly declare.[85]

Many have pointed to the role that the heroic myth of this sort plays in the neoconservative imagination and connected it with Strauss's apparent fear of the West succumbing to nihilism.[86] Thompson, for example, sees in neoconservatism's use of the hero metaphor and its desire for America to embark on grand missions a disdain for liberalism and individual rights. Nietzsche, Heidegger, Strauss, and other critics of liberal individualism may indeed have influenced neoconservatism in direct or indirect ways, as Thompson and others argue. But the general inclination to view abstract and far-off events such as global democracy and bringing an end to tyranny as supremely virtuous, and at the same time to deride local concerns as "prosaic and mundane," is characteristic of democratism. The use of moralizing rhetoric that would call us from our bourgeois torpor fits the pattern of other democratists, who similarly believe that we ought to look beyond everyday matters to a higher, shared cause that can be accomplished through politics. In a 1999 paean to Senator John McCain, Brooks laments that Americans "no longer aggressively push hard-edged creeds" and would rather "enjoy their sport-utility vehicles, their Jewel CDs, and their organic lawn care products." In other words, Americans prefer the business of ordinary living to the frenetic desire to remake the world that drives Washington elites such as Brooks. Brooks reveals the yawning chasm that separates elites such as himself from the rest of Americans, telling his readers, "If you drive around the country, looking into the cultural institutions of the middle class . . . you see a nation that is good-hearted and bourgeois" but "tranquil to a fault." Brooks is of the opposite opinion of G. K. Chesterton, that "the most extraordinary thing in the world is an ordinary man and an ordinary woman and their ordinary children." For Brooks, the life of most Americans may be quaint, but it is morally uninspiring. Instead of attending to a spirit of "patriotism" and a higher calling, Americans preoccupy themselves with their own daily concerns: "When a people turn toward the easy comforts of private life, they inadvertently lose connection with higher, more demanding principles and virtues." Brooks does not have in mind the worship of God, whom many Americans would have identified as that "higher calling," but a civil religion of "muscular progressivism." He imagines the American people finding new life and spirit in a "public philosophy" of "patriotic sentiment, an emotional style and a set of rituals." The end of this patriotism is not simply worship of the nation-state but the inspiration for a new foreign policy fitting of America's greatness. In the dénouement of Brooks's piece, he writes, "America's moral destiny is wrapped up in its status as a superpower. If America ceases to assert itself as the democratic superpower, promoting self-government around the world, it will cease to be the America we love."[87]

The neoconservative belief that Brooks expresses, that democratizing other nations constitutes "more demanding principles and virtues" than the "small-scale morality" of day-to-day life, exemplifies the democratist ethic. Concern with the local and domestic is often derided by democratists as unimportant compared to grand, national missions. "The current mood of squishy tranquility may be a sign of instinctive conservatism," he says, which is to be rejected in favor of a more progressive orientation toward morality.[88] Living the ordinary but difficult domestic life rooted in local concerns is considered to be the essence of the moral life for conservatives of an older Chestertonian or Burkean type, but for Brooks it is the lamentable ethos of Middle America. Brooks as well as Rousseau are of the democratist belief that virtue consists in abstract and romantic longing for a national (perhaps ultimately international) togetherness and feelings of equality and camaraderie—the general will or public interest.

Brooks's article augured the foreign policy that would dominate the Washington consensus after 9/11, yet it does not seem to have made America any better off by the metrics of American domestic peace and prosperity, national security, national unity, or international reputation. On all of these counts, America is decidedly worse off than in the 1990s. "[N]obody is going to identify this decade as a high-water mark of American idealism," Brooks wrote in 1999. Yet many Americans long for the pre-9/11 world, in which American idealism had not driven us into countless and seemingly endless foreign entanglements.[89] It is characteristic of democratism to lament that the nation is not united behind a great international (or domestic) cause that would not simply alter the status quo but fundamentally change human existence as we know it. That democratists often look to the supporting institutions of a civil religion is not surprising. Democracy, in the ideology of democratism, is the Christian eschaton. Just as Christ's coming is expected to usher in a new age, the global democratic revolution is expected to utterly transform life and politics.

"True" Democracy Just around the Corner

One of the trademarks of war democratism, like Soviet communism, is the belief that if victory is elusive and if history continues to march on much as before, fraught with injustices and inequality, it must be due to poor organization and lack of will. Neoconservatives and other democratists are surprised when their foreign policy efforts lead not to democracy but toward its opposite: social backlash in the form of a new authoritarianism and a proliferation of violence.[90] Many in the Bush administration were "beside themselves at the result [of the invasion of Iraq]," David Rose reported in 2006.[91] Similarly, Obama had not expected a new terrorist organization to result from the U.S. invasions in the Middle East. In an interview in 2015, Obama said, "ISIL [the Islamic State of Iraq and the Levant, also known as ISIS] is a direct outgrowth of Al Qaeda in Iraq that grew out of our invasion, which is an example of unintended consequences."[92] The rise of ISIS is just one example of the many unintended consequences of the wars in that region, to say nothing of the U.S. military presence elsewhere involved in the "war on terror," which spans seventy-six countries, or 39% of the world's nations.[93] The unintended consequences of the various missions abroad, especially those of counterterrorism efforts, are impossible to measure, although many have pointed out some of the most obvious results. The Taliban is one noteworthy example of unintended consequences, having first grown out of the mujahideen, a U.S.-backed rebel force that resisted the Soviets during the Soviet-Afghan War of 1979–1989, then turned U.S. enemy during the decades-long intervention in Afghanistan, until finally taking over the country in 2021.[94]

Democratist Idealism and the Proliferation of Violence

The failure of America and its allies to democratize the Middle East and also the belief that democracy is in decline globally (according to Freedom House), ought to raise questions about the vision that has prompted actions like nation-building.[95] In the case of international communism, no practical measures brought the Soviets closer to their vision of a classless society. Rather it stratified Russian society in new ways. The very nature of the communist ideal implies a need for radical social engineering, silencing those who would stand in the way of the glorious vision. Is the goal of global democracy so different? It too seems to require unending violence and occupation of foreign lands. Repeated failures abroad and the proliferation of new sources of political and social chaos suggest the elusive and utopian nature of building democracy through military and cultural intervention. Neoconservatives frequently mention America's "separation from the past and . . . departure into the future" and contrast American foreign policy with the "realpolitik" of other nations in history, but is this accurate ?[96] Krauthammer, when giving the 2004 Irving Kristol Lecture at the American Enterprise Institute for Public Policy Research, opened his talk by saying that, unlike other empires in history, "*we do not hunger for territory.*" Yet he concluded the speech, "This is war, and in war arresting murderers is nice. But you win by taking territory—and leaving something behind."[97] Neoconservatives make it clear that while America's mission is grounded in universal principles, it must make use of the traditional means of warfare in order to accomplish its goals. Ostensibly fueled by noble ideals, the wars in the name of benevolent global hegemony have had consequences as destructive as the wars of our "cynical, Old World counterparts."[98] As of February 2018, the wars in Iraq and Afghanistan, for example, had resulted in 59,592 U.S. and 268,000 Iraqi deaths, including between 180,000 and 202,000 civilian deaths, and 61,889 Afghan deaths, including 31,419 civilian deaths.[99] The financial cost of these wars (including the war in Pakistan) for the United States up to 2018 was estimated to be 4.8 trillion dollars.[100]

Pursuing a grand strategy that even one of its neoconservative proponents admits is "expansive and perhaps utopian" has caused enormous destruction and has had costly consequences for the United States.[101] Neoconservatives claim to be strongly anticommunist and were Cold Warriors until the fall of the Soviet Union, yet their frame of mind bears an uncanny resemblance to that of their erstwhile enemies. Just as the communist cause was subordinated to the revolutionary strategy and tactics of the Bolshevik party, with disastrous results for all but the party's inner circles, so too was the U.S. treatment of Afghans and Iraqis subordinated to "Washington politics" and "American interests," with similar consequences in kind if not degree.[102] The reaction to human suffering of some American politicians with neoconservative leanings has been morbidly reminiscent of dedicated Bolsheviks. Madeleine Albright, for example, U.S. ambassador to the United Nations under President Clinton, famously said in an interview in 1996 that the reported half-million Iraqi children killed as a result of U.S.-led sanctions against Saddam Hussein's regime was "worth it."[103] Even in the absence of such candid admissions, the desire to stay the course despite costly and bloody outcomes indicates the interplay of utopianism and recalcitrance born of a rigid ideological commitment rather than a practical interest in reform.

No closer to the neoconservative vision of global democracy or even a democratic Middle East is the United States than was the Soviet Union to a classless society in the twentieth century. The withdrawal from Afghanistan should have been the coup de grâce of American idealism in foreign policy. But the fact that the orchestrators and cheerleaders of these colossal foreign policy failures have maintained their status as "foreign policy experts," with Boot even named among the "world's leading authorities on armed conflict" by the International Institute for Strategic Studies, suggests that at least among elite circles in American public life democratic interventionism is alive and celebrated as a foreign policy strategy.

History is moving inexorably, these interventionists assume, toward global democracy—"sweeping the world at [an] unprecedented rate"—in a process that is at once natural and historically fated, indeed guided, according to neoconservative thinkers such as Michael Novak, by the hand of God.[104] The "will to freedom" exists universally among peoples and nations, Krauthammer says, and is "the engine of history."[105] Bush often drew on Christian language in his description of U.S. foreign policy aims. In his 2004 State of the Union address he triumphantly proclaimed, "The momentum of freedom in our world is unmistakable, and it is not carried forward by our power alone." "We can trust in that greater power," he added, "who guides the unfolding of the years."[106] According to neoconservatives, U.S. foreign policy stems from universal truth and is not limited by historical contingency or ambitious and self-serving politicians. In an inversion of Christian eschatology, neoconservatives suggest that the imaginative participation in a national mission can provide not only earthly renewal on a global scale but also spiritual fulfillment.[107] Like Brooks, Kristol and Kagan harken to Theodore Roosevelt's message to look beyond everyday life and toward a grand national mission, nothing less than "improv[ing] the world's condition."[108] Americans, and specifically traditional conservatives, neoconservatism insists, need to end their political somnambulism and call for greater global engagement and intervention—nothing short of the transformation of human existence.[109]

Strauss understood well the revolutionary and dangerous implications of the attempt to order politics according to an abstract ideal. The philosopher who contemplates the ideal is bound to see the gross discrepancy between "is" and "ought." "[T]he recognition of universal principles," Strauss says, "forces man to judge the established order, or what is actual here and now, in the light of the natural or rational order; and what is actual here and now is more likely than not to fall short of the universal and unchangeable norm."[110] The idealist who believes, as Strauss does, that the best regime "is not only most desirable; it is also meant to be feasible or possible," sees a need for radical change and may believe that the ideal is worth any cost.[111] In the context of democracy, the need for consent is a major barrier to the rule of wisdom in politics, as Plato's *Republic* and Rousseau's *Social Contract* illustrate. Overcoming the need for consent, while revolutionary, would bring about justice, according to the theory of natural right. "It would be absurd to hamper the free flow of wisdom by any regulations," Strauss says, and "it would be equally absurd to hamper the free flow of wisdom by consideration of the unwise wishes of the unwise."[112] Seeing the clear social and political implications of the doctrine of natural right, he compares it to "dynamite."[113] An elite cadre must somehow appear to raise the political consciousness of the people to its true will for politics to be both *wise* and *legitimate* by modern standards. Brooks's belief that "American purpose can find its voice only in Washington" is an example of this type of democratist interpretation of "representation" that Strauss and others have in mind.[114] The people can find their correct voice only through the mediation of their elites.

Conclusion

In Stanley Kubrick's 1987 film, *Full Metal Jacket*, the colonel tells a discontented subordinate that America is "here to help the Vietnamese, because inside every gook there is an American trying to get out." This was of course a criticism of the type of foreign adventurism that has been analyzed in this chapter, yet over thirty years later the colonel's statement appears to be the genuinely held belief of many so-called experts in U.S. foreign policy. Despite political setbacks (some might say failures) and the suspicion that with its magazine the *Weekly Standard* and its Washington-based think-tank Project for the New American Century, neoconservatism might be dead, its philosophy continues to animate Washington politics. Trump, who campaigned promising to restrain American foreign policy and otherwise limit commitments abroad, still could not help but refer to America's "righteous mission" in his State of the Union address in 2018.[115] The idea of American exceptionalism construed in terms of a "righteous mission" has become so ingrained in the American imagination that passing references to it are hardly noticed. The only prominent candidate in the 2016 election to campaign against nation-building was hardly able to stray from the interventionist path of his neoconservative presidential predecessors. Trump's plans to pull troops out of the Middle East were invariably met with cries of resistance from Democrats and Republicans alike, along with most major media corporations. The 2018 National Defense Strategy abstractly outlined plans for increasing military spending and for deepening the resolve to resist perceived threats to American security, threats that were no longer primarily from terrorism but from "inter-state strategic competition." Few regions of the globe were excluded from the outline of places of strategic importance to U.S. national security. The report named China and the South China Sea and the Indo-Pacific region; Russia and Georgia, Crimea, and eastern Ukraine; North Korea and South Korea and Japan; and Iran and "its neighbors." In summary, the U.S. defense strategy of 2018 proposed, among many other things, "maintaining favorable regional balances of power in the Indo-Pacific, Europe, the Middle East, and the Western Hemisphere."[116] And this was from a presidency which promised to restrain U.S. foreign policy.

Trump proved largely unable to rid Washington, his administration, and perhaps himself of interventionist or internationalist and democratist instincts when it came to grand strategy. If anything, his election at least temporarily strengthened the resolve of the foreign policy establishment in Washington to maintain the status quo. United in common cause against Trump, erstwhile neoconservative and progressive enemies put their differences behind them and together advanced a foreign policy strategy united in its aim.

Stephen Walt analyzes the reasons that liberal hegemony has "remained the default strategy" among the foreign policy elite despite being "sharply at odds with the preferences of most Americans."[117] While the factors Walt mentions, such as political and financial gains for those invested in the status quo, are undoubtedly factors in its perpetuation, this chapter has tried to broaden the picture and show that an interventionist foreign policy in the name of democracy is the practical culmination of the democratist ideology. Liberal hegemony has been a grand strategy in the making in the West since the sentimental humanitarianism of Rousseau became the ethic informing Western politics. Rousseau's philosophy prepared the way for this type of foreign policy thinking among the elites, who, as Walt demonstrates, benefit most from it. Walt's conclusion that the elites have entrenched interests in "[o]pen-ended efforts to remake the world" reflects one of the general findings of this book, that the democratist ideology has served primarily the interests of the powerful, who draw on the ideology's deep rhetorical reserves of language about "freedom" and "equality" to pursue goals that often lead to oppression, greater discrepancies in wealth, sharper political divisions, and devastating wars.

Democratism is both geographically and morally expansive in its vision for humanity. A globalist urge is part of what makes it distinctive. Motivated by the anthropological and epistemological beliefs that all of humanity share the same desire for Western liberal democracy, the democratist ideology manifests in foreign policy as interventionism couched as a moral responsibility. That democratism repeatedly fails to bring about its ends and nevertheless is unwilling to revise its program is evidence of its profoundly ideological nature. Brooks's opinion piece in the *New York Times* in June 2019 reveals the contempt that many liberal internationalists harbor for those who do not share their view. Smugly titled "Voters, Your Foreign Policy Views Stink!," it repeats the neoconservative narrative of the indispensability of America as the world's policeman, warning that "wolves like Putin and Xi" will "fill the void and make bad things happen" without American intervention.[118] That Brooks has maintained this view for decades, despite the quagmires into which it has drawn the United States, suggests the power of the ideology behind it. As he points out, a recent study estimates that only 9.5 percent of voters are "traditional internationalists" and that young people are the most likely "to want the United States to abstain from intervening in human rights abuses."[119] To Brooks this suggests that young people have "lost faith in human nature and human possibility." Another interpretation is that those young people have witnessed the foreign policy failures of Brooks's generation. They have seen the devastating consequences of democratic idealism and witnessed, some firsthand, the creation of new evils following American intervention.

The stark contrast between the violent means and the expected peaceful and democratic end is one of the many paradoxes of democratism. The ostensibly humanitarian mission to help the people of Libya under Muammar Gaddafi, to name one telling example, quickly escalated into a full-scale armed intervention and regime-change mission and resulted in a terribly destructive and ongoing civil war. Just months after Gaddafi's death—an event assumed by liberal internationalists too mark the dawn of a new democratic age in Libya—"the UN came to the conclusion that the human rights situation in Libya was now worse than at any time during Gaddafi's rule."[120] Many look back at life under Saddam with similar nostalgia.

It is difficult to separate the desire for liberation from the violence it necessitates and the power that would fall into the hands of those in charge of the new regime. Cloaked in a general concern for the benighted peoples of the world, the foreign policy of benevolent global hegemony does not hesitate to use force to try to further its ostensibly humanitarian missions. While military-backed intervention in the name of democracy is a hallmark of neoconservatism, more importantly it is a natural outgrowth of democratism. Unable to conceive of a world in which democracy is not the dominant mode of life, democratists are uncomfortable with the idea of peoples and nations choosing another type of government, upheld by norms that are incompatible with liberal democracy. Democratists are convinced that all peoples of globe must, at least deep down, desire the same type of political and economic system that has taken shape in the United States and in many Western European nations. Blaming corrupt reigning elites rather than deeper cultural or religious beliefs that are fundamentally incompatible with Western-style liberal democracy, democratists believe they have a rather straightforward solution: the removal of those elites who are hampering the natural advance of democracy. Wars of intervention may ebb and flow as the electorate wearies of foreign adventurism, but so long as democratism orients its foreign policy, "humanitarian" intervention will continue to guide the thinking of the decision-makers in Washington, London, and Brussels.

8

Conclusion

Imagining what sort of despotism might arise in the democratic age, the nineteenth-century historian and traveler in America Alexis de Tocqueville fears an "immense and tutelary power" that will rise to watch over "an innumerable multitude of men all equal and alike" under the pretext of serving them.[1] The power of this class of overseers, Tocqueville says, "is absolute, detailed, regular, far-seeing, and mild. It would resemble paternal power, if like that, it had for its object to prepare men for manhood; but on the contrary, it seeks only to keep them fixed irrevocably in childhood." This powerful government will take shape, Tocqueville predicts, "in the very shadow of the sovereignty of the people."[2] It will combine centralization with the illusion of popular government, made possible in part by the modern obsession with an abstract idea of equality. Having grown accustomed to conditions in which distinction of any kind is frowned upon, the people will become enervated, lose their will even to govern, and willingly cede their power to the political overclass that promises to rule in their name. Tocqueville sensed that democratic centralism would be accompanied by the trappings of democracy, comforting both the rulers and the ruled. Each person accepts the system "because he sees that it is not a man or a class but the people themselves that hold the end of the chain."[3] Only the pretense of popular rule remains at this late stage of democracy, but according to Tocqueville, the people are complicit in their own demise.

This book has approached the ideology of democratism from the perspective of the "schoolmasters" rather than the multitude. It has not offered an assessment of the extent to which the people have contributed to the rise of this version of democracy—a daunting task. But it is worth asking whether democracy as a form of government, especially of a certain kind, invariably tends toward the type of "administrative despotism" Tocqueville predicts and which this book has investigated. Democracy need not turn totalitarian in order for certain self-proclaimed democrats (with a lowercase "d") to assume the position of overseer. Is Tocqueville correct that, having resigned their actual power,

The Ideology of Democratism. Emily B. Finley, Oxford University Press. © Oxford University Press 2022.
DOI: 10.1093/oso/9780197642290.003.0008

the people "console themselves for being in tutelage by thinking that they themselves have chosen their schoolmasters"? To what degree are the people complicit in abdicating authority in the democratist variant of democracy? That the participants in the Swiss study of deliberative democracy changed their minds in the direction of the study's administrators indicates how easily people defer to those in positions of power, however small.[4] Those who conducted the study would like us to believe that the participants changed their minds because the materials presented were the objective truth, but how can we be certain that this is the case, and that it was not the influence of propaganda that changed minds? Either way, this study is a microcosm of democratist assumptions: the people, on their own, are not up to the task of self-government. Without the "tutelage" of the democratists, to borrow Tocqueville's aptly chosen word, they are ill-informed, unaware of their own best interests, prone to irrational thinking, and unconcerned with the common good. According to the democratist interpretation, real democracy is impossible, despite insistence that it is just around the corner. That is the real democratist paradox.

There is, however, another way to understand democracy. According to this other view, the people en masse are indeed ill-equipped to govern, but it is not because they are irrational or ignorant so much as that certain moral and cultural preconditions are needed for there to be good sense and an inclination for the common good. Moral exertion and deliberation guided by good motives rather than right reasoning in the abstract determines the people's capability for self-government, and morality cannot be taught by experts but must be cultivated by individuals themselves within subsidiary institutions such as the family, local community, and intermediary religious and cultural groups. Figures such as Aristotle, Edmund Burke, Alexander Hamilton, John Adams, James Madison, Alexis de Tocqueville, Orestes Brownson, and Irving Babbitt are qualified supporters of popular government, but they do not claim to be "champions of the people" or to desire direct popular rule. They do not delude themselves about the multitude's capacity for political sagacity. Their beliefs about the capabilities of the people to self-govern are more modest than those of their democratist counterparts. Yet because they do not expect the people to be something other than they are, they also do not believe that revolutionary change is necessary for a functioning democracy to be possible. Because thinkers in this alternate "democratic" tradition are not prone to triumphant proclamations about the sanctity or wisdom of the popular will, they are sometimes derided as elitist, especially by the democratists who fashion themselves the people's *real* champions.

Paradoxically, supposedly elitist figures like Burke, Hamilton, Adams, and others in this line of thinking are democratic in a way that democratists are not. These thinkers, who have a more historically rooted, humbler conception of democracy, do not look to a vanguard of intellectual elites to galvanize the masses to a new way of life.[5] Their historical conceptions of democracy, grounded in an awareness of humankind's dual potentialities for good and evil, result in a political philosophy without pretensions for remaking society. Thinkers in this tradition have the modest aim of reform rather than revolution or transformation.

A look back at democracy's manifold expressions in history helps us to imagine what is really possible and what is probably chimeric. Paradoxically, the type of direct popular democracy that Rousseau, the French revolutionaries, and many democratists glorify appears to promote the variant of democracy that least values the actual will of the people. This plebiscitarian democracy tends toward the centralization of power because it treats citizens as one undifferentiated mass (think of the general will).[6] If citizens represent a single body of interests, then one leader or small cadre of leaders can act as their representative, creating uniform policies to govern them. If, on the other hand, citizens' interests are diverse, competing, and sometimes irreconcilable, then they must have representatives that can channel those interests in meaningful ways politically. The framers of the U.S. Constitution believed this to be the case, and so they advocated for a federated system of states that could protect different geographic and cultural interests; for a bicameral legislature to represent these interests at a more granular level; for an electoral college to give rural and less densely populated areas a voice in national politics; and for three competing branches of government to put additional checks on centralized power—all of this on the assumption that state and local governments would further respect the diverse interests of Americans. Jefferson believed that some of these mechanisms were drawbacks because they thwarted the direct and immediate will of the people, but this book's examination of Jefferson suggests that his vision of direct democracy is less democratic than he imagined.

The U.S. Constitution is not a blueprint for Universal Democracy, but its components represent some ways of facilitating popular rule while trying to prevent too much centralization and the abuse of power. As Aristotle, Brownson, Heinrich Rommen, and others have pointed out, it is fruitless to try to determine the best government in the abstract. Aristotle stressed the role of contingency in assessing the merits of various constitutions: "One sort of constitution may be intrinsically preferable, but there is nothing to prevent another sort from being more suitable in the given case; and indeed this may often happen."[7] He took for granted that one state or person does not prescribe the way of life for another state. "We do not deliberate about all human affairs," Aristotle says in the *Nicomachean Ethics*. "[N]o Spartan, for instance, deliberates about how the Scythians might have the best political system. Rather, each group of human beings deliberates about the actions that they themselves can do."[8] It is best to try to work from certain givens, such as a people's political predisposition, and also, at the most local level, to avoid sweeping claims about how distant peoples ought to live. This was also Brownson's view. "Ordinarily the form of the government practicable for a nation is determined by the peculiar providential constitution of the territorial people," Brownson says, "and a form of government that would be practicable and good in one country may be the reverse in another."[9] Furthermore, Aristotle argues that we ought to aim at a political order that does "not employ a standard of excellence above the reach of ordinary men, or a standard of education requiring exceptional endowments and equipment, or the standard of a constitution which attains an ideal height."[10] The idealism that is at the heart of democratism *encourages* the type of thinking that these figures wish to avoid: it is not shy about prescribing ways that other people ought to live; it tries to legislate from far away; it is universalist in its prescriptions; and it employs a standard of excellence that is not only above the reach of ordinary men and women but also likely outside of epistemic possibility in that it treats human beings as rational abstractions. At best, the defeat of this idealistic vision draws the dreamer into melancholic despair. At worst, it leads him or her into a mad but fruitless pursuit of the ideal. A romantic biopolarity is almost inevitable.

The ultimate emptiness of this democratic idealism is increasingly apparent today. Perhaps the desire to remove the statues of erstwhile democratic heroes such as Jefferson and Lincoln indicates growing awareness of the hollowness of abstract promises about "a new birth of freedom" and that "all men are created equal." The democratist vision of democracy that has been foisted upon Westerners for centuries offers the tantalizing prospect of a new Earth and invites revolt against the existing order, but insofar as its vision is nebulous and unrealizable it is dangerous. Having been encouraged to believe that such abstract ideas of absolute freedom and equality are real possibilities, people begin to despair and grow angry. Many thought leaders have interpreted the rise of anti-Establishment political parties in the United States and Europe to mean that democracy is in peril. Another possibility is that it is not democracy as a form of government that is in danger but the democratist version of it, and hence the power of the democratists.

President of Freedom House Michael J. Abramowitz laments that "right-wing populists gained votes and parliamentary seats in France, the Netherlands, Germany, and Austria during 2017." "While they were kept out of government in all but Austria," Abramowitz says, "their success at the polls helped to weaken established parties on both the right and left." These "right-wing populists," according to Freedom House, are a source of the global democratic "crisis."[11] For those who support the democratist interpretation of democracy, such as Abramowitz, it is entirely consistent to treat the results of popular elections as undemocratic. When contrary to democratism's understanding of what constitutes democracy proper, these election results can be explained away as the work of "populist leaders" and other sinister forces rather than be treated as genuine expressions of the popular will—for good or ill. It may in fact be the case that unmediated popular sovereignty is dangerous, producing deluded and misinformed popular opinion—as history witnesses—but democratism does not criticize this dangerous possibility in democracy *as a form of government.* Instead, democratism proclaims the virtues of pure democracy and popular rule while at the same time pursuing a political vision that is decidedly undemocratic.

Interestingly, Jan-Werner Müller characterizes populism much as I have characterized democratism. Populism, he says, "is a particular moralistic imagi-nation of politics, a way of perceiving the political world that sets a morally pure and fully unified—but . . . ultimately fictional—people against elites who are deemed corrupt or in some other way morally inferior." He goes on to argue that populists are "always antipluralist: populists claim that they, *and only they*, rep-resent the people" and that "[t]he populist core claim also implies that whoever does not really support populist parties might not be part of the proper people to begin with."[12] Müller's criticism seems to extend largely to the leaders of pop-ulist movements rather than the people themselves. These are some of the basic tenets of democratism outlined in this book. For Müller, however, populism is a uniquely modern phenomenon and one that he asserts is distinct from the Rousseauean conception of democracy that he takes to be a theory of genuine democracy. Rousseau's general will "requires actual participation by citizens," Müller asserts. "[T]he populist, on the other hand, can divine the proper will of the people on the basis of what it means, for instance, to be a 'real American.'"[13]

Does not populism as Müller defines it perfectly describe Rousseau's general will? If this modern populism is as Müller characterizes it, then it appears to be yet one more expression in a long line of democratist thinking. However, it may be that Müller and others who associate modern populist movements with "authoritarianism" and "simplistic" views are in fact playing the part of the democratist. Critics of populism tend to dismiss this modern phenomenon as a function of demagogues conspiring to take advantage of popular grievances. This gives the impression that populism is not really a democratic movement at all but the creature of a small coterie of power-seeking elites. Again, this way of disparaging popular sentiment is a quintessential component of democratism. Expressions of the popular will that do not conform to the democratist's expec-tations are dismissed as false and not really representative of the people's desires. But to indict the popular will as such would pose a very serious problem for the critics of populism. It would implicate the very system of government that allowed such views to find expression. The ideology of democratism is defined in part by an unwillingness to criticize democracy while being continually dis-satisfied with actual outcomes. The purpose of mentioning populism here is not to evaluate it as a movement but to highlight the democratist assumptions of some of its critics. If what is called populism has found favor with a plurality or majority of people in the countries in which it has made appearances, as suggested by the success of its candidates at the ballot box, then to dismiss it as undemocratic or dangerous to democracy is, to say the least, paradoxical. These critics ought to consider whether it is democracy itself that is in fact the problem for them.

Jason Brennan represents the quintessential democratist viewpoint in *Against Democracy*, which argues that a knowledgeable elite ought to rule by "epistocracy." Appropriately titled, this book hopes to see less participation in politics from the masses and the greater concentration of power in the hands of certain leaders. Brennan no doubt envisions himself among those with a greater say in politics. While the rest of Americans must be content to have legislation shaped by the people Brennan says are their betters. He hopes that rather than worry about politics, most people will simply continue to distract themselves with "football, NASCAR, tractor pulls, celebrity gossip, and trips to Applebee's." [14,15] That Brennan's bread and circuses should be some of the pastimes of the American heartland illustrates the smug contempt that many democratists hold for ordinary citizens. Those who might not be inclined to defer to the expertise of men such as Brennan are assumed to be backward and ignorant and standing in the way of the democratist paradise. The logic of democratism leads to Brennan's conclusion that "when some citizens are morally unreasonable, ignorant, or incompetent about politics," they ought to be disenfranchised in one way or another.[16] Contrary to Brennan's belief that his theory takes the opposite view of other democratic theorists, who call for greater political engagement and deliberation, his desire for an "epistocracy" is actually nearly identical to many popular democratic theories. It has simply taken deliberative democracy, for example, to its logical and practical conclusion. So many theories of democracy assume the ability of more or less hidden elites to discern the true popular will.

For the democratist, we all can be united in the embrace of the general will—or democratism's interpretation of it. "We are all Georgians," Senator John McCain declared when wishing to defend Georgia against Russian aggression; a few years later he declared, "We are all Ukrainians."[17] Or consider David Brook's assertion that "we are all neoconservatives" and Jefferson's proclamation that "we are all Republicans, we are all Federalists."[18] For the democratist, there are no genuine and meaningful differences among people. All of "our values" are finally reconcilable in the values that democratism holds to be true. Democratism leaves little room for diversity with regard to worldview and other important matters. The "shared recognition of universal rights" demands unquestioning acceptance, lest one be considered extreme, Fascist, or, in the language of yesteryear, "an enemy of the people."[19] Claiming an exclusive right to arbitrate what is reasonable and informed and what is ignorant or "hateful," democratism establishes the criteria for knowledge itself through its command over language and therefore thought. It is an all-encompassing ruling ideology. "[W]hat is essential," Dostoevsky's Grand Inquisitor insists, "is that all may be *together*" in it.[20]

Like the Grand Inquisitor, democratists hope to relieve humanity of the great and "dreadful" burden of freedom and history through elaborate social planning and reorganization.[21] In an attempt to circumvent the human proclivity for selfishness and evil, thinkers such as Rousseau, Maritain, Rawls, Brennan, and many others devise political systems that are supposed to circumvent that facet of human nature that has heretofore made perpetual peace and fraternity impossible: our fallenness. They assume that with the right rational planning and through the proper rational engagement of citizens, the gears of the democratic machine can finally be set in motion. Yet as the democratists "condescend to detailed considerations" of actual political affairs, in the words of Bertrand Russell, many of them discover with Rousseau that "the old problems of eluding tyranny remain."[22] And so they devise ever more elaborate ways of trying to get around the old problem of human nature. It soon becomes apparent that much of the institutional edifice that the democratists try to replace has reappeared in new forms in their own political schemes, from civil religion to a newly stratified society along different, ideological lines.

The foreign policy of democratism puts into particularly sharp relief the democratist's need for power in order to enact the vision. Woodrow Wilson foresaw and pioneered a foreign policy that, beginning with him, would not necessarily respect the desires of the American public and would justify military actions in terms of "liberation" and furthering democracy abroad. Constitutional scholar Louis Fisher lists the many instances in which the Hamiltonian idea that "unity is conducive to energy" was used to justify actions that "resulted in great harm to the nation and its constitutional system" and often gave tremendous power to the executive: "Harry Truman's decision to go North in Korea, resulting in intervention by the Chinese and a costly stalemate; Lyndon Johnson's escalation of the Vietnam War; Richard Nixon's Watergate; Ronald Reagan's Iran-Contra; George W. Bush going to war against Iraq on the basis of six false claims that Saddam Hussein possessed weapons of mass destruction; and Barack Obama using military force to remove Muammar Qaddafi from office, turning Libya into a failed state and a breeding ground for terrorists."[23] All of these instances, with the exception of Nixon's actions, were motivated by the democratist desire to liberate a foreign people and resulted in vast new presidential powers that, according to Fisher, had not been constitutionally delegated. Wilson was especially aware of the role of foreign policy in expanding executive power. C. Eric Schulzke points out that in the 1900 edition of *Congressional Government*, "[Wilson] notes that 'when foreign affairs play a prominent role' in the nation's affairs, the Executive 'must of necessity be its guide.' This 'new leadership,' will have a 'very far-reaching effect on our whole method of government.' "[24]

All of the wars or "military actions" after World War II aimed at foreign libera-tion resulted in an extraordinary increase in power for U.S. presidents.[25] But of the countries listed above, how many were better off after U.S. intervention?

Stephen M. Walt argues that the foreign policy establishment is deeply com-mitted to perpetuating the status quo of liberal hegemony—a consequence of the democratist ideology—because it stands to gain financially and politically.[26] He writes, "A more restrained foreign policy would give the entire foreign policy community less to do, reduce its status and prominence, decrease the impor-tance of teaching foreign policy in graduate schools, and might even lead some prominent philanthropies to devote less money to these topics. In this sense, liberal hegemony and unceasing global activism constitute a full-employment strategy for the entire foreign policy community."[27] I would extend this logic to an assessment of democratism in general. Those who uphold the ideology tend to cry loudest for more power to the people but in practice demand power and resources for themselves. They have much to gain by perpetuating their under-standing of democracy, which requires, first and foremost, that *they* be given the reins of power.

The need for control and a desire to overturn existing regimes—foreign and domestic—suggests that democratist idealism is tied to a lust for power, which is fueled by feelings of righteousness. The U.S. debacle in the Middle East exem-plifies the consequences of a foreign policy motivated by "moral clarity" and natural-right thinking. The conviction that these nations with no experience of anything resembling Western-style democracy could be led by outsiders to such an existence was, as Brooks conceded, childish.[28] Leo Strauss writes that for those who believe in classical natural right, "agreement may produce peace but it cannot produce truth."[29] This is one of the tensions that animates democratism. Feelings of righteousness both create and undermine the desire for global dem-ocratic peace. Wilson's words upon American entrance into the First World War put this dimension of democratism in sharp relief: "Force, Force to the utmost, Force without stint or limit, the righteous and triumphant Force which shall make Right the law of the world, and cast every selfish dominion down in the dust."[30] Indeed the crux of democratism seems to be the belief that "right is more precious than peace."[31] With the advance of military technology and especially drone-use, the increasingly abstract nature of war has made this lofty ideal easier and easier to proclaim.

Democratism's claim that force—even "procedural norms" as a type of coer-cive force—will bring about liberation raises disturbing questions about its deeper motives. Recall Jefferson's words about the birth pangs of freedom: "Rivers of blood must yet flow . . . yet the object is worth rivers of blood, and years of desolation."[32] There is no price too steep for the idealist. The French man of letters Anatole France (1844–1924) observes that the idealist may be "led to the most savage ferocity by the tenderest optimism."[33] Beginning with a vision of glorious new possibilities for humanity, the idealist sooner or later comes to believe that the people he envisions benefiting from his ideas are the very ones who stand in the way of its realization. "[W]hen one starts with the supposition that men are naturally good and virtuous, one inevitably ends by wishing to kill them all," France said.[34]

Robespierre embodies this idea. He cherished Rousseau's ideas and helped to inaugurate a new era of politics in which the interpretation of democracy of the *Social Contract* would prevail among political elites in Western nations. It is easy now to dismiss Robespierre as a caricature, extreme, a fanatical revolutionary little connected with actual democracy, but he believed that he was helping the democratic cause by suppressing what he saw as its enemies. Historian Colin Jones documents the twenty-four hours leading up to Robespierre's public execution: "In the Constituent Assembly between 1789 and 1791, [Robespierre] fearlessly championed the people, fought for individual rather than a property franchise, argued a powerful case for freedom of expression, championed religious toleration, demanded humane judicial reforms, including the abolition of the death penalty, and joined the anti-colonialist cause (which has culminated in the abolition of slavery in February 1794). He made major contributions to debates on the 1793 Constitution, the world's most democratic charter (though currently on hold)."[35] Robespierre genuinely believed that he embodied the people, declaring "Je suis [du] peuple."[36] He may actually have hoped to bring about a better existence for ordinary people.

Robespierre "is painfully sincere in all his words and actions," Jones says, "offering an exemplary model of high-minded action in the style of his great idol, Jean-Jacques Rousseau, the arch-apostle of moral transparency."[37] However, Robespierre's belief in terror as a means to democracy clearly undermined his intentions. "Terror is nothing but prompt, severe, inflexible justice; it is therefore an emanation of virtue," he declared just five months before his own public execution at the hands of the terror he had helped to unleash and justify.[38] His logic, though alarming in its nakedness, conveys the general logic of democratism. In the democratist worldview, virtue and violence are easily reconcilable. The former often necessitates the latter. The ideal of Democracy, or *liberté, égalité, fraternité*, is imagined to be so noble and pure, universal in the goodness it will bestow on humanity, that even violence can be used in its pursuit. Bound up with this idea is the power that must be given the idealist. This is on display in Robespierre's handling of parliamentary procedure: "If one of his own points of order is rejected, [Robespierre] may retort with verbal violence, invoking the loftiest principles and his own emotional disarray at being challenged so stridently, that the speaker has to give way."[39] The idealist fathoms that his or her own path to the regeneration of society is the sole one and demands extraordinary power in its name.

On the other hand, the type of imagination that Babbitt calls "moral" is fundamentally humble. It considers the practical steps required to achieve the goals of liberty and equality. It asks what, concretely, is the goal, and at what cost. It considers whether a particular vision is an actual possibility given the circumscribed nature of human existence, or whether the goal is simply a lofty abstraction. The moral imagination is cultivated through an awareness of history and rejects idealism as a dangerous invitation to violence and coercion. It looks to past events to furnish examples of future possibilities. This type of imagination results in an understanding of politics in general and democracy in particular that is modest in its ambitions. It eschews grand theories and systems promising to ameliorate the human condition and to solve once and for all the historical challenge of politics. Its foreign policy is limited in aim, always having in mind the complexity of foreign cultures and the law of unintended consequences.

The Italian philosopher Benedetto Croce, writing at the turn of the twentieth century, was alarmed by the metaphysical speculation and ahistoricism that seemed to have become dominant in philosophy. Seeming to anticipate the dangerous consequence of such abstract theorizing for politics, especially in his home country, Croce says that practical action informed by a philosophy that is "outside and above history" "may be noble at least in its intention, or ignoble; it may want to 'réorganiser la société,' as with August Comte, or it may want to revolutionize and rationalize society, as with Karl Marx, or it may want to use its means to keep the people quiet and servile, as with other philosophers: but the incongruity is always the same."[40] The incongruity, that is, between the ideal and existing reality. For the idealist, reality must be made to conform to the vision, however painful it might be. Croce seems to have it right that ahistorical philosophies claiming to address issues of "supreme" importance over other "minor" and particular concerns often serve the interests of those who would be the "directors and reformers of society and the State."[41] His belief is not unlike that of Russell, who saw in the idea of a general will an empty abstraction made to order for abuse.

Hailing the voice of the people, democratists actually look to an enlightened elite not to lead the people to the best version of themselves but to encourage their own views from the people, which almost always means requiring the people to abandon their historically evolved practices. Claes G. Ryn, who puts forth a historical, constitutional view of democracy, argues against this type of democratist elitism. "Truly cosmopolitan thinkers or leaders who see disturbing weaknesses in a people that they would like to see changed would not demand that the people abandon their historical heritage for a wholly different way of life assumed to be inherently superior. Fruitful, authentic change can only result from the particular society trying to be more fully itself, by living up to and in the process also revising its own *highest standards*."[42] Ryn argues that for a rationalistic and ahistorical thinker like the democratist "[t]o call upon a people to discard what made them what they are and to insist on a supposedly superior uni-culture is to rob them of a source of identity and self-respect. A people cannot genuinely reform without building on its own strengths, without in a sense, being itself. Imposing on it an allegedly universal culture inimical to its traditions can produce only mechanical, inorganic change."[43]

Some may respond that while certain democratists may seem to advocate a "uni-culture" through their uncompromising insistence on *their* interpretation of democracy, surely others, such as the deliberative democracy theorists, for example, are not guilty of this. It is true that deliberative democracy seems to allow communities to find their own norms through dialogue, but, as this book has shown, the deliberative theorists' parameters for acceptable discussion have already determined the culture that is acceptable: some variant of secular, neoliberal culture. Deliberative democracy has come up repeatedly in this book because it demonstrates that democratism can assume different forms, some of which are subtle and democratic in appearance. That the theories of Rawls and Habermas are more subtle than others in advancing a particular normative vision, one favoring a kind of proceduralism, does not place them outside the democratist tradition.

Proclaiming that the voice of the people is supreme—something that has become de rigueur for those seeking political power in the democratic age—helps to create the impression that the actions of the democratists are always democratic. The Rousseauean concept of the general will, which set democratism on its general course, also makes "possible the mystic identification of a leader with his people, which has no need of confirmation by so mundane an apparatus as the ballot-box," as Russell remarked.[44] Claiming to speak on behalf of the general will, democratism has been a source of great influence for its purveyors. Because its representatives claim that they alone represent the voice of the people, democratism discourages discussion that would call into question its actions and motives. "Either you are with us, or you are with the terrorists," in the words of George W. Bush.[45]

Despite rhetorical posturing, democratism aims not for direct democracy, as its proponents claim, but for *directed* democracy of a particular type. The word "democracy" and corresponding language about freedom and equality have provided cover for what are actually undemocratic sentiments, actions, and ideas and have helped democratism to escape notice as a comprehensive ideology with hugely ambitious, transformative goals. This ideology has exerted enormous influence and explains a great deal about modern political developments in the West. This book has sought to illustrate and explain the nature of democratism by analyzing in depth the thought, rhetoric, and actions of prominent philosophers, politicians, religious, intellectuals, and politicians who exemplify it. Through an extended examination of the ideas, assumptions, and subtleties in the political philosophies of representative figures, this work has tried to demonstrate that to the other great political "isms" must be added another of equal scope and internal coherence: democratism. Previously understood as a regime type among others with, at best, limited potential for good in the concrete, the idea of democracy has here been transformed in the imagination and thought of many prominent Western intellectuals into an ideal for a new way of life. Guided by this hypostatized, idealistic notion of democracy, many have pursued and continue to pursue legislation and foreign and domestic policies that promise to liberate, equalize, and democratize. Indistinguishable from a dream of equality and togetherness, democratism conveys a vision of liberation from constraints and injustices, a new existence that it promises is just around the corner. Additional "surges," greater organization, increased "awareness," and more education are supposed finally to bring about "true" democracy. With its "assurance of things hoped for and conviction of things not seen," democratism has all the earmarks of a type of faith.[46]

One of the great ironies of the modern democratic age is that while democracy has been given pride of place among regime types for the first time in history—in no small part due to the legacy of Rousseau—democracy's most outspoken advocates and theorists focus on ways dramatically to alter or circumvent the popular will. Many thinkers before the democratic age who are by no means "democrats" in the modern sense of the term were arguably more interested than democratists in letting the beliefs of the actual population exert real political influence. Aristotle, Cicero, and Aquinas are but three representatives of an older Western tradition of political philosophy who come to mind. They knew the weaknesses and limitations of human beings, not least those of the common people, and yet, as champions of what they regarded as the common good, they thought it proper for government to respect and accommodate the interest of the masses rather than the other way around. By putting forth the idea that human beings are inherently good and have an unlimited capacity to rule themselves wisely and as equals, many "democrats" have laid the groundwork for and advanced a concentration of power that monarchs of old never could have dreamed possible.

One of the effects of democratism has been to build into actual democratic societies a chronic distrust of current practices and beliefs as well as a barely concealed contempt for actual popular opinions that do not conform to democratist notions of the Good. It is suggestive of a glaring deficiency, a far-reaching solipsism, in the contemporary academy that the many dubious and yet highly influential beliefs that this book has identified and connected have not previously been brought into the open for critical examination. A certain myopia has protected the ideology of democratism from uncomfortable scrutiny.

The findings of this book are, admittedly, disturbing, even astounding. It has been amply demonstrated that the political mind of the Western world has been decisively imprinted by an ideology that in the name of democracy *undermines* actual popular rule, that contains a very large amount of chimerical idealistic dreaming, engages in more or less conscious intellectual deception, and includes a heavy ingredient of arrogance. Democratism's claim to moral and intellectual superiority reveals remarkable conceit. Democratists are not content to recommend limited reforms of existing democracies; this is partly because they are deeply uncomfortable with the diversity of beliefs and ways of life that are a part of genuinely pluralistic, democratic societies. They feel the need to turn to abstract theory, in which complexity, uncertainty, and human fallibility give way to neat and satisfying formulas. Having their own abstract, idealistic vision, democratists set aside as largely irrelevant the historical experience and concrete, particular circumstances that otherwise inform the people's thinking that they are trying to transform.

At the very end of this study it seems proper to try to pinpoint what might be the most characteristic or defining aspect of democratism. That this ideology contains a blend of modern abstract rationalism and romantic dreaming has been shown, and this paradoxical mixture accounts for its predominant moral-intellectual dynamic. But perhaps the most telling attribute of democratism is its more or less hidden elitism—the belief of democratists that they possess special knowledge about the true way to conduct politics and can speak authoritatively about how to transform society. Supremely confident in their own interpretation of Right, democratists do not hesitate to make sweeping proclamations about the ways in which society must change. In this philosophy are all of the seeds of modern, democratic tyranny.

NOTES

Chapter 1

1. "[F]rom him came, / As from the Pythian's mystic cave of yore, / Those oracles which set the world in flame, / Nor ceased to burn till kingdoms were no more." Lord Byron, *Childe Harold's Pilgrimage* (H.C. Baird, 1854), 151, 153.
2. Robert Nisbet, *The Present Age: Progress and Anarchy in Modern America* (Indianapolis, Indiana: Liberty Fund, 1988), 54.
3. Jacob L. Talmon, *Political Messianism: The Romantic Phase* (New York: Frederick A. Praeger Publishing, 1960), 127.
4. Quoted in James Farr and David Lay Williams, eds., *The General Will: The Evolution of a Concept* (New York: Cambridge University Press, 2015), editors' introduction, xvi.
5. Ernst Cassirer, *The Question of Jean-Jacques Rousseau*, 2nd edition, ed. Peter Gay (New Haven, Connecticut: Yale University Press, 1989), 76.
6. Jean-Jacques Rousseau, *Rousseau, Judge of Jean-Jacques: Dialogues*, trans. Judith Bush et al. (Hanover, New Hampshire: University Press of New England, 1990), 213.
7. Gerald Gaus explores four different interpretations of Rousseau's general will, but they all share the idea that for Rousseau, "a properly constituted democracy could express the will or judgment of the people." See Gerald Gaus, "Does Democracy Reveal the Voice of the People? Four Takes on Rousseau," *Australasian Journal of Philosophy*, Vol. 75, no. 2 (1997), 141–162.
8. Judith Shklar, "General Will," in *The Dictionary of the History of Ideas: Studies of Selected Pivotal Ideas*, Vol. 2, ed. Philip Wiener (New York: Charles Scribner's Sons, 1973), 275.
9. Farr and Williams, *The General Will*, xv–xvi.
10. Ibid., xvi.
11. Aristotle, *Politics*, ed. Ernest Barker (New York: Oxford University Press, 1958), Book I-II, 1252a–1253b.
12. See *Leviathan*, Part II in *Of Commonwealth*, Ch. XVII, in which Hobbes states that human beings are naturally asocial and that they unite "all their wills by plurality of voices unto one will" to form a commonwealth. Thomas Hobbes, *Leviathan*, ed. A. P. Martinich (Toronto: Broadview Publishing, 2005), 128.
13. Ibid.
14. Ibid., 129.
15. See John Locke, *Second Treatise of Government*, ed. C. B. Macpherson (Indianapolis, Indiana: Hackett Publishing, 1980), 8.
16. Ibid., 45–46.
17. Ibid., 47.
18. For the continuity between Hobbes and Locke (and earlier, natural-law thinkers) and Rousseau, see Robert Derathé, *Le Rationalisme de J.-J. Rousseau* and *Jean-Jacques Rousseau et la science politique de son temps* (Paris: Presses Universitaires, 1950).

19. The introduction of money as a means of exchange generates wealth disparity. See Locke, *Second Treatise of Government*, 23.

20. Jean-Jacques Rousseau, *On the Social Contract*, in *The Basic Political Writings*, 2nd ed., trans. Donald A. Cress (Indianapolis, Indiana: Hackett Publishing Company, 2011), 164.

21. Gay, "Introduction" to Cassirer, *The Question of Jean-Jacques Rousseau*, 26.

22. Rousseau, *On the Social Contract*, 164.

23. Derathé, *Le Rationalisme de J.-J. Rousseau*, 169, 176, quoted in Gay, "Introduction" to Cassirer, *The Question of Jean-Jacques Rousseau*, 26.

24. Rousseau, *On the Social Contract*, 167.

25. David Lay Williams, "The Substantive Elements of Rousseau's General Will," in Farr and Williams, *The General Will*, 219.

26. Quoted in ibid., 220.

27. Ibid., 220.

28. Rousseau, *On the Social Contract*, 173.

29. Ibid.

30. Quoted in Patrick Riley, "The General Will before Rousseau: The Contributions of Arnauld, Pascal, Malebranche, Bayle, and Bossuet," in Farr and Williams, *The General Will*, 14.

31. Quoted in ibid., 15.

32. Ibid., 11.

33. Diderot, in the essay "Natural Rights," writes that "the general will in each individual is a pure act of understanding that reasons in the silence of the passions about what man can demand of his fellow man and about what his fellow man can rightfully demand of him." Moreover, the general will is "always good" and "never falls into error." See Denis Diderot, "Natural Rights," in *The Encyclopedia of Diderot and d'Alembert: Collaborative Translation Project*, trans. Stephen J. Gendzier (Ann Arbor: Michigan Publishing, University of Michigan Library, 2009), http://hdl.handle.net/2027/spo.did2222.0001.313 (accessed February 8, 2019); originally published as "Droit naturel," in *Encyclopédie ou Dictionnaire raisonné des sciences, des arts et des métiers*, Vol. 5 (Paris, 1755), 115–116.

34. I have borrowed this phrase from Patrick Riley's titular work, *The General Will before Rousseau: The Transformation of the Divine into the Civic* (Princeton, New Jersey: Princeton University Press, 1986).

35. Ibid., 14.

36. Quoted in ibid., 16.

37. Alberto Postigliola, "De Malebranche à Rousseau: Les Apories de la Volonté Générale et la Revanche du 'Raisonner Violent,'" in Riley, "The General Will before Rousseau," 57.

38. Riley, "The General Will before Rousseau," 57.

39. David Lay Williams, *Rousseau's Social Contract: An Introduction* (New York: Cambridge University Press, 2014), 247–248.

40. Joshua Cohen, *Rousseau: A Free Community of Equals* (New York: Oxford University Press, 2010), 10.

41. Ibid., 179n12.

42. Rousseau, *On the Social Contract*, 173.

43. Ibid.

44. Quoted in Williams, *Rousseau's Social Contract*, 246.

45. See Williams, "The Substantive Elements of Rousseau's General Will," 228–230.

46. Ibid., 227.

47. See Jean-Jacques Rousseau, *Discourse on Political Economy*, in *The Basic Political Writings*, 2nd ed., trans. Donald A. Cress (Indianapolis, Indiana: Hackett Publishing Company, 2011), 127.

48. Ibid., 58.

49. Williams, "The Substantive Elements of Rousseau's General Will," 221.

50. Ibid., 222.

51. Rousseau, *On the Social Contract*, 167.

52. Ibid., 159.

53. Ibid., 167.

54. Rousseau, *Discourse on Political Economy*, 128.

55. Ibid., 132.

56. Rousseau, *On the Social Contract*, 182.

57. Ibid., 181.

58. Ibid.

59. Hobbes, *Leviathan*, 129.

60. See Plato, *Republic*, trans. G. M. A. Grube (Indianapolis, Indiana: Hackett Publishing Co., 1992), 414b–415d.

61. Rousseau, *On the Social Contract*, 182.

62. Ibid., 183.

63. Rousseau, *Discourse on the Origin and Foundations of Inequality among Men*, in *The Basic Political Writings*, 2nd ed., trans. Donald A. Cress (Indianapolis, Indiana: Hackett Publishing Company, 2011), 32.

64. Rousseau, *On the Social Contract*, 183.

65. Rousseau, *Rousseau, Judge of Jean-Jacques*, 23.

66. See Frederick Neuhouser, *Rousseau's Theodicy of Self-Love: Evil, Rationality, and the Drive for Recognition* (New York: Oxford University Press, 2008), 21–22.

67. Rousseau, *Discourse on the Origin and Foundations of Inequality*, 55.

68. Rousseau, *On the Social Contract*, 188.

69. F. C. Green, *Jean-Jacques Rousseau: A Critical Study of His Life and Writings* (Cambridge: Cambridge University Press, 1955), 280–281.

70. Thomas Jefferson to Roger C. Weightman, June 24, 1826. Available at the Library of Congress digital archive: https://www.loc.gov/exhibits/declara/rcwltr.html.

71. Woodrow Wilson, *Leaders of Men*, ed. T. H. Vail Motter (Princeton, New Jersey: Princeton University Press, 1952), 24.

72. Letter to Malesherbes in Jean-Jacques Rousseau, *The Collected Writings of Rousseau*, Vol. 5, trans. Christopher Kelley (Hanover, New Hampshire: Dartmouth College, 1995), 575.

73. Letter to Beaumont in Jean-Jacques Rousseau, *The Collected Writings of Rousseau*, Vol. 9, trans. Christopher Kelley and Judith R. Bush (Hanover, New Hampshire: Dartmouth College, 2001), 28.

74. Rousseau, *On the Social Contract*, 161; emphasis added. By "real relations," Rousseau means property.

75. Rousseau, "Discourse on the Origin of Inequality," 69.

76. Letter to Beaumont, in Rousseau, *The Collected Writings of Rousseau*, Vol. 9, 28.

77. Rousseau, *Discourse on the Sciences and Arts*, 14.

78. Rousseau, *Discourse on Political Economy*, 128.

79. Rousseau, *On the Social Contract*, 171.

80. Ibid., 172.

81. Ibid., 166.

82. 1 Corinthians 12:19.

83. Rousseau, *On the Social Contract*, 167.

84. 1 Corinthians 12:26.

85. Bertrand de Jouvenel, *The Ethics of Redistribution* (Indianapolis, Indiana: Liberty Fund, 1990), 15.

86. See John Rawls, *A Theory of Justice: Original Edition* (Cambridge, Massachusetts: The Belknap Press of Harvard University Press, 1971) and *Political Liberalism: Expanded Edition* (New York: Columbia University Press, 2005).

87. De Jouvenel, *The Ethics of Redistribution*, 14.

88. Rousseau, *Discourse on the Sciences and the Arts*, 14.

89. Eric Voegelin, "Ersatz Religion," in *Science, Politics and Gnosticism* (Wilmington, Delaware: ISI Books, 2007), 75. For all of Voegelin's insight into the phenomenon of gnosticism, he never mentions its connection with the philosophy of Rousseau. In fact, Voegelin is mostly silent on Rousseau. In his voluminous corpus he mentions Rousseau in fewer than a dozen passages. See Carolina Armenteros, "Rousseau in the Philosophy of Eric Voegelin," paper delivered at American Political Science Association Annual Meeting, 2011.

90. Voegelin, "Ersatz Religion," 100.

91. Rousseau, Discourse on the Origin and Foundations of Inequality among Men, 46.

92. Ibid., 74.

93. Ibid., 100n.ix.

94. Rousseau, *On the Social Contract*, 172.

95. Rousseau, *Discourse on the Origin and Foundations of Inequality among Men*, 46.

96. Jean-Jacques Rousseau, *Reveries of the Solitary Walker*, trans. Peter France (New York: Penguin Books, 2004), 27.

97. Letter to Malesherbes in Rousseau, *The Collected Writings of Rousseau*, Vol. 5, 575.

98. See Rousseau, *Rousseau, Judge of Jean-Jacques; Reveries;* and *The Confessions*, trans. J. M. Cohen (New York: Penguin Books), 1953.

99. Rousseau, *Discourse on the Origin and Foundations of Inequality among Men*, 48, 51.

100. Rousseau, *Reveries*, 43, 31; Rousseau, *Rousseau, Judge of Jean-Jacques*, 246

101. Rousseau, *Reveries*, 37.

102. Rousseau, *Discourse on the Origin and Foundations of Inequality among Men*, 100n.ix. For examples of Rousseau's belief that "men" in the abstract are good but living and breathing human beings are often bad, see Rousseau, *Reveries*, 37, 50, and 55.

103. Bryan Garsten, "Benjamin Constant's Liberalism," in Farr and Williams, *The General Will*, 383.

104. This is not the place to attempt to dissect the substantive differences between liberalism and democratism, but suffice to say that democratism draws special attention to the concept of the popular will in understandings of legitimacy and government, whereas liberalism as a concept is much more sprawling and with many more contributors, not all of whom hold an ideological view of liberalism, whereas democratism specifically references the *ideological* component of democratic thinking.

105. Quoted in Riley, "The General Will before Rousseau," 16.

106. Rousseau, *On the Social Contract* 178. At one point Rousseau says that "there is only one good government possible for a state" (193).

107. Ibid., 193.

108. Rousseau, *Reveries*, 27.

109. An address, April 6, 1918, in Arthur Link, *The Papers of Woodrow Wilson* (Princeton, New Jersey: Princeton University Press, 1984), Vol. 47, 270.

110. Rousseau *Discourse on the Origin and Foundations of Inequality among Men* ,41.

111. Maritain represents a Christian thinker who *does* believe that Christianity calls for a specific political order, namely democracy. I examine Maritain as a democratist in chapter 5 of this book.

112. Garsten, "Benjamin Constant's Liberalism," 387.

113. Benjamin Constant, *Principles of Politics Applicable to All Governments* (Indianapolis, Indiana: Liberty Fund, 2003), 19.

114. To be sure, Patrick Riley notes Alberto Postigliola's observation that Rousseau adopts Malebranche's metaphysical categorization of the general will without accounting for human finitude. Riley, "The General Will before Rousseau," 56–57.

115. Nelson Lund, *Rousseau's Rejuvenation of Political Philosophy: A New Introduction* (London: Palgrave Macmillan, 2016), 5.

Chapter 2

1. Edmund Burke, *Reflections on the Revolution in France*, ed. J. G. A. Pocock (Indianapolis, Indiana: Hackett Publishing Co., 1987), 49.

2. A number of works have addressed aspects of what I term "democratism." Those that suggest the possibility of regarding a certain view of democracy as an ideology include Claes G. Ryn, *Democracy and the Ethical Life: A Philosophy of Politics and Community*, 2nd ed. (Washington, DC: The Catholic University of America Press, 1990), first published in 1978, *The New Jacobinism: America as Revolutionary State*, 2nd expanded ed. (Bowie, Maryland: National Humanities Institute, 2011), first published in 1991, and *America the Virtuous: The Crisis of Democracy and the Quest for Empire* (New Brunswick, New Jersey: Transaction Publishers, 2003); Ryszard Legutko, *The Demon in Democracy: Totalitarian Temptations in Free Societies*, trans. Teresa Adelson (New York: Encounter Books, 2016); Peter Collins, *Ideology after the Fall of Communism* (New York: Boyars/Bowerdean, 1992); Michael P. Federici, *The Rise of*

Right-Wing Democratism in Postwar America (Westport, Connecticut: Praeger Publishers, 1991); Richard M. Gamble, *The War for Righteousness: Progressive Christianity, the Great War, and the Rise of the Messianic Nation* (Wilmington, Delaware: ISI Books, 2003); Patrick Deneen, *Democratic Faith* (Princeton, New Jersey: Princeton University Press, 2005) and *Why Liberalism Failed* (New Haven, Connecticut: Yale University Press, 2018); Irving Babbitt, *Democracy and Leadership* (Indianapolis, Indiana: Liberty Fund, 1979); and Edmund Burke's classic work, *Reflections on the Revolution in France*. While many of these works refer to or assume the general phenomenon of democratism, none concentrates on this subject in order to examine and define its central beliefs and trace an intellectual and political history of the ideology.

3. James Burnham, *Congress and the American Tradition* (Chicago: Henry Regnery Co., 1959), 41.

4. Erik Ritter Von Kuehnelt-Leddihn, *The Menace of the Herd or Procrustes at Large* (Milwaukee, Wisconsin: Bruce Publishing Company, 1943), 28, 10 (written under the name Francis Stuart Campbell).

5. Ryn, *America the Virtuous*, 16.

6. Irving Babbitt, *Rousseau and Romanticism* (New Brunswick, New Jersey: Transaction Publishers, 2004), 75, first published in 1919.

7. Jefferson to James Madison. *The Papers of Thomas* Jefferson, Volume 15: 27 March 1789 to 30 November 1789 (Princeton University Press, 1958), 394.

8. The "idyllic" imagination, Babbitt says, is universal or an ideal type. For an extended discussion of this type of epistemological role of the imagination, see Claes G. Ryn, *Will, Imagination, and Reason: Babbitt, Croce and the Problem of Reality* (New Brunswick, New Jersey: Transaction Publishers, 1997), first published in 1986.

9. The following sketch outlining some of the salient differences between democratism and republicanism is meant to demonstrate that the fundamental assumptions behind democratism are very different from those informing republicanism of the classical variety. Illustrating some of the major differences between these two ideas will help to place democratism in historical and intellectual context and also help to define democratism. It should go without saying that this account of republicanism is far from comprehensive. To engage with the voluminous literature on republicanism is hardly possible here and would detract from the major purpose at hand: defining democratism.

10. Federalist No. 10, in George W. Carey and James McClellan, eds., *The Federalist: The Gideon Edition* (Indianapolis, Indiana: Liberty Fund, 2001), 46.

11. Thomas Jefferson to John Taylor, May 28, 1816. All references to Jefferson's correspondence can be found at https://founders.archives.gov/, which maintains a digitized archive of all of Thomas Jefferson's letters and is fully searchable.

12. See *Social Contract*, Book II, Ch. 3: Jean-Jacques Rousseau, "On the Social Contract," in *The Basic Political Writings*, 2nd ed., ed. Donald A. Cress (Indianapolis, Indiana: Hackett Publishing Co., 2011), 173.

13. Quentin Skinner, *Liberty before Liberalism* (New York: Cambridge University Press, 1998), 1–2.

14. Ibid., 4.

15. Ibid., 4–5.

16. For a full discussion of Hobbes's understanding of liberty see Quentin Skinner, *Thomas Hobbes and Republican Liberty* (New York: Cambridge University Press, 2008), esp. 154–158.

17. Quoted in ibid., 161.

18. Book II, Ch. 1: Aristotle, *Nicomachean Ethics*, trans. Martin Ostwald (Upper Saddle River, New Jersey: Prentice Hall, 1999), 33.

19. Jean-Jacques Rousseau, *Emile or On Education*, trans. Allan Bloom (New York: Basic Books, 1979), 213.

20. Contrast the relationship of the *Émile* to the *Social Contract* with the relationship of Aristotle's *Nicomachean Ethics* to the *Politics*. In the *Émile*, Rousseau is concerned with eliciting the child's natural goodness through his education. In the *Ethics*, Aristotle believes that an ethical character must be formed and shaped by preexisting institutions such as the family and society. Herein lies one of the roots of the two different political philosophies.

21. Jefferson to James Madison. *The Papers of Thomas* Jefferson, Volume 15: 27 March 1789 to 30 November 1789 (Princeton University Press, 1958), 394.

22. See Matthew Cantirino, "The Dictatress and the Decisionmakers," *Humanitas*, Vol. 35, Nos. 1–2 (2022): 116.

23. Alexis de Tocqueville, *Democracy in America*, trans. Harvey C. Mansfield and Delba Winthrop (Chicago: University of Chicago Press, 2000), 6.

24. John Quincy Adams, "An Address Delivered at the Request of a Committee of the Citizens of Washington; On the Occasion of Reading the Declaration of Independence, On the Fourth of July, 1821," quoted in Cantirino, "The Dictatress and the Decisionmakers," 117.

25. Adams, "An Address Delivered at the Request of a Committee of the Citizens of Washington."

26. Rousseau, "On the Social Contract," 156.

27. Babbitt, *Democracy and Leadership*, 154.

28. Ibid., 294.

29. Rousseau, "On the Social Contract," 177.

30. It is especially ironic that the latest class of people to be considered enemies of democracy are the "populists," since historically the term "populism" has referred to popular, grassroots political movements that eschew political elitism.

31. Rousseau, "On the Social Contract," 177.

32. Jefferson to James Monroe, March 7, 1801. Available at https://founders.archives.gov/documents/Jefferson/01-33-02-0166.

Chapter 3

1. This chapter, in a certain respect, turns the thesis—a thesis that now seems rather quaint and dated—of Jean M. Yarbrough's 1998 book *American Virtues* on its head. Yarbrough says, "By exploring in a serious and critical way Jefferson's understanding of the virtues that modern republicanism encourages and on which it depends, we may be in a better position to address some of the most pressing moral and political problems of our own day." See Jean M. Yarbrough, *American Virtues: Thomas Jefferson on the Character of a Free People* (Lawrence: University Press of Kansas, 1998), xx.

2. Jefferson preferred the terminology of "republicanism" rather than "democracy," often associating the latter word—following from the ancient philosophers—with mob rule. Yet the very evolution of "Jeffersonian democracy" as a salutary concept demonstrates that the word has undergone significant change since Jefferson's time. Jefferson, along with others, helped to further the idea that direct popular rule should be the standard for republicanism. This chapter explores Jefferson's understanding of what is now commonly referred to as "democracy"—popular rule with minimal mediation or "filtration" through representatives. As this book argues, the abstract terms matter far less than the concrete reality that gives them their life and meaning. Whether one lauds democracy or republicanism is inconsequential. Only a close examination of the system of beliefs behind these abstractions reveals their meaning, and especially what *kind* of democrat one is. For Jefferson's relationship with "democracy" per se, see Peter S. Onuf, "Jefferson and American Democracy," in *A Companion to Thomas Jefferson*, ed. Francis D. Cogliano (Blackwell, 2012), 397.

3. See Jean-Jacques Rousseau, "On the Social Contract," in *The Basic Political Writings*, 2nd ed., ed. Donald A. Cress (Indianapolis, Indiana: Hackett Publishing Co., 2011), 173. Thomas Jefferson had a copy of Rousseau's *Social Contract* in his library at Monticello. See Emily Millicent Sowerby, ed., *Catalogue of the Library of Thomas Jefferson*, 5 vols. (1952–1959), vol. 3, no. 2338. And as an avid Francophile interested in French politics, he must have been quite familiar with the Genevan's theory of republicanism, which in so many ways mirrored his own.

Many have compared Jefferson to Rousseau. To mention just a few: for a pointed comparison of Jefferson's and Rousseau's democratic inclinations, see Claes G. Ryn, *Democracy and the Ethical Life: A Philosophy of Politics and Community,* 2nd ed. (Washington, DC: The Catholic University of America Press, 1990), chap. 11, "Constitutionalism versus Plebiscitarianism," and chap. 12, "The General Will." Ryn compares Jefferson's desire that "every form of government were so perfectly contrived, that the will of the majority could always be obtained, fairly and without impediment," to Rousseau's General Will and his belief that "any law which the people has not ratified in person is void; it is not law at all" (183, 117–118). Others, including Will and Ariel Durant, have commented on Rousseau's influence over Jefferson's writing of the Declaration of Independence. See Will Durant and Ariel Durant, *The Story of Civilization: Rousseau and Revolution*, vol. 10 (New York: Simon & Schuster, 1967), 891. Jason Robles in "An Honest Heart and a Knowing Head: A Study of the Moral, Political, and Educational Thought of Jean-Jacques Rousseau and Thomas Jefferson" (doctoral thesis, University of Colorado, 2012) argues that "the Jeffersonian vision of republican government 'of the people, by the people, and for the people'—sits comfortably alongside Rousseau's theory" (iii). Conor Cruise O'Brien compares Jefferson's desire for Britain to be forcibly "freed" by revolutionary France to Rousseau's idea that people might be "forced to be free" under the General Will. O'Brien also observes that although Jefferson, so far as the author is aware, never explicitly acknowledged a debt to Rousseau, we should not "understand from that, that the debt was not there." For "Jefferson, always keenly alert, in his long march to the presidency, to considerations of political advantage and disadvantage, must have been well aware that to acknowledge a debt to Rousseau would have been politically damaging." See Conor Cruise O'Brien, "Rousseau, Robespierre, Burke, Jefferson, and the French Revolution," in *The Social Contract and the First and Second Discourses: Jean-Jacques Rousseau*, ed. Susan Dunn (New Haven, Connecticut: Yale University Press, 2002), 306–8.

4. Richard K. Matthews, *The Radical Politics of Thomas Jefferson: A Revisionist View* (Lawrence: University Press of Kansas, 1984), 15.

5. Jefferson to John Taylor, May 28, 1816.

6. Ibid. In considering the legacy of "Jeffersonian democracy," it means little that Jefferson refused to think of himself as a "democrat" proper, no doubt due to the connotation of mob rule that had been associated with democracy since antiquity

7. Ibid.

8. Jefferson to David Hartley, July 2, 1787.

9. Query XIX in Thomas Jefferson, *Notes on the State of Virginia*, ed. William Peden (Chapel Hill: University of North Carolina Press, 1955), 164–165.

10. Ibid.

11. Jefferson to John Jay, August 23, 1785.

12. Jefferson to David Williams, November 14, 1803.

13. Jefferson to Horatio G. Spafford, March 17, 1817.

14. Adams would escape from the "rattle-gabble" of the streets of Boston to his family farm, which "put the mind into a stirring, thoughtful mood." Even Hamilton, otherwise very different from Jefferson, admits that farming "has *intrinsically a strong claim to pre-eminence over every other kind of industry*," producing "a state most favourable to the freedom and independence of the human mind." James Madison too calls husbandry "pre-eminently suited to the comfort and happiness of the individual." George Washington, hailed as an American Cincinnatus, fondly reflects, "To see plants rise from the earth and flourish by the superior skill and bounty of the laborer fills the contemplative mind with ideas which are more easy to be conceived than expressed." Carl J. Richard, *The Founders and the Classics* (Cambridge, Massachusetts: Harvard University Press, 1995), 165; Alexander Hamilton, "Report on Manufactures," in Morton J. Frisch, ed., *Selected Writings and Speeches of Alexander Hamilton* (Washington, DC: American Enterprise Institute, 1985), 280.

15. Jefferson to James Madison, December 20, 1787.

16. Gordon Wood and Louis Hartz, for example, see the imprint of John Locke on the American Revolution. See Gordon S. Wood, *The Radicalism of the American Revolution* (Vintage Books, 1991) and Louis Hartz, *The Liberal Tradition in America* (San Diego, California: Harcourt Brace and Co., 1991).

17. Jefferson to Adamantios Coray, October 31, 1823.

18. Jefferson to William Johnson, June 12, 1823.

19. Jefferson, first inaugural address, March 4, 1801.

20. Cf. Locke, *Second Treatise of Government*, Ch. V, "Of Property," esp. §42: "[T]he increase of lands, and the rights employing of them, is the great art of government"; Ch. VIII, "Of the Beginning of Political Societies," esp. §95: John Locke, *Second Treatise of Government*, ed. C. B. Macpherson (Indianapolis, Indiana: Hackett Publishing, 1980), 26, 52.

21. Jefferson to Pierre Samuel Du Pont de Nemours, April 4, 1816.
22. St. John de Crèvecoeur, "Letters from an American Farmer: Letter III" (1782).
23. Jefferson to Joseph Priestley, March 21, 1801.
24. Jefferson to François D'Ivernois, February 6, 1795.
25. Jefferson, *Notes on the State of Virginia*, Query XIX.
26. Jefferson to John Taylor, May 28, 1816.
27. See Patricia U. Bonomi, *Under the Cope of Heaven: Religion, Society, and Politics in Colonial America* (New York: Oxford University Press, 2003), 274.
28. Jefferson to William Short, August 4, 1820.
29. Edmund Burke, *Reflections on the Revolution in France*, ed. J. G. A. Pocock (Indianapolis, Indiana: Hackett Publishing Co., 1987), 30.
30. Jefferson to Joseph Priestley, March 21, 1801.
31. Ernest Lee Tuveson, *Redeemer Nation: The Idea of America's Millennial Role* (Chicago: University of Chicago Press, 1980), 109.
32. Jean-Jacques Rousseau, "Discourse on Inequality," in *The Basic Political Writings*, ed. Donald A. Cress (Indianapolis, Indiana: Hackett Publishing Co., 2011), 66.
33. Jefferson, *Notes on the State of Virginia*, Query XIX, 165.
34. Tuveson, *Redeemer Nation*, 109.
35. Irving Babbitt, *Democracy and Leadership* (Indianapolis, Indiana: Liberty Fund, 1979), 139.
36. Ibid.
37. The comparison with Rousseau might be continued here with Rousseau's *Émile*, the titular character of which looks to his tutor for direction. Paradoxically, an enlightened educator is necessary to coax from the boy the virtues of spontaneity and natural goodness. Having received this education, Émile, in the end, chooses to live in the country, away from the degrading life of the city, and in what may be called a quasi-natural state.
38. Jefferson to Thomas Cooper, August 14, 1820; Jefferson to Peter Carr, August 10, 1787.
39. Jefferson to Peter Carr, August 10, 1787.
40. Jefferson to John Adams, August 1, 1816.
41. Jefferson to Pierre Samuel Dupont de Nemours, April 24, 1816.
42. Jefferson to Joseph C. Cabell, September 10, 1817.
43. Jefferson to Charles Yancey, January 6, 1816.
44. Jefferson to Levi Lincoln, January 1, 1802.
45. See Paul Zummo, "Thomas Jefferson's America: Democracy, Progress, and the Quest for Perfection" (doctoral dissertation, The Catholic University of America, 2008), esp. chap. 1.
46. Cameron Addis, "Jefferson and Education," *The Journal of Southern History*, Vol. 72, No. 2 (2006): 457.
47. Robert K. Faulkner, "Spreading Progress: Jefferson's Mix of Science and Liberty," *The Good Society*, Vol. 79, No. 1 (2008): 26. See also Silvio A. Bedini, *Thomas Jefferson, Statesman of Science* (New York: Macmillan Publishing Company, 1990).
48. Quoted by Cassirer, *The Question of Jean-Jacques Rousseau*, 127.
49. Quoted by Joyce Appleby, "Commercial Farming and the 'Agrarian Myth' in the Early Republic," *The Journal of American History*, Vol. 68, No. 4 (March 1982): 833; Jefferson to Benjamin Rush, January 16, 1811.
50. Jefferson to Samuel Kercheval, July 12, 1816.
51. Ibid.
52. Hannah Arendt, *On Revolution* (Penguin Classics, 2006), 241.
53. See Francis Bacon, *Novum Organum* (1620), Book I, XXXI. Available in the public domain and can be accessed at: https://oll.libertyfund.org/title/bacon-novum-organum
54. For a retelling of this episode, see Alan Taylor, *Thomas Jefferson's Education* (New York: W. W. Norton & Co., 2019), 246–49.
55. Jefferson to Adams, October 28, 1813.
56. Jefferson to Pierre Samuel DuPont de Nemours, April 15, 1811.
57. Mark Andrew Holowchak, *Thomas Jefferson's Philosophy of Education: A Utopian Dream* (New York: Routledge, 2014), xvii.
58. Taylor, *Thomas Jefferson's Education*, 193.
59. Ibid., 214.

60. Ibid., 258–259.
61. Jefferson to Thomas Cooper, November 2, 1822.
62. Taylor, *Thomas Jefferson's Education*, 259.
63. Jefferson indeed had hoped that the University of Virginia would produce a new generation that would eventually abolish slavery. See Taylor, *Thomas Jefferson's Education*, 214.
64. Jefferson to Thomas Cooper, November 2, 1822.
65. Jefferson uses this phrase on several occasions. See Jefferson to George Rogers Clark, December 25, 1780, and Jefferson to James Madison, April 27, 1809.
66. Jefferson to Roger Weightman, June 24, 1826.
67. Ibid.
68. Jefferson to Robert R. Livingston, April 18, 1802.
69. Peter S. Onuf, "Prologue: Jefferson, Louisiana, and American Nationhood," in *Empires of the Imagination: Transatlantic Histories of the Louisiana Purchase*, ed. Peter J. Kastor and François Weil (Charlottesville: University of Virginia Press, 2009), 32.
70. Quoted in Robert W. Tucker and David C. Hendrickson, *Empire of Liberty: The Statecraft of Thomas Jefferson* (New York: Oxford University Press, 1990), 157.
71. Jefferson to John Breckinridge, August 12, 1803.
72. Tucker and Hendrickson, *Empire of Liberty*, 159.
73. Walter A. McDougall, *The Tragedy of U.S. Foreign Policy: How America's Civil Religion Betrayed the National Interest* (New Haven, Connecticut: Yale University Press, 2016), 57.
74. Anthony F. C. Wallace, *Jefferson and the Indians: The Tragic Fate of the First Americans* (Cambridge, Massachusetts: Belknap Press, 1999), 206.
75. Christian B. Keller, "Philanthropy Betrayed: Thomas Jefferson, the Louisiana Purchase, and the Origins of Federal Indian Removal Policy," *Proceedings of the American Philosophical Society*, Vol. 144, No. 1 (2000): 42.
76. Jefferson to John Adams, September 4, 1823.
77. For an account of the history of Jefferson's dealings with the Native Americans, see Wallace, *Jefferson and the Indians*, chapter 7, "President Jefferson's Indian Policy," pp. 206–240. For Jefferson's use of deception and salami tactics, see esp. 221–23.
78. Jefferson, "Memorandum for Henry Dearborn," December 29, 1802.
79. Jefferson to William Henry Harrison, February 27, 1803.
80. Andrew Jackson, Second Annual Message to Congress, December 6, 1830, National Archives, https://www.archives.gov/historical-docs/todays-doc/index.html?dod-date=1206, accessed September 10, 2021. For the relationship between Jefferson's Indian removal policies and Jackson's, see Keller, "Philanthropy Betrayed," 39–66; Peter S. Onuf, "We Shall All Be Americans: Thomas Jefferson and the Indians," *Indiana Magazine of History*, Vol. 95, No. 2 (1999): 103–141; Harold Hellenbrand, "Not 'to Destroy but to Fulfill': Jefferson, Indians, and Republican Dispensation," *Eighteenth-Century Studies*, Vol. 18, No. 4 (Autumn 1985): 523–549.
81. Jefferson to William Henry Harrison, February 27, 1803.
82. Jefferson to William Ludlow, September 6, 1824. Robert Nisbet sheds light on and traces this notion of progress in the comparative method of Comte, Spencer, Tylor, and others in *The Making of Modern Society* (Sussex: Wheatsheaf Books, 1986), 72–74.
83. Peter S. Onuf, "Thomas Jefferson's Christian Nation," in *Religion, State, and Society: Jefferson's Wall of Separation in Comparative Perspective*, ed. R. Fatton and R. Ramazini (New York: Palgrave Macmillan, 2009), 23.
84. In this respect Jefferson follows in the footsteps of John Locke, who undertook a similar venture in *The Reasonableness of Christianity*, ed. I. T. Ramsey (Stanford, California: Stanford University Press, 2005).
85. Jefferson to Joseph Priestley April 9, 1803.
86. Justin D. Garrison, "Friedrich Nietzsche: The Hammer Goes to Monticello," in *Critics of Enlightenment Rationalism*, ed. Gene Callahan and Kenneth B. McIntyre (New York: Palgrave Macmillan, 2020), 69.
87. Ibid., 68–69. See Jefferson to Joseph Priestley, March 21, 1801.
88. Jefferson to Gideon Granger, May 3, 1801.
89. Jefferson to Benjamin Galloway, February 2, 1812.

90. Jefferson to John Taylor, June 4, 1798.
91. Jefferson to Roger C. Weightman, June 24, 1826.
92. Jefferson to Peter Carr, August 10, 1787.
93. Jefferson to Joseph Priestley, March 21, 1801.
94. Jefferson to John Taylor, June 4, 1798.
95. Jefferson to John Taylor, May 28, 1816.
96. Jefferson to Horatio Gates, March 8, 1801.
97. Richard Hofstadter, *The Idea of a Party System: The Rise of Legitimate Opposition in the United States, 1780–1840* (Berkeley: University of California Press, 1972), 205, quoted in David N. Mayer, *The Constitutional Thought of Thomas Jefferson* (Charlottesville: University Press of Virginia, 1994), 123.
98. Mayer, *The Constitutional Thought of Thomas Jefferson*, 123.
99. See Jefferson to Benjamin Galloway, February 2, 1812.
100. Jefferson to David Hall, July 6, 1802.
101. Jefferson to Richard Rush, October 20, 1820.
102. Henry Adams, *The History of the United States during the Administrations of Thomas Jefferson* (New York: Library of America, 1986), 101.
103. Jefferson to Richard Rush, October 20, 1820.
104. Jefferson, unaddressed letter, March 18, 1793.
105. Jefferson to François D'Ivernois, February 6, 1795.
106. Jefferson to William Short, January 3, 1793.
107. Adams, *The History of the United States*, 100.
108. Jefferson to William Smith, November 13, 1787.

Chapter 4

1. For a history of this type of foreign policy thinking in America, see Walter A. McDougall, *Promised Land, Crusader State: The American Encounter with the World since 1776* (New York: Houghton Mifflin Company, 1997) and *The Tragedy of U.S. Foreign Policy: How America's Civil Religion Betrayed the National Interest* (New Haven, Connecticut: Yale University Press, 2016).
2. John Quincy Adams, "An Address Delivered at the Request of the Citizens of Washington; on the Occasion of Reading the Declaration of Independence, on the Fourth of July, 1821," quoted in McDougall in *Promised Land, Crusader State*, 36.
3. See Ernest Lee Tuveson, *Redeemer Nation: The Idea of America's Millennial Role* (Chicago: University of Chicago Press, 1968), viii; McDougall *Promised Land, Crusader State*, 118; Ralph Henry Gabriel, *The Course of American Democratic Thought* (New York: Ronald Press Co., 1940), 339; Richard Gamble, *The War for Righteousness: Progressive Christianity, the Great War, and the Rise of the Messianic Nation* (Wilmington, Delaware: ISI Books, 2003), 111.
4. Gabriel, *The Course of American Democratic Thought*, 339.
5. McDougall, *Promised Land, Crusader State*, 118.
6. Woodrow Wilson, "A Campaign Address in Jersey City, New Jersey," in Arthur S. Link, ed. *The Papers of Woodrow Wilson*, 69 vols. (Princeton: Princeton University Press, 1966–1994), 24: 443. May 25, 1912.
7. Woodrow Wilson, First Inaugural Address, March 4, 1913.
8. The influence of the social gospel movement on Wilson has been well documented. See Tuveson, *Redeemer Nation*, 173–175; Gamble, *The War for Righteousness*; McDougall, *Promised Land, Crusader State*, Ch. 6; Milan Babík, *Statecraft and Salvation: Wilsonian Liberal Internationalism as Secularized Eschatology* (Waco, Texas: Baylor University Press, 2013), Ch. 6; Gregory S. Butler, "Visions of a Nation Transformed: Modernity and Ideology in Wilson's Political Thought," *Journal of Church and State*, Vol. 39 (Winter 1997); Lloyd E. Ambrosius, *Wilsonian Statecraft: Theory and Practice of Liberal Internationalism during World War I* (Wilmington, Delaware: Scholarly Resources, 1991), 3. Much work has also been done to show the tremendous impact that Wilson's liberal Protestant faith had on his politics: this theme is variously treated in Butler, "Visions of a Nation Transformed"; Babík, *Statecraft and Salvation*; Gamble's *War for Righteousness*; Jan Willem Schulte Nordholt, *Woodrow Wilson: A Life for World Peace* (Berkeley: University of California Press, 1991), 46. Various Wilson

biographers have mentioned the centrality of Wilson's faith to his politics, including Ray Standard Baker, *Woodrow Wilson: Life and Letters* (Garden City, New York: Doubleday, 1927–1939), 1:68; Arthur Link, *Higher Realism of Woodrow Wilson* (Nashville: Vanderbilt University Press, 1971), 4 (among many other places). Ronald J. Pestritto documents the influence of Hegel and German Idealism on Wilson's thinking in *Woodrow Wilson and the Roots of Modern Liberalism* (Lanham, Maryland: Rowman and Littlefield, 2005), 1–33.

9. Quoted in Gamble, *The War for Righteousness*, 61.
10. Gamble, *The War for Righteousness*, 58.
11. Babík, *Statecraft and Salvation*, 21. See Augustine, *City of God*, trans. Marcus Dodd (Peabody, Massachusetts: Hendrickson Publishing Company, 2009). Tuveson says the expectation that human suffering and strife could permanently give way to peace and brotherhood "reversed the attitude dominant in Christianity for many centuries" (*Redeemer Nation*, 12).
12. Catholicism, too, had come under the influence of a new, progressive theology that many traditional Catholics condemned as heretical "modernism" and "Americanism." See, for example, Pope Leo XIII's letter "Testem Benevolentiae nostrae" to Cardinal James Gibbons, Archbishop of Baltimore, January 22, 1899. https://www.papalencyclicals.net/leo13/l13te ste.htm.
13. Butler, "Visions of a Nation Transformed," 43.
14. Woodrow Wilson, "The Modern Democratic State," in *The Papers of Woodrow Wilson* (Princeton, New Jersey: Princeton University Press, 1966–1994), 5:71.
15. Ibid., 5:63–78.
16. Ibid., 5:70.
17. Woodrow Wilson, *Constitutional Government in the United States* (New York: Columbia University Press, 1908).
18. Wilson, "The Modern Democratic State," 5:75, emphasis in original.
19. Ibid., 5:76.
20. Similarly, while Wilson claims philosophical kinship with Edmund Burke, there is little that Wilson has in common with the Irishman. Many have argued that Wilson's alleged conservatism and fondness for Burke have been greatly exaggerated. August Heckscher, *Woodrow Wilson* (New York: Scribner, 1991), 112; Babík, *Statecraft and Salvation*, 166–169; Butler, "Visions of a Nation Transformed," 46–49. Scholars have noted the connection between Wilson and Rousseau. Robert Nisbet sees in Wilson a "Rousseauian vision" of a nationalized community: *The Present Age*, 51–54. Irving Babbitt in *Democracy and Leadership* (Indianapolis, Indiana: Liberty Fund, 1979), 295–296 finds Wilson's "sentimental imperialism" inspired by a Rousseauean "idyllic imagination." Ethan M. Fishman notes the similarities between the two idealists' sense of limitlessness in *The Prudential Presidency: An Aristotelian Approach to Presidential Leadership* (Westport, Connecticut: Praeger, 2001), 51–52.
21. Wilson, "The Modern Democratic State," 5:76.
22. Jean-Jacques Rousseau, "On the Social Contract," in *The Basic Political Writings*, 2nd ed., ed. Donald A. Cress (Indianapolis, Indiana: Hackett Publishing Co., 2011), 171.
23. Ibid., 173.
24. Wilson, "The Modern Democratic State," 5:80.
25. Rousseau, "On the Social Contract," 164.
26. Wilson, "The Modern Democratic State," 5:75.
27. Ibid., 5:83.
28. Ibid.
29. Ibid., 5:84.
30. "Leaders of Men" was originally a commencement speech that Wilson delivered on numerous occasions. It was later published as an essay.
31. Wilson, "The Modern Democratic State," 5:83.
32. Wilson, *The New Freedom*, ed. William Bayard Hale. (New York: Doubleday, Page and Company, 1913), 10.
33. Woodrow Wilson, *Leaders of Men*, ed. T. H. Vail Motter (Princeton, New Jersey: Princeton University Press, 1952), 44–45.
34. Wilson, *Constitutional Government*, 68.
35. Rousseau, "On the Social Contract," 182.

36. Wilson, *Leaders of Men,* 29.

37. Ibid.

38. Ibid., 33.

39. Babbitt, *Democracy and Leadership,* 218. Babbitt is here quoting the famous words of Napoleon.

40. Wilson, *Leaders of Men,* 33.

41. McDougall, *Promised Land, Crusader State,* 128.

42. Wilson, *Leaders of Men,* 26, emphasis in original.

43. Woodrow Wilson, *Congressional Government* (Baltimore, Maryland: Johns Hopkins University Press, 1956), 210.

44. Wilson, *Leaders of Men,* 26.

45. Wilson, *Congressional Government,* 209–210.

46. Jeffrey K. Tulis, *The Rhetorical Presidency* (Princeton, New Jersey: Princeton University Press, 1987), 120.

47. Woodrow Wilson, "Cabinet Government in the United States" (August 1879), in *The Public Papers of Woodrow Wilson: College and State,* Vols. 1–2 (New York: Harper and Brothers, 1925–1927), 1:33–34.

48. Ibid., 1:35. Several scholars have termed this aspect of Wilson's presidency "crisis leadership." Tulis, *The Rhetorical Presidency,* 126; C. Eric Schulzke, "Wilsonian Crisis Leadership, the Organic State, and the Modern Presidency," *Polity,* Vol. 37, No. 2 (April 2005): 262–285.

49. Wilson, "Cabinet Government in the United States," 1:34; Woodrow Wilson, *A History of the American People* (New York: Harper and Brothers Publishers, 1902), 299; Schulzke, "Wilsonian Crisis Leadership," 275.

50. Wilson, *Constitutional Government,* 67, emphasis added.

51. Wilson, "Cabinet Government in the United States," 1:35.

52. Wilson, *Constitutional Government,* 65.

53. James MacGregor Burns, *The Power to Lead* (New York: Simon and Schuster, 1984), 190.

54. Wilson, "The Modern Democratic State," 5:72.

55. Ibid., 5:73.

56. Quoted in Niels Aage Thorson, *The Political Thought of Woodrow Wilson* (Princeton, New Jersey: Princeton University Press, 1988), 185.

57. Wilson, *Leaders of Men,* 39.

58. Wilson, *The New Freedom,* 54.

59. Wilson, First Inaugural Address, March 4, 1914.

60. See Gamble, *The War for Righteousness,* 76–77.

61. McDougall, *Promised Land, Crusader State,* 132. See, for example, Link, *Higher Realism of Woodrow Wilson* and Thomas A. Bailey, *Woodrow Wilson and the Lost Peace* (Chicago: Quadrangle Books, 1963). On the other hand, Paul Johnson, *Modern Times: The World from the Twenties to the Nineties* (New York: Perennial Classics Ed., 2001), 22 believes that Wilson desired moral authority through neutrality. McDougall also believes this.

62. Quoted in Gamble, *The War for Righteousness,* 138.

63. McDougall, *Promised Land, Crusader State,* 191; Wilson, "Declaration of Neutrality" delivered before the U.S. Senate, August 19, 1914.

64. McDougall, *The Tragedy of U.S. Foreign Policy,* 148.

65. Ibid., 157.

66. Rodney Carlisle, "The Attacks on U.S. Shipping That Precipitated American Entry into World War I," *The Northern Mariner,* Vol. 17, No. 3 (July 2007): 43.

67. McDougall, *Promised Land, Crusader State,* 135.

68. McDougall, *The Tragedy of U.S. Foreign Policy,* 148.

69. Wilson, "War Message to Congress," 309. Publicly available at the National Archives website, archives.gov.

70. Carlisle points out that most secondary scholarship about Wilson's neutrality and decision to go to war neglects the actual casus belli. Most accounts make little or no mention of the specific U.S. ships sunk in the U-boat campaign, and some make no mention of any ship losses. See Carlisle, "The Attacks on U.S. Shipping," 42n1.

71. Wilson, "War Message to Congress," 309; Carlisle, "The Attacks on U.S. Shipping," 63.

72. See, for example, William Kristol and Robert Kagan, "Introduction: National Interest and Global Responsibility," in *Present Dangers: Crisis and Opportunity in American Foreign and Defense Policy*, ed. Robert Kagan and William Kristol (New York: Encounter Books, 2000), 3–24.

73. Wilson, "War Message to Congress," 309.

74. Riezler's diary, April 18, 1915, quoted in Johnson, *Modern Times*, 107.

75. Wilson's letter to Chairman Edwin Webb of the House Judiciary Committee, in "Wilson Demands Press Censorship," *New York Times*, May 23, 1917.

76. Peter Conolly-Smith, "'Reading between the Lines': The Bureau of Investigation, the United States Post Office, and Domestic Surveillance during World War I," *Social Justice*, Vol. 36, No. 1 (2009): 16.

77. Amendment to the Espionage Act, 65th Congress, Session II, Ch. 75 (1918). For a discussion of civil liberties under Wilson, see H. C. Peterson and Gilbert C. Fite, *Opponents of War, 1917–1918* (Madison: University of Wisconsin Press, 1957); Harry N. Scheiber, *The Wilson Administration and Civil Liberties, 1917–1921* (Ithaca, New York: Cornell University Press, 1960); Zechariah Chafee Jr., *Free Speech in the United States* (Cambridge, Massachusetts: Harvard University Press, 1954); Geoffrey R. Stone, *Perilous Times: Free Speech in Wartime from the Sedition Act of 1798 to the War on Terrorism* (New York: W. W. Norton, 2005), 135–235; Mitchell Newton-Matza, *The Espionage and Sedition Acts: World War I and the Image of Civil Liberties* (New York: Routledge, 2017).

78. Quoted in Conolly-Smith, "'Reading between the Lines,'" 10.

79. Ibid., 13.

80. Ibid., 12.

81. Geoffrey R. Stone, "Mr. Wilson's First Amendment," in *Reconsidering Woodrow Wilson: Progressivism, Internationalism, War, and Peace*, ed. John Milton Cooper Jr. (Baltimore, Maryland: Johns Hopkins University Press, 2008), 196.

82. Stone, "Mr. Wilson's First Amendment," 196–198.

83. Quoted in Benjamin A. Kleinerman, "'In the Name of National Security' Executive Discretion and Congressional Legislation in the Civil War and World War I," in *The Limits of Constitutional Democracy*, ed. Jeffrey K. Tulis and Stephen Macedo (Princeton, New Jersey: Princeton University Press, 2010), 93.

84. Wilson, "Address on Flag Day," June 14, 1917. This document is publicly available at The American Presidency Project at https://www.presidency.ucsb.edu/documents/address-flag-day.

85. Woodrow Wilson, speech at the opening of the Third Liberty Loan Campaign, delivered in the Fifth Regiment Armory, Baltimore, April 6, 1918, in Arthur Link, *The Papers of Woodrow Wilson* (Princeton, New Jersey: Princeton University Press, 1984), 47:270.

86. Ross Gregory, "To Do Good in the World: Woodrow Wilson and America's Mission," in *Makers of American Diplomacy*, ed. Frank J. Merli and Theodore A. Wilson (New York: Charles Scribner's Sons, 1974), 363.

87. Johnson, *Modern Times*, 24–25.

88. Henry Kissinger, *Diplomacy* (New York: Simon & Schuster, 1994), 235.

89. Quoted in Johnson, *Modern Times*, 31.

90. Johnson, *Modern Times*, 32.

91. Wilson, *Leaders of Men*, 50.

92. Henry Cabot Lodge discusses the failure of the League in the Senate and mentions the "steady advance of opposition" to the League "among the mass of the American people . . . [that] became stronger day by day as, owing to the debate, the average American came to understand the questions to be decided." Henry Cabot Lodge, *The Senate and the League of Nations* (New York: Charles Scribner's Sons, 1925), 179.

93. Quoted in Gerhard Schulz, *Revolutions and Peace Treaties: 1917–1920*, trans. Marian Jackson (London: Methuen & Co., 1972), 189.

94. Ibid., 182.

95. Ibid., 183.

96. Johnson, *Modern Times*, 14.

97. Wilson, "Address on Flag Day," June 14, 1917.

98. Woodrow Wilson, address at Cheyenne, Wyoming, September 24, 1919. The American Presidency Project: https://www.presidency.ucsb.edu/documents/address-the-princess-theater-cheyenne-wyoming.

99. Babbitt, *Democracy and Leadership*, 122.

100. Ibid., 103.

101. Jean-Jacques Rousseau, *The Confessions*, trans. J. M. Cohen (New York: Penguin Books, 1953), 398

102. Nordholt, *Woodrow Wilson*, 52.

103. Quoted in Tuveson, *Redeemer Nation*, 211.

104. Wilson, "Americanism and the Foreign Born," May 10, 1915; Wilson, speech at the opening of the Third Liberty Loan Campaign, both in Link, *Papers*, 47:270; Wilson's words to Frank Cobb, quoted in Johnson, *Modern Times*, 14.

105. Wilson at Oakland, September 18, 1919, quoted in Tuveson, *Redeemer Nation*, 210–211. Babík says that "Wilson's international political utopianism derived in significant measure from his religious utopianism: his scripturally inspired belief that history was a redemptive process, with America as the providentially appointed savior of humanity" (*Statecraft and Salvation*, 3).

106. Wilson, speech at the opening of the Third Liberty Loan Campaign in Link, *Papers*, 47:270.

107. Thomas Carlyle, *The French Revolution: A History*, 3 vols. (Boston: Dana Estes & Company, 1985), 2:56.

Chapter 5

1. The sociologist and philosopher Daniel Bell assumes that liberal democracy cannot be ideological. See his *The End of Ideology: On the Exhaustion of Political Ideas in the Fifties* (Cambridge, Massachusetts: Harvard University Press, 2000; originally published 1960), in which he claims that systematic ideologies are now petering out and giving way to a postideological world.

2. Maritain, Jacques. *Man and the State*. (Washington, DC: The Catholic University of America Press, 1998; first published in 1951), 108.

3. Ibid., 60.

4. Ibid., 61.

5. Ibid., 59.

6. Ibid., 59.

7. Ibid., 59.

8. Jacques Maritain, *Christianity and Democracy*, in *Christianity and Democracy and The Rights of Man and Natural Law*, trans. Doris C. Anson (San Francisco, California: Ignatius Press, 1986), 46.

9. Jacques Maritain, *Ransoming the Time*, trans. Harry Lorin Binsse (New York: Scribner's Sons, 1941), 18.

10. Heinrich Rommen, *The State in Catholic Thought* (St. Louis, Missouri: B. Herder Book Co., 1950), 501.

11. Maritain, *Ransoming the Time*, 17.

12. Ibid., 18.

13. Ibid., 21.

14. Ibid., 21.

15. Ibid., 27.

16. Ibid., 24.

17. Erik Ritter Von Kuehnelt-Leddihn, *Liberty or Equality: The Challenge of Our Times*, ed. John P. Hughes (Auburn, Alabama: The Mises Institute, 2014), 90.

18. Maritain, *Man and the State*, 172.

19. Ibid., 104–105.

20. Thomas Aquinas, *Summa Theologica* 2.2, Question 66, Article 7.

21. Pope Paul VI, *Gaudium et Spes*, December 7, 1965, introduction §4. This document is publicly available through the digital Vatican archives: https://www.vatican.va/archive/hist_councils/ii_vatican_council/documents/vat-ii_const_19651207_gaudium-et-spes_en.html.

22. Ibid., Part I, Ch. 2, §26.

23. Pope John XXIII, *Pacem in Terris*, April 11, 1963, §§11–27. https://www.vatican.va/content/john-xxiii/en/encyclicals/documents/hf_j-xxiii_enc_11041963_pacem.html.

24. Ibid., §§41, 42–43.

25. Maritain, *Christianity and Democracy*, 111.

26. See Karl Marx and Friedrich Engels, *The Communist Manifesto*, ed. L. M. Findlay (Ontario: Broadview Press, 2004) and Karl Marx and Friedrich Engels, *The German Ideology*, ed. C. J. Arthur (New York: International Publisher Co., 1970).

27. Pope John Paul II, *Sollicitudo Rei Socialis* §41.1, in J. Michael Miller, ed., *The Encyclicals of John Paul II* (Huntington, Indiana: Our Sunday Visitor Publishing Division, 2001), 411.

28. John Paul II, *Evangelium Vitae*, §70. https://www.vatican.va/content/john-paul-ii/en/encyclicals/documents/hf_jp-ii_enc_25031995_evangelium-vitae.html

29. Maritain, *Christianity and Democracy*, 18.

30. Ibid., 4–5.

31. Ibid., 12.

32. Ibid., 12–13.

33. Book of Revelation, Ch. 21.

34. Maritain, *Man and the State*, 114–115.

35. Ibid., 201. The idea of constructing a world government persisted into the 1990s. The model of world government—the Hutchins report or Committee to Frame a World Constitution—that Maritain admired in *Man and the State*, again, received attention a half-century later. In the December 1995 issue of the *University of Chicago Magazine*, the intellectual home of the Committee, there appeared an article expressing renewed hope that such a scheme for global politics could finally come to fruition. The author writes that "the committee's dream of a world order guaranteeing universal justice beyond the proclivities of nationalism and national self-interest may not seem so quixotic as it did in the days of the incipient Cold War." He points to some elements of the draft constitution that have already been enacted in various ways, such as the North American Free Trade Agreement and the European Union, two institutions whose political utility is currently undergoing serious political reexamination. The article, appropriately titled "Drafting Salvation," reveals the continual ebb and flow of democratist optimism. See John W. Boyer, "Drafting Salvation," *University of Chicago Magazine*, December 1995, accessible at http://magazine.uchicago.edu/archives.

36. Maritain, *Man and the State*, 214, 215–216.

37. Ibid., 214, 215.

38. Ibid., 207.

39. Ibid., 208.

40. Ibid., 199.

41. Ibid., 207–208.

42. Marx and Engels, *The Communist Manifesto*, 62–69.

43. Pope Paul VI, *Gaudium et Spes*, Introduction, §5.

44. Jacques Maritain, *Integral Humanism, Freedom in the Modern World, and A Letter on Independence*, ed. Otto Bird (Notre Dame, Indiana: University of Notre Dame Press, 1996), 181n8.

45. Ibid., 181.

46. Ibid., 182.

47. Ibid., 177–178.

48. Maritain, *Man and the State*, 199.

49. Ibid., 213.

50. Maritain, *Christianity and Democracy*, 41.

51. Ibid., 38.

52. Maritain, *Man and the State*, 50–51. Compare this with Wilson's statement that, together with America, all nations "are entering or nearing the adult age of their political development." See Woodrow Wilson, "The Modern Democratic State," in *The Papers of Woodrow Wilson* (Princeton, New Jersey: Princeton University Press, 1966–1994), 5:74.

53. Maritain, *Man and the State*, 142.

54. Ibid., 141.

55. Maritain, *Christianity and Democracy*, 48, 13.

56. UNESCO, *Human Rights, Comments and Interpretations* (Paris: PHS, 1949), 2.

57. Thaddeus J. Kozinski, *The Political Problem of Religious Pluralism* (Lanham, Maryland: Lexington Books, 2010), 69.

58. Ibid.

59. Maritain, *Man and the State*, 176.

60. Aurel Kolnai, "Between Christ and the Idols of Modernity: A Review of Jacques Maritain's *Man and the State*," in *Privilege and Liberty and Other Essays in Political Philosophy*, ed. Daniel J. Mahoney (Lanham, Maryland: Lexington Books, 1999), 180.

61. Ibid.

62. Ibid.

63. Jacques Maritain, *The Peasant of the Garonne*, trans. Michael Cudahy and Elizabeth Hughes (New York: Holt, Rinehart and Winston, 1968), 201.

64. Ibid.

65. Eric Voegelin, "Ersatz Religion," in *Science, Politics and Gnosticism* (Wilmington, Delaware: ISI Books, 2007), 75.

66. Maritain, *The Peasant of the Garonne*, 203.

67. Ibid., 204.

68. Voegelin, "Ersatz Religion," 83.

69. Orestes Brownson, *The American Republic: Its Constitution, Tendencies, and Destiny* (New York: P. O'Shea, 1866), 184.

70. Ibid., 181.

71. Ibid., 181–182.

72. Rommen, *The State in Catholic Thought*, 477.

73. Brownson, *The American Republic*, 183.

74. Rommen, *The State in Catholic Thought*, 478.

75. Brownson, *The American Republic*, 186.

76. Ibid., 274–275.

77. Ibid., 272–273.

78. Ibid., 185.

79. Maritain, *Man and the State*, 202.

80. Ibid., 199.

81. Kolnai, "Between Christ and the Idols of Modernity," 179.

82. Ibid., 178–179.

83. Pope Francis, Laudato si', §219. Accessible at https://www.vatican.va/content/dam/france sco/pdf/encyclicals/documents/papa-francesco_20150524_enciclica-laudato-si_en.pdf.

84. Ibid., §231.

85. Ibid., §220.

86. See Michael Novak, "The Achievement of Jacques Maritain," in *Catholic Social Thought and Liberal Institutions: Freedom with Justice* (New Brunswick, New Jersey: Transaction Publishers, 1989) also reveals the continuity of Novak's thought with Maritain's.

87. Brownson, *The American Republic*, 186.

88. Maritain, *Man and the State*, 216.

Chapter 6

1. Andre Bächtiger, John S. Dryzek, Jane Mansbridge, and Mark Warren, "Deliberative Democracy: An Introduction," in *The Oxford Handbook of Deliberative Democracy*, ed. Andre Bächtiger et al., (New York: Oxford University Press, 2018), 2.

2. Many deliberative democrats self-consciously draw on Rousseau's political ideals. For a review of the philosophical origins of deliberative democracy, see Simone Chambers, "The Philosophical Origins of Deliberative Ideals," in *The Oxford Handbook of Deliberative Democracy*, 55–69.

3. Ibid.

4. Bächtiger et al., "Deliberative Democracy," 2.

5. "Remarks by the President at Presentation of the National Medal of the Arts and the National Humanities Medal," White House, September 29, 1999, https://clintonwhitehouse4.archi ves.gov/WH/New/html/19990929.html.

6. The National Conversation at the Wilson Center, https://www.wilsoncenter.org/the-natio nal-conversation-the-wilson-center, accessed 9/21/2017.

7. Second-generation deliberative democrats broaden the notion of rationality to include "differing styles of communication such as narrative and rhetoric" and to account for the role of emotion in discourse. See Bächtiger et al., "Deliberative Democracy," 3.

8. The argument of communitarians such as Michael Walzer is that Rawls fails to account sufficiently for historical community norms in his conception of political justice. See Michael Walzer, *Spheres of Justice: A Defense of Pluralism and Equality* (New York: Basic Books, Inc., 1983).

9. Joshua Cohen, "Procedure and Substance in Deliberative Democracy," in *Philosophy and Democracy: An Anthology*, ed. Thomas Christiano (New York: Oxford University Press, 2003), 21.

10. Bächtiger et al., "Deliberative Democracy," 2.

11. Cohen, "Procedure and Substance in Deliberative Democracy," 21.

12. Dennis F. Thompson, "Deliberative Democratic Theory and Empirical Political Science," *Annual Review of Political Science,* Vol. 11 (2008): 498.

13. Seyla Benhabib, "Liberal Dialogue versus a Critical Theory of Discursive Legitimation," in *Liberalism and the Moral Life*, ed. Nancy L. Rosenblum (Cambridge, Massachusetts: Harvard University Press, 1996), 143.

14. Bruce Ackerman, "Why Dialogue?," *The Journal of Philosophy*, Vol. 86, No. 1 (January 1989): 10.

15. Jürgen Habermas, "Discourse Ethics: Notes on a Program of Philosophical Justification," in *Moral Consciousness and Communicative Action*, trans. Christian Lenhardt and Shierry Weber Nicholsen (Cambridge, Massachusetts: MIT Press, 1990), 91.

16. Benhabib, "Liberal Dialogue versus a Critical Theory of Legitimacy," 150.

17. John Rawls, "The Idea of Public Reason Revisited," *The University of Chicago Law Review*, Vol. 64, No. 3 (Summer 1997): 769.

18. Derek W. M. Barker, Noëlle McAfee, David W. McIvor, "Introduction," in *Democratizing Deliberation: A Political Theory Anthology*, ed. Derek W. M. Barker, Noëlle McAfee, David W. McIvor (Dayton, Ohio: Kettering Foundation Press, 2012), 4. Others, however, have dismissed deliberative democracy "as irrelevant when it comes to 'understanding democratic politics on a national scale.'" Quoted in Bächtiger et al., "Deliberative Democracy," 1.

19. Bächtiger et al., "Deliberative Democracy," 3.

20. Habermas defines communicative action as the process by which "one actor seeks *rationally* to *motivate* another by relying on the illocutionary binding/bonding (*Bindungseffekt*) of the offer contained in his speech act." See Habermas, "Discourse Ethics," 58. See also, Habermas, *The Theory of Communicative Action* in two volumes, trans. Thomas McCarthy (Boston: Beacon Press, 1984–1985).

21. Jürgen Habermas, "Three Normative Models of Democracy," *Constellations*, Vol. 1, No. 1 (1994): 7.

22. Habermas, "Discourse Ethics," 58.

23. Ibid., 67.

24. Ibid., 58.

25. Ibid., 63.

26. Ibid., 66, emphasis in original.

27. Habermas, "Three Normative Models of Democracy," 4–5.

28. Cf. Edmund Burke, *Reflections on the Revolution in France*, ed. J. G. A. Pocock (Indianapolis, Indiana: Hackett Publishing Co., 1987).

29. Habermas, "Three Normative Models of Democracy," 5, emphasis added.

30. Thomas McCarthy, "Kantian Constructivism and Reconstructivism: Rawls and Habermas in Dialogue," *Ethics*, Vol. 105, no. 1 (October 1994): 47.

31. Ibid.

32. Rawls, "The Idea of Public Reason Revisited," 772.

33. Ibid., 773.
34. Some, including Rawls, contend that *Political Liberalism* is intended to be the historical application of the metaphysics of *A Theory of Justice*. Richard Rorty, for example, argues that *Political Liberalism* demonstrates the historical nature of justice as fairness: *Objectivity, Relativism, and Truth: Philosophical Papers*, Vol. 1 (New York: Cambridge University Press, 1991).
35. Cohen, "Reflections on Habermas on Democracy," in *Ratio. Juris*, Vol. 12 Issue 4 (December 1999): 387.
36. Jürgen Habermas, *Between Facts and Norms: Contributions to a Discourse Theory of Law and Democracy*, trans. William Rehg (Cambridge, Massachusetts: MIT Press, 1996), 304; Cohen, "Reflections on Habermas on Democracy," 400.
37. For the relationship between deliberation democracy and Mill, see Amy Gutmann and Dennis Thompson, *Why Deliberative Democracy?* (Princeton, New Jersey: Princeton University Press, 2004), 9; Chambers, "The Philosophical Origins of Deliberative Ideals," 60.
38. Cohen, "Reflections on Habermas on Democracy," 387.
39. Ackerman, "Why Dialogue?," 17–18.
40. Amy Gutmann and Dennis Thompson, "Moral Conflict and Political Consensus," *Ethics*, Vol. 101, No. 1 (October 1990): 78.
41. Thompson, "Deliberative Democratic Theory and Empirical Political Science," 509.
42. Ibid., 506.
43. Ibid.
44. Bächtiger et al., "Deliberative Democracy," 6.
45. Simone Chambers explains, "When Rousseau suggests that deliberation might undermine the general will . . . he is not, according to this reading, rejecting the core ideals of deliberative democracy; instead he is suggesting that deliberation must be insulated from factionalism and certain types of disagreements, that is, those in which citizens reason from self and group interests rather than from the common good" ("The Philosophical Origins of Deliberative Ideals," 57).
46. Cohen, "Procedure and Substance in Deliberative Democracy," 18.
47. See James MacGregor Burns, *The Deadlock of Democracy* (Englewood Cliffs, New Jersey: Prentice Hall, 1963).
48. Bächtiger et al., "Deliberative Democracy," 5.
49. Gutmann and Thompson, "Moral Conflict and Political Consensus," 86.
50. Robert J. Lacey, *American Pragmatism and Democratic Faith* (DeKalb: Northern Illinois University Press, 2008), 21.
51. Ibid.
52. Gutmann and Thompson, "Moral Conflict and Political Consensus," 77. See J. Knight and J. Johnson, "What Sort of Political Equality Does Democratic Deliberation Require?," in *Deliberative Democracy*, ed. J. Bohman and W. Rehg (Cambridge, Massachusetts: MIT Press, 1997), 280, 292.
53. André Bächtiger, Marco Steenbergen, Thomas Gautschi, and Seraina Pedrini, "Deliberation in Swiss Direct Democracy: A Field Experiment on the Expulsion Initiative," *National Centres of Competence in Research (NCCR) Newsletter*, February 2011, 5.
54. Ibid., 6–7.
55. Ibid., 5.
56. Paul Quirk, William Bendix, and Andre Bächtiger, "Institutional Deliberation," in *The Oxford Handbook of Deliberative Democracy*, ed. Andre Bächtiger et al. (New York: Oxford University Press), 287.
57. Amy Gutmann and Dennis Thompson, "Reflections on Deliberative Democracy: When Theory Meets Practice," in *The Oxford Handbook of Deliberative Democracy*, ed. Andre Bächtiger et al. (New York: Oxford University Press), 905–906.
58. Chambers, "The Philosophical Origins of Deliberative Ideals," 60.
59. Quoted in ibid.
60. Gutmann and Thompson, "Moral Conflict and Political Consensus," 77.
61. Gutmann and Thompson, "Reflections on Deliberative Democracy," 904–905.
62. Bächtiger et al., "Deliberation in Swiss Direct Democracy," 5.

63. Michael Saward, "Rawls and Deliberative Democracy," in *Democracy as Public Deliberation: New Perspectives*, ed. Maurizio Passerin D'Entreves (New York: Manchester University Press, 2002), 117.

64. Ibid.

65. John Rawls, *Political Liberalism: Expanded Edition* (New York: Columbia University Press, 2005), 225, quoted in Saward, "Rawls and Deliberative Democracy," 115.

66. Rawls, *Political Liberalism*, 225, quoted in Saward, "Rawls and Deliberative Democracy," 115.

67. John Rawls, *A Theory of Justice*, rev. ed. (Cambridge, Massachusetts: The Belknap Press of Harvard University Press, 1999), 107; Rawls, "The Idea of Public Reason Revisited," 774.

68. Rawls, "The Idea of Public Reason Revisited," 774.

69. For a discussion of Rawls's defense of the welfare state, see Stephen Nathanson, *Economic Justice* (New York: Pearson, 1997), "Rawls's Defense of the Liberal Democratic Welfare State," 81–99, esp. 92–93. In *Justice as Fairness: A Restatement* (Cambridge, Massachusetts: The Belknap Press, 2001; second edition), Rawls does state that justice requires property ownership or liberal socialism, but this separates Rawls from, say, communists or full-blown socialists, rather than from welfare state capitalism, which he seems to endorse.

70. John Rawls, *A Theory of Justice: Original Edition* (Cambridge, Massachusetts: The Belknap Press of Harvard University Press, 1971), 87.

71. Rawls, "The Idea of Public Reason Revisited," 773–774.

72. Habermas, "Three Normative Models of Democracy," 6.

73. For a treatment of deliberative democracy's tendency for ahistoricism and rationalism, see Ryan Holston, "Deliberation in Context: Reexamining the Confrontation between the Discourse Ethics and Neo-Aristotelianism," *Telos*, Vol. 181 (Winter 2017): 151–175.

74. Bächtiger et al., "Deliberative Democracy," 1.

75. Gutmann and Thompson, "Reflections on Deliberative Democracy," 900.

76. Gutmann and Thompson, "Moral Conflict and Political Consensus," 77.

77. Stefan Rummens, "Deliberation and Justice," in *The Oxford Handbook of Deliberative Democracy*, ed. Andre Bächtiger et al. (New York: Oxford University Press), 136.

78. Quoted in Monique Deveaux, "Deliberative Democracy and Multiculturalism," in *The Oxford Handbook of Deliberative Democracy*, ed. Andre Bächtiger et al. (New York: Oxford University Press), 161, 163.

79. Ibid., 161.

80. Ibid., 163.

81. Benhabib, "Liberal Dialogue versus a Critical Theory of Legitimacy," 150.

82. Andrew March and Alicia Steinmetz, "Religious Reasons in Public Deliberation," in *The Oxford Handbook of Deliberative Democracy*, ed. Andre Bächtiger et al. (New York: Oxford University Press), 208.

83. Quoted in Jeffrey Flynn, "Communicative Power in Habermas's Theory of Democracy," *European Journal of Political Theory* 3 (4) 2004: 446.

84. Even Rawls admits that his assumptions about individuals embodying these abstract concepts are for hypothetical purposes and that real people often fall short of these ideals. See Rawls, *A Theory of Justice: Original Edition*, 443 and Rawls, *Political Liberalism*, 20.

85. St. Paul Letter to the Romans 7:15–19 (New Revised Standard Version).

86. See Plato, *Republic*, trans. G. M. A. Grube (Indianapolis, Indiana: Hackett Publishing Co., 1992), Book III for his "myth of the metals" and his understanding of the central importance of myth, song, lyric, rhetoric, art, and poetry for the formation of young minds in the city.

87. Rawls, *A Theory of Justice: Original Edition*, 87.

88. Ibid., 87–88.

89. Ibid., 88.

90. See Thompson, "Deliberative Democratic Theory and Empirical Political Science," 498–500.

91. Ibid., 500.

92. Michael X. Delli Carpini, Fay Lomax Cook, and Lawrence R. Jacobs, "Public Deliberation, Discursive Participation, and Citizen Engagement: A Review of the Empirical Literature," *Annual Review of Political Science*, Vol. 7 (2004): 325.

93. Thompson, "Deliberative Democratic Theory and Empirical Political Science," 509, 506.

94. Patrick Deneen, *Democratic Faith* (Princeton, New Jersey: Princeton University Press, 2005), 27.

95. Habermas, *Between Facts and Norms*, 318.

96. Thompson, "Deliberative Democratic Theory and Empirical Political Science," 500.

97. Rousseau, *The Social Contract*, in *The Basic Political Writings* (Indianapolis: Hacket Publishing, 2011), 199. Book III, Ch. 4.

98. Thompson, "Deliberative Democratic Theory and Empirical Political Science," 500.

99. Rawls, *A Theory of Justice: Original Edition*, 87.

100. Plato, *Republic*, 95.

101. See Zach Beauchamp, "The Anti-Liberal Moment," *Vox*, September 9, 2019, https://www. vox.com/policy-and-politics/2019/9/9/20750160/liberalism-trump-putin-socialism-reactionary, accessed September 10, 2019. That the popular, left-wing *Vox* magazine has documented recent criticisms against liberalism of the Lockean and Rawlsian sorts is a testament to the rather widespread discontent.

102. Barker et al, "Introduction," 7.

103. Jean-Jacques Rousseau, "On the Social Contract," in *The Basic Political Writings*, 2nd ed., trans. Donald A. Cress (Indianapolis, Indiana: Hackett Publishing Co., 2011), Book II, Ch. 5., 167.

104. "Mark Zuckerberg and Jack Dorsey Testimony Transcript Hearing November 17, [2020]," , Transcript Library, rev.com/blog/transcripts/mark-zuckerberg-jack-dorsey-testimony-transcript-senate-tech-hearing-november-17.

Chapter 7

1. George W. Bush, Second Inaugural Address, January 20, 2005. The primary source documents of George W. Bush cited in this chapter can be found at https://georgewbush-whitehouse.archives.gov/index.html.

2. John Mearsheimer, *The Great Delusion: Liberal Dreams and International Realities* (New Haven, Connecticut: Yale University Press, 2018), 153.

3. See ibid., esp. Ch. 3, in which Mearsheimer analyzes political liberalism. Stephen M. Walt, *The Hell of Good Intentions: America's Foreign Policy Elite and the Decline of U.S. Primacy* (New York: Farrar, Straus and Giroux, 2018).

4. Mearsheimer, *The Great Delusion*, 217.

5. This is a reference to C. Bradley Thompson with Yaron Brook, *Neoconservatism: An Obituary for an Idea* (Boulder, Colorado: Paradigm Publishers, 2010).

6. Max Boot, "I'm No Democrat—but I'm Voting Exclusively for Democrats to Save Our Democracy," *Washington Post*, October 11, 2021, https://www.washingtonpost.com/opini ons/2021/10/11/im-no-democrat-im-voting-exclusively-democrats-save-our-democr acy/, accessed November 2, 2021.

7. Irving Kristol defined neoconservatism as a "persuasion" on numerous occasions. For a collection of his essays that mention the term, see Irving Kristol, *The Neo-conservative Persuasion: Selected Essays, 1942–2009* (New York: Basic Books, 2011)

8. Deal W. Hudson, *Sed Contra: The Neocon Question*, July 1, 2003, https://www.crisismagaz ine.com/2003/sed-contra-the-neocon-question, accessed March 10, 2018.

9. A great deal of scholarship and journalism has investigated the connection between the neoconservatives and Strauss and the Straussians. Two of the most prominent scholars indicting Strauss for the rise of neoconservatism are Shadia Drury and C. Bradley Thompson. See Shadia Drury, *Leo Strauss and the American Right* (New York: St. Martin's Press, 1999) and Thompson and Brook, *Neoconservatism*. Strauss's students have responded to these claims with works of their own: see Catherine H. Zuckert and Michael P. Zuckert, *The Truth about Leo Strauss: Political Philosophy and American Democracy* (Chicago: University of Chicago Press, 2014); Peter Minowitz, *Straussophobia: Defending Leo Strauss and Straussians against Shadia Drury and Other Accusers* (Lanham, Maryland: Lexington Books, 2009).

10. For a detailed list of many of the Straussians involved in the Bush and Reagan administrations, see Kenneth R. Weinstein, "Philosophic Roots, The Role of Leo Strauss, and the War in Iraq," in *The Neocon Reader*, ed. Irwin Stelzer (New York: Grove Press, 2004), 204–205.

11. Leo Strauss, *Natural Right and History* (Chicago: University of Chicago Press, 1953), 11.
12. Ibid., 15.
13. Ibid., 11.
14. See Book III of Plato's *Republic*.
15. Strauss, *Natural Right and History*, 133.
16. Ibid., 141–142.
17. Leo Strauss, "On Classical Political Philosophy," in *The Rebirth of Classical Political Rationalism*, ed. Thomas Pangle (Chicago: University of Chicago Press, 1989), 55.
18. Strauss, *Natural Right and History*, 133.
19. Strauss, "On Classical Political Philosophy," 55.
20. Strauss, *Natural Right and History*, 144.
21. Strauss, "On Classical Political Philosophy," 55, 50.
22. Strauss, *Natural Right and History*, 141, 142.
23. See, for example, Thompson and Brook, *Neoconservatism*. While Thompson makes a compelling case for the influence of Strauss on many neoconservatives, especially Strauss's student Irving Kristol, Thompson's argument appears to be heavily influenced by his own Straussian background. Thompson emphasizes the Straussian methodology at the expense of other powerful cultural influences that span the ideological spectrum and affect neoconservatives and the Left alike.
24. See Louis Hartz, *The Liberal Tradition in America* (San Diego, California: Harcourt Brace and Co., 1991) and especially Robert Kagan, *Dangerous Nation* (New York: Vintage Books, 2006).
25. Kagan, *Dangerous Nation*, 42.
26. J. Hector St. John de Crèvecoeur, Letter III, 1782, https://avalon.law.yale.edu/18th_cent ury/letter_03.asp.
27. Kagan, *Dangerous Nation*, 42.
28. Charles Krauthammer, "Democratic Realism: An American Foreign Policy for a Unipolar World," Irving Kristol Lecture at American Enterprise Institute for Public Policy Research, January 1, 2004, 14.
29. See, for example, Russell Kirk, *The Roots of American Order* (Wilmington, Delaware: ISI, 2003); George W. Carey, *In Defense of the Constitution* (Indianapolis, Indiana: Liberty Fund, 1995); Claes G. Ryn, *Democracy and the Ethical Life* (Washington, DC: The Catholic University of America Press, 1990), 154–165.
30. John Quincy Adams, "An Address Delivered at the Request of a Committee of the Citizens of Washington; On the Occasion of Reading the Declaration of Independence, On the Fourth of July, 1821," (Washington, DC: Davis and Force, 1821), 29.
31. Allan Bloom, "Rousseau: The Turning Point," in *Giants and Dwarfs: Essays 1960–1990* (New York: Simon & Schuster, 1990), 208.
32. William Kristol and Robert Kagan stress the role of regime-change in "Introduction: National Interest and Global Responsibility," in *Present Dangers: Crisis and Opportunity in American Foreign and Defense Policy*, ed. William Kristol and Robert Kagan (New York: Encounter Books, 2000).
33. Strauss, *Natural Right and History*, 18.
34. Kagan, *Dangerous Nation*, 40.
35. Ibid.
36. Condoleezza Rice, "The President's National Security Strategy," in *The Neocon Reader*, ed. Irwin Steelier (New York: Grove Press, 2004), 85.
37. Krauthammer, "Democratic Realism," 14, quoting John F. Kennedy.
38. William Kristol and Robert Kagan, "Toward a Neo-Reaganite Foreign Policy," *Foreign Affairs*, Vol. 75, No. 4 (July 1996): 20.
39. Krauthammer, "Democratic Realism," 14.
40. Kristol and Kagan, "Introduction," 22.
41. Max Boot, "American Imperialism? No Need to Run Away from the Label," *USA Today*, May 5, 2003. Thomas Donnelly and William Kristol also employ this Jeffersonian epithet in the title of their article in the *Weekly Standard*: "An Empire for Liberty," *Weekly Standard*, October 2, 2017.
42. Boot, "American Imperialism?".

43. Max Boot, "We Didn't Kick Britain's Ass to Be This Kind of Country: Donald Trump's Abandonment of Human Rights Is a Repudiation of the Country's Founding Principles," *Foreign Policy*, July 3, 2017.

44. George W. Bush, speech at Whitehall Palace, London, November 20, 2003.

45. George W. Bush, "Address before a Joint Session of Congress on the State of the Union," January 31, 2006.

46. George H. W. Bush, "Address before a Joint Session of Congress on the State of the Union," January 29, 1991.

47. Rice, "The President's National Security Strategy," 83.

48. Bush, Second Inaugural Address.

49. Kristol and Kagan, "Introduction," 20.

50. Kagan, "Power and Weakness," 14–15; Kristol and Kagan, "Introduction," 23.

51. Daniel Bell and Irving Kristol, "What Is the Public Interest?," *The Public Interest*, Vol. 1, No. 1 (Fall 1965): 5.

52. George W. Bush, Speech to United Nations General Assembly, September 21, 2004.

53. Ralph Peters, "Stability, America's Enemy," *Parameters*, Winter 2001-2002, 6.

54. Michael A. Ledeen, *The War against the Terror Masters: Why It Happened, Where We Are Now, How We'll Win* (New York: Truman Talley Books, 2003), 213.

55. Mission statement from USAID website: https://www.foreignassistance.gov/, accessed February 21, 2018.

56. https://www.foreignassistance.gov/categories/Education-Social-Services, accessed February 21, 2018. Cf. John Locke, *Second Treatise of Government*, ed. C. B. Macpherson (Indianapolis, Indiana: Hackett Publishing, 1980), 26, 52, Ch. V, "Of Property," esp. §42: "[T]he increase of lands, and the rights employing of them, is the great art of government"; and Ch. VIII, esp. §95: "Of the Beginning of Political Societies."

57. John McCain, speech at the Republican National Convention, August 29, 2012. Transcript available at: https://www.politico.com/story/2012/08/john-mccain-rnc-speech-transcript-080399.

58. The Afghan Women and Children Relief Act, 22 USC 2374, passed December 12, 2001, authorized educational and healthcare measures that would benefit women in Afghanistan. In 2002 the U.S.-Afghan Women's Council was formed to provide education and microfinance programs to women in Afghanistan. This organization was to "help promote partnerships between the public and private sectors, as between the two countries and governments concerned," and its "key function" was to "mobilize and bring together resources, expertise, and networking capabilities across governments, NGOs, and private companies—and target them specifically toward practical projects for women." See U.S. Department of State archive, https://2001-2009.state.gov/g/wi/rls/46289.htm and https://2001-2009.state.gov/g/wi/rls/10684.htm, accessed August 13, 2019. Projects such as the Iraqi Women's Gift Fund combined government support and funding from U.S. corporations and private citizens to help with the "economic and political empowerment of Iraqi women." U.S. Department of State archive, https://2001-2009.state.gov/g/wi/rls/72237.htm, accessed August 13, 2019.

59. Quoted in Nadje Al-Ali and Nicola Pratt, *What Kind of Liberation?* (Berkeley: University of California Press, 2009), 63.

60. Ibid.

61. See, for example, Michaele L. Ferguson, "'W' Stands for Women: Feminism and Security Rhetoric in the Post-9/11 Bush Administration," *Politics and Gender*, Vol. 1, No. 1 (March 2005): 9–38; Al-Ali and Pratt, *What Kind of Liberation?*; Barbara Finlay, *Bush and the War on Women: Turning Back the Clock on Women's Progress* (New York: Zed Books, 2006); Kim Berry, "The Symbolic Use of Afghan Women in the War on Terror," *Humboldt Journal of Social Relations*, Vol. 27, No. 2 (2003): 137–160; Jennifer L. Fluri and Rachel Lehr, *The Carpetbaggers of Kabul and Other American-Afghan Entanglements: Intimate Development, Geopolitics, and the Currency of Gender and Grief* (Athens: University of Georgia Press, 2017), Ch. 4, "'Conscientiously Chic': The Production and Consumption of Afghan Women's Liberation."

62. Many have pointed out the ideological motives for the Soviet "liberation" of women in Central Asia. Some of the major works include Gregory Massell, *The Surrogate Proletariat* (Princeton,

New Jersey: Princeton University Press, 1974); Douglas Northrop, *Veiled Empire: Gender and Power in Stalinist Central Asia* (Ithaca, New York: Cornell University Press, 2004); Marianne Kamp, *The New Woman in Uzbekistan: Islam, Modernity and Unveiling under Communism* (Seattle: University of Washington Press, 2006). For a comparison of the U.S. and Soviet treatment of Muslim women, see Emily B. Finley, "Women's Liberation in Sino, Soviet, and American State-Building: Theory and Practice," *Humanitas*, Vol. 35, Nos. 1–2 (2022).

63. Ferguson, "'W' Stands for Women," 28.

64. U.S. Department of State archive, https://2001-2009.state.gov/g/wi/rls/10684.htm, accessed August 13, 2019.

65. George W. Bush, "Remarks by the First Lady and the President on Efforts to Globally Promote Women's Human Rights," The East Room of the White House, March 12, 2004.

66. Richard Holbrooke, "Is U.S. Economy Recovering?," Interview with Fareed Zakaria GPS, October 24, 2010.

67. Among other places, this is referenced in *Time* magazine's "Person of the Year" 2007: Joe Klein, "Runners-Up: David Petraeus," *Time*, December 19, 2007.

68. John McCain, speech at the Republican National Convention.

69. Chuck Hagel, "Leaving Iraq, Honorably," *Washington Post*, November 26, 2006.

70. "U.S. Policy on Iraq," an interview with Henry Kissinger, November 19, 2006, on *BBC Sunday Morning with Andrew Marr*.

71. Kosh Sadat and Stanley McChrystal, "Staying the Course in Afghanistan: How to Fight the Longest War," *Foreign Affairs*, November–December 2017. Available at: https://www.foreign affairs.com/articles/asia/2017-10-16/staying-course-afghanistan.

72. On October 1, 2009, at the International Institute for Strategic Studies in London, General McChrystal, breaking the tradition that military officials not recommend national strategy, gave a speech calling for another surge of U.S. troops. "Surges" continued under President Trump, who authorized Secretary of Defense James Mattis to deploy additional troops. As of January 2018, fourteen thousand additional troops were deployed to Afghanistan with the prospect of more being sent. See Greg Jaffe and Missy Ryan, "Up to 1,000 More U.S. Troops Could Be Headed to Afghanistan This Spring," *Washington Post*, January 21, 2018, https://www.washingtonpost.com/world/national-security/up-to-1000-more-us-troops-could-be-headed-to-afghanistan-this-spring/2018/01/21/153930b6-fd1b-11e7-a46b-a3614530bd8 7_story.html?utm_term=.fb7b6dee379c. Accessed February 19, 2018. Trump continued to give the Central Intelligence Agency the authority to use drone strikes to kill suspected terrorists, a practice that Obama initiated. See Gordon Lubold and Shane Harris, "Trump Broadens CIA Power to Launch Drone Strikes," *Wall Street Journal Online*, March 13, 2017, https://www.wsj.com/articles/trump-gave-cia-power-to-launch-drone-strikes-1489444 374?mod=rss_US_News, accessed February 19, 2018.

73. For a thorough account of the thoughts and actions of many in the Johnson administration, especially those closest to the decision-making, see David Halberstam, *The Best and the Brightest* (New York: Ballantine Books, 1992).

74. Memorandum for the President from George Ball, "A Compromise Solution in South Vietnam," July 1, 1965, in Mike Gravel, ed., *The Pentagon Papers*, Vol. 4 (Boston: Beacon Press, 1971), 615–619.

75. Ralph Peters, "Wishful Thinking and Indecisive Wars," *The Journal of International Security Affairs*, No. 16 (Spring 2009), http://archive.is/mqqb, accessed February 16, 2018.

76. Ibid.

77. Arthur Brooks, "For Iraqis to Win, the U.S. Must Lose," in *The New York Times*, May 11, 2004. https://www.nytimes.com/2004/05/11/opinion/for-iraqis-to-win-the-us-must-lose.html.

78. Sadat and McChrystal, "Staying the Course in Afghanistan."

79. Ibid.

80. See Martin Malia, *The Soviet Tragedy: A History of Socialism in Russia, 1917–1991* (New York: Free Press, 1994), Ch. 4, "A Regime Is Born: War Communism, 1918–1921." For a convincing argument about the similarities between communism and liberal democracy, see Ryszard Legutko, *The Demon in Democracy: Totalitarian Temptations in Free Societies*, trans. Teresa Adelson (New York: Encounter Books, 2016).

81. Kristol and Kagan, "Introduction," 18.

82. Ibid., 17.

83. Robert Kagan, "Power and Weakness," *Policy Review*, No. 113 (June–July 2002): 8.

84. Ibid., 8, 16; Boot, "American Imperialism?". According to a report released in 2016 by the U.S. director of national intelligence, between January 20, 2009, and December 31, 2015, drone strikes killed 2,372 to 2,581 combatants and 64 to 116 noncombatants *outside* of Afghanistan, Iraq, and Syria (https://www.dni.gov/index.php/newsroom/reports-publi cations/item/1741-summary-of-information-regarding-u-s-counterterrorism-strikes-outs ide-areas-of-active-hostilities, accessed February 19, 2018). The Bureau of Investigative Journalism reports that the number of civilians killed was between 380 and 801 for that time period, and the total number killed was 2,753 (https://www.thebureauinvestigates.com/stor ies/2016-07-01/obama-drone-casualty-numbers-a-fraction-of-those-recorded-by-the-bur eau, accessed February 19, 2018). The Bureau of Investigative Journalism reports that these figures represent ten times more drone strikes in "the covert war on terror" during Obama's presidency than Bush's (https://www.thebureauinvestigates.com/stories/2017-01-17/oba mas-covert-drone-war-in-numbers-ten-times-more-strikes-than-bush, accessed February 19, 2018).

85. Kristol and Kagan, "Toward a Neo-Reaganite Foreign Policy," 32.

86. See Thompson and Brook, *Neoconservatism*, Ch. 4, "The Road to Nihilism," and Ch. 10, "National-Greatness Conservatism"; Drury, *Leo Strauss and the American Right*, 11–19. Jason Ralph, *America's War on Terror: The State of the 9/11 Exception from Bush to Obama* (New York: Oxford University Press, 2013), 8–10;

87. David Brooks, "Politics and Patriotism: From Teddy Roosevelt to John McCain," *Weekly Standard*, April 26, 1999.

88. Ibid.

89. Ibid.

90. The Watson Institute at Brown University "Cost of War" project has summarized as of April 2015, "In Afghanistan, the return to power of discredited warlords, the marginalization of other groups, and the concentration of power in the presidency have contributed to a gov-ernment that does not represent the interests of large numbers of Afghans. Afghan women remain cut out of political decisions, and many suffer violations of basic human rights such as health care, food, housing, and security. . . . The Iraqi government lacks political and eco-nomic inclusion, does not provide basic security for its citizens, and has regressed towards authoritarianism in recent years. The government's failure to provide basic security for its citizens and to protect rule of law has contributed to widespread gender violence against Iraqi women, though the international community has been silent about these issues." http://wat son.brown.edu/costsofwar/costs/social, accessed February 15, 2018.

91. See David Rose, "Neo Culpa," *Vanity Fair*, December 5, 2006. https://www.vanityfair.com/ news/2007/01/neocons200701.

92. Barack Obama, interview with *Vice News*, March 10, 2015. See also Jason Hanna, "Here's How ISIS Was Really Founded," CNN, August 13, 2016.

93. Watson Institute, "Current United States Counterterror War Locations," http://watson. brown.edu/costsofwar/papers/map/counterterrorwarlocations, accessed February 15, 2018.

94. The Taliban slowly increased their hold over the country until taking over. See "Fivefold Increase in Terrorism Fatalities since 9/11, Says Report," *The Guardian*, November 17, 2014; Idrees Ali, "Taliban Increases Influence, Territory in Afghanistan: U.S. Watchdog," Reuters, October 31, 2017; Ken Dilanian, "Taliban Control of Afghanistan Highest since U.S. Invasion," NBC News, January 29, 2016; Vanda Felbab-Brown testimony before the Subcommittee on Terrorism, Nonproliferation, & Trade of the House Foreign Affairs Committee on Afghanistan's terrorism resurgence: "Afghanistan's terrorism resurgence: Al-Qaida, ISIS, and beyond," Brookings, April 27, 2017, https://www.brookings.edu/testimonies/afghanistans-terrorism-resurgence-al-qaida-isis-and-beyond/, accessed February 15, 2018.

95. Freedom House, "Freedom in the World 2017," https://freedomhouse.org/report/freedom-world/freedom-world-2017, accessed February 15, 2018.

96. Kagan, *Dangerous Nation*, 40.

97. Krauthammer, "Democratic Realism," 2, 17, emphasis in original.

98. Boot, "We Didn't Kick Britain's Ass to Be This Kind of Country."

99. According to the U.S. Department of Defense count on February 13, 2018, Iraq Body Count Project, https://www.iraqbodycount.org/, accessed February 13, 2018. Also see CNN report by Ben Westcott, October 31, 2017. This report relied on data from the Watson Institute at Brown University, Stanford, and the Special Inspector General for Afghanistan Reconstruction, https://www.cnn.com/2017/08/21/asia/afghanistan-war-explainer/index.html, accessed February 13, 2018.

100. According to the Watson Institute at Brown University "Costs of War" project: "This figure includes: direct Congressional war appropriations; war-related increases to the Pentagon base budget; veterans care and disability; increases in the homeland security budget; interest payments on direct war borrowing; foreign assistance spending; and estimated future obligations for veterans' care. This total omits many other expenses, such as the macroeconomic costs to the U.S. economy; the opportunity costs of not investing war dollars in alternative sectors; future interest on war borrowing; and local government and private war costs." Watson Institute, "Costs of War," http://watson.brown.edu/costsofwar/costs/econo mic, accessed February 13, 2018.

101. Krauthammer, "Democratic Realism," 15. For domestic missed opportunity costs, see Watson Institute, "Cost of War," http://watson.brown.edu/costsofwar/costs/economic/economy, accessed February 22, 2018; for the effect of war on intangibles domestically, see Lisa Graves, "Burdens of War: The Consequences of the U.S. Military Response to 9/11: The Costs to Civil Liberties and the Rule of Law in the U.S.," Watson Institute, http://watson.brown.edu/costsofwar/costs/economic/economy, accessed February 22, 2018.

102. See Norah Niland, "Democratic Aspiration and Destabilizing Outcomes in Afghanistan," Watson Institute, http://watson.brown.edu/costsofwar/files/cow/imce/papers/2014/COW%20Niland%2061615.pdf, accessed February 22, 2018. Although Niland's conclusions, ironically, mirror those of many neoconservatives (she blames the "drawdown of U.S. and NATO troops" and an "inappropriate model of democracy" for failures in Afghanistan), her project conveys the sinister motives and expected consequences of U.S. foreign policy in Afghanistan.

103. Madeleine Albright, interview by Leslie Stahl, CBS's 60 Minutes, May 12, 1996, https://www.youtube.com/watch?v=FbIX1CP9qr4, accessed February 22, 2018.

104. Kristol and Kagan, "Introduction," 20. See Michael Novak, Catholic Social Thought and Liberal Institutions: Freedom with Justice (New York: Routledge, 2017).

105. Krauthammer, "Democratic Realism," 14.

106. George W. Bush, "Address before a Joint Session of the Congress on the State of the Union," January 20, 2004.

107. See Kristol and Kagan's discussion of "national greatness" in "Toward a Neo-Reaganite Foreign Policy," 32.

108. Kristol and Kagan, "Introduction," 23.

109. Ibid., 22. See also Kristol and Kagan, "Toward a Neo-Reaganite Foreign Policy," 18–19; Brooks, "Politics and Patriotism."

110. Strauss, Natural Right and History, 13.

111. Ibid., 139.

112. Ibid., 140–141. Note that Strauss is recounting not merely Plato's understanding of natural right but also his own. Strauss says, "The classical natural right doctrine [in] its original form, if fully developed, is identical with the doctrine of the best regime" (144).

113. Ibid., 153.

114. David Brooks, "A Return to National Greatness: A Manifesto for a Lost Creed," Weekly Standard, March 3, 1997.

115. Donald Trump, "State of the Union Address," January 30, 2018, https://www.whitehouse.gov/briefings-statements/president-donald-j-trumps-state-union-address/, accessed February 26, 2018.

116. https://dod.defense.gov/Portals/1/Documents/pubs/2018-National-Defense-Strategy-Summary.pdf

117. Walt, The Hell of Good Intentions, 16.

118. David Brooks, "Voters, Your Foreign Policy Views Stink!," *New York Times*, June 13, 2019, https://www.nytimes.com/2019/06/13/opinion/foreign-policy-populism.html, accessed November 26, 2019.

119. Ibid.

120. Patrick C. R. Terry, "The Libya Intervention (2011): Neither Lawful, nor Successful," *The Comparative and International Law Journal of Southern Africa*, Vol. 48, No. 2 (July 2015): 179.

Chapter 8

1. Alexis de Tocqueville, *Democracy in America*, trans. Harvey C. Mansfield and Delba Winthrop (Chicago: University of Chicago Press, 2000), 663.

2. Ibid., 663, 664.

3. Ibid., 665.

4. See André Bächtiger, Marco Steenbergen, Thomas Gautschi, and Seraina Pedrini, "Deliberation in Swiss Direct Democracy: A Field Experiment on the Expulsion Initiative," *The National Centres of Competence in Research (NCCR) Newsletter*, February 2011.

5. Claes G. Ryn identifies two different and opposing types of democracy: plebiscitary and constitutional. The former he characterizes as Rousseauan and democratist in nature; the latter is consonant with the American system devised by the framers. For a fuller analysis of the dichotomy between the Rousseauean understanding of democracy and the Burkean or American constitutional understanding, see Claes G. Ryn, *Democracy and the Ethical Life: A Philosophy of Politics and Community*, 2nd ed. (Washington, DC: The Catholic University of America Press, 1990), esp. Ch. XI, "Constitutionalism versus Plebiscitarianism."

6. For a thoroughgoing discussion of plebiscitarian democracy, see ibid.

7. See Aristotle, *Politics*, ed. Ernest Barker (New York: Oxford University Press, 1958), IV, xi, §20, p. 184.

8. See Aristotle, *Nicomachean Ethics*, trans. Terrence Irwin (Indianapolis, Indiana: Hackett Publishing Company, 1999), Book III, Ch. 3, §12, p. 35.

9. Orestes Brownson, *The American Republic: Its Constitution, Tendencies, and Destiny* (New York: P. O'Shea, 1866), 183.

10. Aristotle, *Politics*, IV, xi, §1, p. 180.

11. Michael J. Abramowitz, "Democracy in Crisis," Freedom House, https://freedomhouse.org/report/freedom-world/freedom-world-2018#anchor-one, accessed May 16, 2018.

12. Jan-Werner Müller, *What Is Populism?* (Philadelphia: University of Pennsylvania Press, 2017), 3.

13. Ibid., 29.

14. Jason Brennan, *Against Democracy* (Princeton, New Jersey: Princeton University Press, 2016), 5.

15. Ibid., 3.

16. Ibid., 17.

17. John McCain, interview, *Time*, March 3, 2014.

18. Jefferson, First Inaugural Address. Available at https://avalon.law.yale.edu/19th_century/jefinau1.asp.

19. Abramowitz, "Democracy in Crisis."

20. Fyodor Dostoevsky, *The Brothers Karamazov* (New York: Modern Library, 1996), 282.

21. Ibid.

22. Bertrand, Russell *The History of Western Philosophy* (New York: Simon & Schuster, 1972), 700.

23. Louis Fisher, "Unconstitutional Wars from Truman Forward," *Humanitas*, Vol. 30, Nos. 1–2 (2017): 15.

24. C. Eric Schulzke, "Wilsonian Crisis Leadership, the Organic State, and the Modern Presidency," *Polity*, Vol. 37, No. 2 (April 2005): 273.

25. Barack Obama refused to call American military intervention in Libya "war" because of the "limited nature, scope, and duration" of the planned operations. See Fisher, "Unconstitutional Wars from Truman Forward," 19–20.

26. The definition of the "foreign policy community" on which I rely is Walt's: "those *individuals and organizations that actively engage on a regular basis with issues of international affairs. This definition incorporates both formal government organizations and the many groups and individuals that deal with foreign policy as part of their normal activities."* Stephen M. Walt, *The Hell of Good Intentions: America's Foreign Policy Elite and the Decline of U.S. Primacy* (New York: Farrar, Straus and Giroux, 2018), 95, emphasis in original.

27. Ibid., 112.

28. The following represent a few examples documenting the results of the U.S. intervention in the Middle East: Toby Dodge, "The Ideological Roots of Failure: The Application of Kinetic Neo-liberalism to Iraq," *International Affairs*, Vol. 86, No. 6 (November 1, 2010): 1269–1286; Barbara J. Falk, "1989 and Post–Cold War Policymaking: Were the 'Wrong' Lessons Learned from the Fall of Communism?," *International Journal of Politics, Culture, and Society*, Vol. 22, No. 3 (September 2009): 291–313; David Beetham, "The Contradictions of Democratization by Force: The Case of Iraq," *Democratisation*, Vol. 16, No. 3 (2009): 443–454; Peter Bergen, *The Longest War: The Enduring Conflict between America and Al-Qaeda* (New York: Free Press, 2011); Norah Niland, "Democratic Aspiration and Destabilizing Outcomes in Afghanistan," Watson Institute, October 15, 2014, http://watson.brown.edu/costsofwar/files/cow/imce/papers/2014/COW%20Niland%2061615.pdf, accessed February 22, 2018; Patrick C. R. Terry, "The Libya Intervention (2011): Neither Lawful, nor Successful," *The Comparative and International Law Journal of Southern Africa*, Vol. 48, No. 2 (July 2015): 162–182.

29. Leo Strauss, *Natural Right and History* (Chicago: University of Chicago Press, 1953), 11.

30. Woodrow Wilson, address, April 6, 1918, in Arthur Link, *The Papers of Woodrow Wilson*, Vol. 47 (Princeton, New Jersey: Princeton University Press, 1984), 270.

31. Woodrow Wilson, "War Message to Congress," April 2, 1917, in Albert Fried, ed., *A Day of Dedication: The Essential Writings and Speeches of Woodrow Wilson* (New York: Macmillan Co., 1965), 309.

32. Thomas Jefferson to John Adams, September 4, 1823.

33. Irving Babbitt, *Democracy and Leadership* (Indianapolis, Indiana: Liberty Fund, 1979), 104.

34. Ibid.

35. Colin Jones, *The Fall of Robespierre: 24 Hours in Revolutionary Paris* (London: Oxford University Press, 2021), 34.

36. Ibid., 29.

37. Ibid., 36.

38. See Maximilien Robespierre, "On the Principles of Political Morality That Should Guide the National Convention in the Domestic Administration of the Republic," February 5, 1794, in *Robespierre: Virtue and Terror*, ed. Jean Ducange, trans. John Howe (New York: Verson, 2007), 108–125.

39. Jones, *The Fall of Robespierre*, 37.

40. Benedetto Croce, *History as the Story of Liberty* (Indianapolis, Indiana: Liberty Fund, 2000), 160.

41. Ibid., 159.

42. Claes G. Ryn, "A More Complete Realism: Grand Strategy in a New Key," *Humanitas*, Vol. 35, Nos. 1–2 (2022): 19. This is an idea that is more fully developed in Ryn's *Democracy and the Ethical Life*.

43. Ryn, "A More Complete Realism," 20.

44. Russell, *The History of Western Philosophy*, 700.

45. George W. Bush, address to a joint session of Congress, September 20, 2001.

46. Hebrews 11:1.

WORKS CITED

Abramowitz, Michael J. "Democracy in Crisis." Freedom House. https://freedomhouse.org/rep ort/freedom-world/freedom-world-2018#anchor-one, accessed May 16, 2018.

Ackerman, Bruce. "Why Dialogue?" *The Journal of Philosophy*, Vol. 86, No. 1 (January 1989): 5–22.

Addis, Cameron. "Jefferson and Education," *The Journal of Southern History*, Vol. 72, No. 2. 2006.

Al-Ali, Nadje, and Nicola Pratt. *What Kind of Liberation?* Berkeley: University of California Press, 2009.

Ambrosius, Lloyd E. *Wilsonian Statecraft: Theory and Practice of Liberal Internationalism during World War I*. Wilmington, Delaware: Scholarly Resources, 1991.

Appleby, Joyce. "Commercial Farming and the 'Agrarian Myth' in the Early Republic." *The Journal of American History*, Vol. 68, No. 4 (March 1982): 833–849.

Arendt, Hannah. *On Revolution*. Penguin Classics. 2006.

Aristotle. *Nicomachean Ethics*, trans. Martin Ostwald. Upper Saddle River, New Jersey: Prentice Hall, 1999.

Aristotle. *Politics*. Edited by Ernest Barker. New York: Oxford University Press, 1958.

Armenteros, Carolina. "Rousseau in the Philosophy of Eric Voegelin," paper delivered at American Political Science Association Annual Meeting, 2011.

Augustine. *The Political Writings*. Edited by Henry Paolucci. Washington, DC: Regnery Publishing, Inc., 1962.

Augustine. *City of God*. Translated by Marcus Dodd. Peabody, Massachusetts: Hendrickson Publishing Company, 2009.

Babbitt, Irving. *Democracy and Leadership*. Indianapolis, Indiana: Liberty Fund, 1979; originally published in 1924.

Babbitt, Irving. *Rousseau and Romanticism*. New Brunswick, New Jersey: Transaction Publishers, 2004; originally published in 1919.

Bächtiger, Andre, John S. Dryzek, Jane Mansbridge, and Mark Warren. "Deliberative Democracy: An Introduction." In *The Oxford Handbook of Deliberative Democracy*, ed. by Andre Bächtiger et al. Oxford University Press Online Publication, 2018.

Bächtiger, André, Marco Steenbergen, Thomas Gautschi, and Seraina Pedrini, "Deliberation in Swiss Direct Democracy: A Field Experiment on the Expulsion Initiative." In *The National Centres of Competence in Research (NCCR) Newsletter*. February 2011.

Bacon, Francis. *Novum Organum* (1620). Available in the public domain and can be accessed at: https://oll.libertyfund.org/title/bacon-novum-organum.

Babík, Milan. *Statecraft and Salvation: Wilsonian Liberal Internationalism as Secularized Eschatology*. Waco, Texas: Baylor University Press, 2013.

Bailey, Thomas A. *Woodrow Wilson and the Lost Peace*. Chicago: Quadrangle Books, 1963.

Baker, Ray Standard. *Woodrow Wilson: Life and Letters.* Garden City, New York: Doubleday, 1927–1939.

Banning, Lance. *The Jeffersonian Persuasion: Evolution of a Party Ideology.* Ithaca, New York: Cornell University Press, 1978.

Barker, Derek W. M., Noëlle McAfee, and David W. McIvor, eds. *Democratizing Deliberation: A Political Theory Anthology.* Dayton, Ohio: Kettering Foundation Press, 2012.

Bedini, Silvio A. *Thomas Jefferson: Statesman of Science.* New York: Macmillan Publishing Co., 1990.

Beauchamp, Zach. "The Anti-Liberal Moment." *Vox,* September 9, 2019. https://www.vox.com/policy-and-politics/2019/9/9/20750160/liberalism-trump-putin-socialism-reactionary.

Beetham, David. "The Contradictions of Democratization by Force: The Case of Iraq." *Democratisation,* Vol. 16, No. 3 (2009): 443–454.

Beiner, R., and W. J. Booth, eds. *Kant and Political Philosophy.* New Haven, Connecticut: Yale University Press, 1993.

Bell, Daniel. *The End of Ideology: On the Exhaustion of Political Ideas in the Fifties.* Cambridge, Massachusetts: Harvard University Press, 2000, originally published 1960.

Bell, Daniel, and Irving Kristol. "What Is the Public Interest?" *The Public Interest,* Vol. 1, No. 1 (Fall 1965): 1–5.

Benhabib, Seyla. "Liberal Dialogue versus a Critical Theory of Discursive Legitimation." In *Liberalism and the Moral Life,* ed. Nancy L. Rosenblum. Cambridge, Massachusetts: Harvard University Press, 1996.

Bergen, Peter. *The Longest War: The Enduring Conflict between America and Al-Qaeda.* New York: Free Press, 2011.

Berns, Walter. *Making Patriots.* Chicago: University of Chicago Press, 2001.

Berry, Kim. "The Symbolic Use of Afghan Women in the War on Terror." *Humboldt Journal of Social Relations,* Vol. 27, No. 2 (2003): 137–160.

Bloom, Allan. *Giants and Dwarfs: Essays 1960–1990.* New York: Simon & Schuster, 1990.

Bonomi, Patricia U. *Under the Cope of Heaven: Religion, Society, and Politics in Colonial America.* New York: Oxford University Press, 2003.

Boot, Max. "We Didn't Kick Britain's Ass to Be This Kind of Country: Donald Trump's Abandonment of Human Rights Is a Repudiation of the Country's Founding Principles." *Foreign Policy,* July 3, 2017. https://foreignpolicy.com/2017/07/03/we-didnt-kick-britains-ass-to-be-this-kind-of-country/.

Boot, Max. "I'm No Democrat—but I'm Voting Exclusively for Democrats to Save Our Democracy." *Washington Post,* October 11, 2021, https://www.washingtonpost.com/opinions/2021/10/11/im-no-democrat-im-voting-exclusively-democrats-save-our-democracy/

Boyer, John W. "Drafting Salvation," *University of Chicago Magazine,* December 1995.

Jason Brennan, *Against Democracy.* Princeton, New Jersey: Princeton University Press, 2016.

Brownson, Orestes. *The American Republic: Its Constitution, Tendencies, and Destiny.* New York: P. O'Shea, 1866.

Burke, Edmund. *Reflections on the Revolution in France.* Edited by J. G. A. Pocock. Indianapolis, Indiana: Hackett Publishing Co., 1987; originally published in 1790.

Burke, Edmund. *Further Reflections on the Revolution in France.* Edited by Daniel E. Ritchie. Indianapolis, Indiana: Liberty Fund, 1992.

Burnham, James. *Congress and the American Tradition.* Chicago: Henry Regnery Co., 1959.

Burns, James MacGregor. *The Power to Lead.* New York: Simon and Schuster, 1984.

Burns, James MacGregor. *The Deadlock of Democracy.* Englewood Cliffs, New Jersey: Prentice Hall, 1963.

Bush, George W. Second Inaugural Address, January 20, 2005. https://www.npr.org/templates/story/story.php?storyId=4460172.

Butler, Gregory S. "Visions of a Nation Transformed: Modernity and Ideology in Wilson's Political Thought," *Journal of Church and State,* Vol. 39. Winter 1997.

Byron, George Gordon. *Childe Harold's Pilgrimage.* H.C. Baird, 1854.

Calhoun, Frederick S. *Power and Principle: Armed Intervention in Wilsonian Foreign Policy*. Kent, Ohio: Kent State University Press, 1986.

Cantirino, Matthew. "The Dictatress and the Decisionmakers," *Humanitas*, Vol. 35, Nos. 1–2 2022.

Cappon, Lester J. *The Adams-Jefferson Letters*. Chapel Hill: Omohundro Institute and University of North Carolina Press, 1988.

Carey, George W., and James McClellan, eds. *The Federalist: The Gideon Edition*. Indianapolis, Indiana: Liberty Fund, 2001.

Carey, George W. *In Defense of the Constitution*. Indianapolis, Indiana: Liberty Fund, 1995.

Carlisle, Rodney. "The Attacks on U.S. Shipping That Precipitated American Entry into World War I." *The Northern Mariner*, Vol. 17, No. 3 (July 2007): 41–66.

Carlyle, Thomas. *The French Revolution: A History*, 3 vols. Boston: Dana Estes & Company, 1985.

Cassirer, Ernst. *The Question of Jean-Jacques Rousseau*, 2nd edition. Edited by Peter Gay. New Haven, Connecticut: Yale University Press, 1989.

Chafee Jr., Zechariah. *Free Speech in the United States*. Cambridge, Massachusetts: Harvard University Press, 1954.

Christiano, Thomas, ed. *Philosophy and Democracy: An Anthology*. New York: Oxford University Press, 2003.

Clinton, Bill. "Remarks by the President at Presentation of the National Medal of the Arts and the National Humanities Medal," White House, September 29, 1999, https://clintonwhitehouse4.archives.gov/WH/New/html/19990929.html.

Cohen, Joshua. *Rousseau: A Free Community of Equals*. New York: Oxford University Press, 2010.

Cohen, Joshua. "Procedure and Substance in Deliberative Democracy." In *Philosophy and Democracy: An Anthology*, ed. Thomas Christiano. New York: Oxford University Press, 2003.

Cohen, "Reflections on Habermas on Democracy." In *Ratio. Juris*, Vol. 12, No. 4 (December 1999): 385–416.

Collins, Peter. *Ideology after the Fall of Communism*. New York: Boyars/Bowerdean, 1992.

Conolly-Smith, Peter. "'Reading between the Lines': The Bureau of Investigation, the United States Post Office, and Domestic Surveillance during World War I." *Social Justice*, Vol. 36, No. 1 (2009): 7–24.

Constant, Benjamin. *Principles of Politics Applicable to All Governments*. Indianapolis, Indiana: Liberty Fund, 2003.

Cooper Jr., John Milton, ed. *Reconsidering Woodrow Wilson: Progressivism, Internationalism, War, and Peace*. Baltimore, Maryland: Johns Hopkins University Press, 2008.

Croce, Benedetto. *History as the Story of Liberty*. Indianapolis, Indiana: Liberty Fund, 2000; first published in 1938.

Croce, Benedetto. *The Philosophy of Giambattista Vico*. Translated by R. G. Collingwood. New Brunswick, New Jersey: Transaction Publishers, 2002.

Croce, Benedetto. *History as the Story of Liberty*. Indianapolis, Indiana: Liberty Fund, 2000.

Croce, Benedetto. *Aesthetic: As Science of Expression and General Linguistic*. Translated by Douglas Ainslie. New Brunswick, New Jersey: Transaction Publishers, 1995.

Dahl, Robert. *How Democratic Is the American Constitution?* New Haven, Connecticut: Yale University Press, 2003.

Deane, Herbert A. *The Political and Social Ideas of St. Augustine*. New York: Columbia University Press, 1963.

de Jouvenel, Bertrand. *The Ethics of Redistribution*. Indianapolis, Indiana: Liberty Fund, 1990.

Delli Carpini, Michael X., Fay Lomax Cook, and Lawrence R. Jacobs. "Public Deliberation, Discursive Participation, and Citizen Engagement: A Review of the Empirical Literature." *Annual Review of Political Science*, Vol. 7 (2004): 315–344.

Deneen, Patrick. *Democratic Faith*. Princeton, New Jersey: Princeton University Press, 2005.

Deneen, Patrick. *Why Liberalism Failed*. New Haven, Connecticut: Yale University Press, 2018.

de Crèvecoeur, J. Hector St. John. Letters From an American Farmer. https://avalon.law.yale.edu/subject_menus/letters.asp.

D'Entreves, Maurizio Passerin, ed. *Democracy as Public Deliberation: New Perspectives.* New York: Manchester University Press, 2002.

Derathé, Robert. *Le Rationalisme de J.-J. Rousseau* and *Jean-Jacques Rousseau et la science politique de son temps.* Paris: Presses Universitaires, 1950.

Deveaux, Monique. "Deliberative Democracy and Multiculturalism." In *The Oxford Handbook of Deliberative Democracy*, ed. Andre Bächtiger et al. New York: Oxford University Press.

Diderot, Denis. "Natural Rights." In *The Encyclopedia of Diderot and d'Alembert: Collaborative Translation Project*, translated by Stephen J. Gendzier. Ann Arbor: Michigan Publishing, University of Michigan Library, 2009, 115–116.

Dixon, William J. "Democracy and the Peaceful Settlement of International Conflict." *American Political Science Review*, Vol. 88 (March): 14–32.

Dodge, Toby. "The Ideological Roots of Failure: The Application of Kinetic Neo-liberalism to Iraq." *International Affairs*, Vol. 86, No. 6 (November 1, 2010): 1269–1286.

Dostoevsky, Fyodor. *The Brothers Karamazov.* New York: Modern Library, 1996.

Drury, Shadia. *Leo Strauss and the American Right.* New York: St. Martin's Press, 1999.

Dryzek, John S. "Theory, Evidence, and the Tasks of Deliberation." In *Deliberation, Participation and Democracy: Can the People Govern*, ed. Shawn W. Rosenberg. New York: Palgrave Macmillan, 2007, pp. 237–250.

Durant, Will and Ariel Durant, *The Story of Civilization: Rousseau and Revolution*, vol. 10. New York: Simon & Schuster, 1967.

Falk, Barbara J. "1989 and Post–Cold War Policymaking: Were the 'Wrong' Lessons Learned from the Fall of Communism?" *International Journal of Politics, Culture, and Society*, Vol. 22, No. 3 (September 2009): 291–313.

Farr, James and David Lay Williams, eds. *The General Will: The Evolution of a Concept.* New York: Cambridge University Press, 2015.

Faulkner, Robert K. "Spreading Progress: Jefferson's Mix of Science and Liberty." *The Good Society*, Vol. 79, No. 1 (2008): 26–32.

Feasby, Colin. "Libman v. Quebec (A.G.) and the Administration of the Process of Democracy under the *Charter*: The Emerging Egalitarian Model." *McGill Law Journal*, Vol. 44 (1999).

Federici, Michael P. *The Rise of Right-Wing Democratism in Postwar America.* Westport, Connecticut: Praeger Publishers, 1991.

Ferguson, Michaele L. "'W' Stands for Women: Feminism and Security Rhetoric in the Post-9/11 Bush Administration." *Politics and Gender*, Vol. 1, No. 1 (March 2005): 9–38.

Finlay, Barbara. *Bush and the War on Women: Turning Back the Clock on Women's Progress.* New York: Zed Books, 2006.

Finley, Emily B. "Women's Liberation in Sino, Soviet, and American State-Building: Theory and Practice," *Humanitas*, Vol. 35, Nos. 1–2 (2022).

Fisher, Louis. "Unconstitutional Wars from Truman Forward." *Humanitas*, Vol. 30, Nos. 1–2 (2017): 5–29.

Fried, Albert, ed. *A Day of Dedication: The Essential Writings and Speeches of Woodrow Wilson.* New York: Macmillan Co., 1965.

Frisch, Morton J., ed. *Selected Writings and Speeches of Alexander Hamilton.* Washington, DC: American Enterprise Institute, 1985.

Fluri, Jennifer L. and Rachel Lehr. *The Carpetbaggers of Kabul and Other American-Afghan Entanglements: Intimate Development, Geopolitics, and the Currency of Gender and Grief.* Athens: University of Georgia Press, 2017.

Flynn, Jeffrey. "Communicative Power in Habermas's Theory of Democracy." *European Journal of Political Theory*, Vol. 3, No. 4 (2004): 433–454.

Fukuyama, Francis. *The End of History and the Last Man.* New York: Avon Books, 1992.

Gabriel, Ralph Henry. *The Course of American Democratic Thought.* New York: Ronald Press Co., 1940.

Gamble, Richard M. *In Search of the City on a Hill: The Making and Unmaking of an American Myth.* New York: Bloomsbury Academic, 2012.

Gamble, Richard M. *The War for Righteousness: Progressive Christianity, the Great War, and the Rise of the Messianic Nation.* Wilmington, Delaware: ISI Books, 2013.

Garrison, Justin D. *"An Empire of Ideals": The Chimeric Imagination of Ronald Reagan.* New York: Routledge, 2013.

Garrison, Justin D. "Friedrich Nietzsche: The Hammer Goes to Monticello." In *Critics of Enlightenment Rationalism,* ed. Gene Callahan and Kenneth B. McIntyre. New York: Palgrave Macmillan, 2020, pp. 61–78.

Gravel, Mike, ed. *The Pentagon Papers.* Vol. 4. Boston: Beacon Press, 1971.

Green, F. C. *Jean-Jacques Rousseau: A Critical Study of His Life and Writings.* Cambridge: Cambridge University Press, 1955.

Gregg, Gary, ed. *Vital Remnants.* Wilmington, Delaware: ISI Books, 1999.

Gregory, Horace. "Our Writers and the Democratic Myth." *The Bookman,* August 1932, 377–382.

Gutmann, Amy, and Dennis Thompson. "Moral Conflict and Political Consensus." *Ethics,* Vol. 101, No. 1 (October 1990): 64–88.

Gutmann Amy, and Dennis Thompson. *Why Deliberative Democracy?* Princeton, New Jersey: Princeton University Press, 2004.

Gutmann Amy, and Dennis Thompson. "Reflections on Deliberative Democracy: When Theory Meets Practice." In *The Oxford Handbook of Deliberative Democracy,* ed. Andre Bächtiger et al. New York: Oxford University Press.

Habermas, Jürgen. *Between Facts and Norms: Contributions to a Discourse Theory of Law and Democracy.* Translated by William Rehg. Cambridge, Massachusetts: MIT Press, 1996.

Habermas, Jürgen. "Three Normative Models of Democracy." *Constellations,* Vol. 1, No. 1 (1994).

Habermas, Jürgen. *Moral Consciousness and Communicative Action.* Translated by Christian Lenhardt and Shierry Weber Nicholsen. Cambridge, Massachusetts: MIT Press, 1990.

Habermas, Jürgen. *The Theory of Communicative Action* in two volumes. Translated by Thomas McCarthy. Boston: Beacon Press, 1984–1985.

Halberstam, David. *The Best and the Brightest.* New York: Ballantine Books, 1992.

Harland, Michael. *Democratic Vanguardism: Modernity, Intervention, and the Making of the Bush Doctrine.* Lanham, Maryland: Lexington Books, 2013.

Hartz, Louis. *The Liberal Tradition in America.* San Diego, California: Harcourt Brace and Co., 1991; originally published in 1955.

Hellenbrand, Harold. "Not 'to Destroy but to Fulfill': Jefferson, Indians, and Republican Dispensation." *Eighteenth-Century Studies,* Vol. 18, No. 4 (Autumn 1985): 523–549.

Henretta, James A. "Families and Farms: *Mentalité* in Pre-Industrial America." *William and Mary Quarterly,* Vol. 35 (January 1978): 3–32.

Hitchens, Christopher. *Thomas Jefferson: Author of America.* New York: Harper Collins, 2005.

Hobbes, Thomas. *Leviathan.* Edited by A. P. Martinich. Toronto: Broadview Publishing, 2005.

Holowchak, Mark Andrew. *Thomas Jefferson's Philosophy of Education: A Utopian Dream.* New York: Routledge, 2014.

Holston, Ryan. "Deliberation in Context: Reexamining the Confrontation between the Discourse Ethics and Neo-Aristotelianism." *Telos,* Vol. 181 (Winter 2017): 151–175.

Hudson, Deal W. *Sed Contra: The Neocon Question.* July 1, 2003. https://www.crisismagazine.com/2003/sed-contra-the-neocon-question

Jefferson, Thomas. *Notes on the State of Virginia.* Edited by William Peden. Chapel Hill: University of North Carolina Press, 1955.

Jefferson, Thomas. *Jefferson's "Bible": The Life and Morals of Jesus of Nazareth.* American Book Distributors, 1997.

Johnson, Paul. *Modern Times: The World from the Twenties to the Nineties.* New York: Perennial Classics Ed., 2001.

Jones, Colin. *The Fall of Robespierre: 24 Hours in Revolutionary Paris.* London: Oxford University Press, 2021.

Kagan, Robert. *Dangerous Nation.* New York: Vintage Books, 2006.

Kagan, Robert. "Power and Weakness." In *Policy Review,* No. 113. June–July 2002.

Kamp, Marianne. *The New Woman in Uzbekistan: Islam, Modernity and Unveiling under Communism.*
     Seattle: University of Washington Press, 2006.

Keller, Christian B. "Philanthropy Betrayed: Thomas Jefferson, the Louisiana Purchase, and the
     Origins of Federal Indian Removal Policy." *Proceedings of the American Philosophical Society*,
     Vol. 144, No. 1 (March 2000): 39–66.

Kirk, Russell. *The Politics of Prudence.* Wilmington, Delaware: ISI Books, 1993.

Kirk, Russell. *The Roots of American Order.* Wilmington, Delaware: ISI, 2003.

Kissinger, Henry. *Diplomacy.* New York: Simon & Schuster, 1994.

Knight, J., and J. Johnson. "What Sort of Political Equality Does Democratic Deliberation Require?"
     In *Deliberative Democracy*, ed. J. Bohman and W. Rehg. Cambridge, Massachusetts: MIT
     Press, 1997.

Kolnai, Aurel. "Between Christ and the Idols of Modernity: A Review of Jacques Maritain's *Man
     and the State.*" In *Privilege and Liberty and Other Essays in Political Philosophy*, ed. Daniel J.
     Mahoney (Lanham, Maryland: Lexington Books, 1999.

Kozinski, Thaddeus J. *The Political Problem of Religious Pluralism.* Lanham, Maryland: Lexington
     Books, 2010.

Krauthammer, Charles. "Democratic Realism: An American Foreign Policy for a Unipolar World."
     Irving Kristol Lecture at American Enterprise Institute for Public Policy Research, January
     1, 2004.

Kristol, William, and Robert Kagan. "Toward a Neo-Reaganite Foreign Policy." *Foreign Affairs*, Vol.
     75, No. 4 (July 1996).

Kristol, William, and Robert Kagan, eds. *Present Dangers: Crisis and Opportunity in American
     Foreign and Defense Policy.* New York: Encounter Books, 2000.

Kristol, Irving. *The Neo-conservative Persuasion: Selected Essays, 1942–2009.* New York: Basic
     Books, 2011.

Lacey, Robert J. *American Pragmatism and Democratic Faith.* DeKalb: Northern Illinois University
     Press, 2008.

Lawrence, Michael A. "Justice-as-Fairness as Judicial Guiding Principle: Remembering John
     Rawls and the Warren Court." *Brooklyn Law Review*, Vol. 81 (2016).

Ledeen, Michael A. *The War against the Terror Masters: Why It Happened. Where We Are Now. How
     We'll Win.* New York: Truman Talley Books, 2003.

Legutko, Ryszard. *The Demon in Democracy: Totalitarian Temptations in Free Societies.* Translated
     by Teresa Adelson. New York: Encounter Books, 2016.

Lenin, Vladimir. *What Is to Be Done? Burning Questions of Our Movement.* New York: International
     Publishers, 1929.

Link, Arthur. *Higher Realism of Woodrow Wilson.* Nashville, Tennessee: Vanderbilt University
     Press, 1971.

Link, Arthur. *The Papers of Woodrow Wilson.* Princeton, New Jersey: Princeton University Press,
     1966–1994.

Lipset, Seymour Martin. *Political Man: The Social Bases of Politics.* New York: Doubleday, 1960.

Locke, John. *Second Treatise of Government.* Edited by C. B. Macpherson. Indianapolis,
     Indiana: Hackett Publishing, 1980.

Locke, John. *The Reasonableness of Christianity.* Edited by I. T. Ramsey. Stanford, California: Stanford
     University Press, 2005.

Lodge, Henry Cabot. *The Senate and the League of Nations.* New York: Charles Scribner's
     Sons, 1925.

Lund, Nelson. *Rousseau's Rejuvenation of Political Philosophy: A New Introduction.* London: Palgrave
     Macmillan, 2016.

MacIntyre, Alasdair. *After Virtue.* Notre Dame, Indiana: University of Notre Dame Press, 1981.

MacIntyre, Alasdair. "Does Applied Ethics Rest on a Mistake? *The Monist*, Vol. 67, No. 4
     (1984): 498–513.

Mahoney, Daniel J., ed. *Privilege and Liberty and Other Essays in Political Philosophy.* Lanham,
     Maryland: Lexington Books, 1999.

Makarenky, Jay. "Fair Opportunity to Participate: The *Charter* and the Regulation of Electoral Speech." *The Canadian Political Science Review*, Vol. 3, No. 2 (June 2009).

Malia, Martin. *The Soviet Tragedy: A History of Socialism in Russia, 1917–1991*. New York: Free Press, 1994.

Mannheim, Karl. *Ideology and Utopia: An Introduction to the Sociology of Knowledge*. Translated by Louis Wirth and Edward Shils. New York: Harcourt, Brace & World, Inc., 1936.

March, Andrew, and Alicia Steinmetz. "Religious Reasons in Public Deliberation." In *The Oxford Handbook of Deliberative Democracy*, ed. Andre Bächtiger et al. New York: Oxford University Press.

Maritain, Jacques. *Man and the State*. Washington, DC: The Catholic University of America Press, 1998; first published in 1951.

Maritain, Jacques. *Christianity and Democracy*, in *Christianity and Democracy and The Rights of Man and Natural Law*. Translated by Doris C. Anson. San Francisco, California: Ignatius Press, 1986; first published in 1943.

Maritain, Jacques. *Ransoming the Time*. Translated by Harry Lorin Binsse. New York: Scribner's Sons, 1941.

Maritain, Jacques. *The Peasant of the Garonne*. Translated by Michael Cudahy and Elizabeth Hughes. New York: Holt, Rinehart and Winston, 1968.

Maritain, Jacques. *Integral Humanism, Freedom in the Modern World, and A Letter on Independence*. Edited by Otto Bird. Notre Dame, Indiana: University of Notre Dame Press, 1996.

Marx, Karl, and Friedrich Engels. *The Communist Manifesto*. Edited by L. M. Findlay. Ontario: Broadview Press, 2004.

Marx, Karl, and Friedrich Engels. *The German Ideology*. Edited by C. J. Arthur. New York: International Publisher Co., 1970.

Massell, Gregory. *The Surrogate Proletariat*. Princeton, New Jersey: Princeton University Press, 1974.

Matthews, Richard K. *The Radical Politics of Thomas Jefferson: A Revisionist View*. Lawrence: University Press of Kansas, 1984.

McCarthy, Thomas. "Kantian Constructivism and Reconstructivism: Rawls and Habermas in Dialogue." *Ethics*, Vol. 105, No. 1 (October 1994): 44–63.

McCoy, Drew R. *The Elusive Republic: Political Economy in Jeffersonian America*. Chapel Hill, 1980.

McDougall, Walter A. *Promised Land, Crusader State: The American Encounter with the World since 1776*. New York: Houghton Mifflin Company, 1997.

McDougall, Walter A. *The Tragedy of U.S. Foreign Policy: How America's Civil Religion Betrayed the National Interest*. New Haven, Connecticut: Yale University Press, 2016.

Mearsheimer, John. *The Great Delusion: Liberal Dreams and International Realities*. New Haven, Connecticut: Yale University Press, 2018.

Miller, J. Michael, ed. *The Encyclicals of John Paul II*. Huntington, Indiana: Our Sunday Visitor Publishing Division, 2001.

Minowitz, Peter. *Straussophobia: Defending Leo Strauss and Straussians against Shadia Drury and Other Accusers*. Lanham, Maryland: Lexington Books, 2009.

Müller, Jan-Werner. *What Is Populism?* Philadelphia: University of Pennsylvania Press, 2017.

Nathanson, Stephen. *Economic Justice*. New York: Pearson, 1997.

Neuhouser, Frederick. *Rousseau's Theodicy of Self-Love: Evil, Rationality, and the Drive for Recognition*. New York: Oxford University Press, 2008.

Newton-Matza, Mitchell. *The Espionage and Sedition Acts: World War I and the Image of Civil Liberties*. New York: Routledge, 2017.

Nisbet, Robert. *The Quest for Community*. San Francisco, California: Institute for Contemporary Studies, 1990.

Nisbet, Robert. *The Making of Modern Society*. Sussex: Wheatsheaf Books, 1986.

Nisbet, Robert. *The Present Age: Progress and Anarchy in Modern America*. Indianapolis, Indiana: Liberty Fund, 1988.

Nordholt, Jan Willem Schulte. *Woodrow Wilson: A Life for World Peace*. Berkeley: University of California Press, 1991.

Northrop, Douglas. *Veiled Empire: Gender and Power in Stalinist Central Asia*. Ithaca, New York: Cornell University Press, 2004.

Novak, Michael, "The Achievement of Jacques Maritain." In *Catholic Social Thought and Liberal Institutions: Freedom with Justice*. New Brunswick, New Jersey: Transaction Publishers, 1989.

O'Brien, Conor Cruise. "Rousseau, Robespierre, Burke, Jefferson, and the French Revolution." In *The Social Contract and the First and Second Discourses: Jean-Jacques Rousseau*, ed. Susan Dunn. New Haven, Connecticut: Yale University Press, 2002, 306–308.

Onuf, Peter S. "We Shall All Be Americans: Thomas Jefferson and the Indians." *Indiana Magazine of History*, Vol. 95, No. 2 (June 1999): 103–141.

Onuf, Peter S. "Prologue: Jefferson, Louisiana, and American Nationhood." In *Empires of the Imagination: Transatlantic Histories of the Louisiana Purchase*, ed. Peter J. Kastor and François Weil. Charlottesville: University of Virginia Press, 2009.

Onuf, Peter S. "Jefferson and American Democracy." In *A Companion to Thomas Jefferson*, ed. Francis D. Cogliano. Blackwell, 2012.

Paine, Thomas. *Common Sense and Related Writings*. Edited by Thomas P. Slaughter. New York: Bedford/St. Martin's Press, 2000.

Pangle, Thomas, ed. *The Rebirth of Classical Political Rationalism*. Chicago: University of Chicago Press, 1989.

Pestritto, Ronald J. *Woodrow Wilson: The Essential Political Writings*. Lanham, Maryland: Lexington Books, 2005.

Pestritto, Ronald J. *Woodrow Wilson and the Roots of Modern Liberalism*. Lanham, Maryland: Rowman and Littlefield, 2005.

Peters, Ralph. "Stability, America's Enemy." *Parameters*, Winter 2001–2002: 5–20.

Peters, Ralph. "Wishful Thinking and Indecisive Wars." *The Journal of International Security Affairs*, No. 16 (Spring 2009).

Peterson, H. C., and Gilbert C. Fite. *Opponents of War, 1917–1918*. Madison: University of Wisconsin Press, 1957.

Plato. *Republic*. Translated by G. M. A. Grube. Indianapolis, Indiana: Hackett Publishing Co., 1992.

Pope Francis, Laudato si'. Accessible at https://www.vatican.va/content/dam/francesco/pdf/encyclicals/documents/papa-francesco_20150524_enciclica-laudato-si_en.pdf.

Pope Leo XIII. "Testem Benevolentiae nostrae," letter to Cardinal James Gibbons, Archbishop of Baltimore, January 22, 1899. https://www.papalencyclicals.net/leo13/l13teste.htm.

Pope Paul VI, *Gaudium et Spes*, December 7, 1965. https://www.vatican.va/archive/hist_counc ils/ii_vatican_council/documents/vat-ii_const_19651207_gaudium-et-spes_en.html.

Pope John XXIII, *Pacem in Terris*, April 11, 1963, §§11–27. https://www.vatican.va/content/john-xxiii/en/encyclicals/documents/hf_j-xxiii_enc_11041963_pacem.html.

Pope John Paul II. *Evangelium Vitae*. https://www.vatican.va/content/john-paul-ii/en/encyclic als/documents/hf_jp-ii_enc_25031995_evangelium-vitae.html.

Quirk, Paul, and William Bendix, and Andre Bächtiger. "Institutional Deliberation." In *The Oxford Handbook of Deliberative Democracy*, ed. Andre Bächtiger et al. New York: Oxford University Press.

Ralph, Jason. *America's War on Terror: The State of the 9/11 Exception from Bush to Obama*. New York: Oxford University Press, 2013.

Rawls, John. "The Idea of Public Reason Revisited." *The University of Chicago Law Review*, Vol. 64, No. 3 (Summer 1997): 765–807.

Rawls, John. *Political Liberalism: Expanded Edition*. New York: Columbia University Press, 2005.

Rawls, John. *Justice as Fairness: A Restatement*. Cambridge, Massachusetts: The Belknap Press, 2001; second edition.

Rawls, John. *A Theory of Justice*. Rev. ed. Cambridge, Massachusetts: The Belknap Press of Harvard University Press, 1999.

Rawls, John. *A Theory of Justice: Original Edition*. Cambridge, Massachusetts: The Belknap Press of Harvard University Press, 1971.

Rice, Condoleezza. "The President's National Security Strategy." In *The Neocon Reader*, ed. Irwin Steelier. New York: Grove Press, 2004.

Richard, Carl J. *The Founders and the Classics: Greece, Rome and the American Enlightenment*. Cambridge, Massachusetts: Harvard University Press, 1994.

Riley, Patrick. *The General Will before Rousseau: The Transformation of the Divine into the Civic*. Princeton, New Jersey: Princeton University Press, 1986.

Robespierre, Maximilien. *Robespierre: Virtue and Terror*. Edited by Jean Ducange, trans. John Howe. New York: Verson, 2007.

Robles, Jason. "An Honest Heart and a Knowing Head: A Study of the Moral, Political, and Educational Thought of Jean-Jacques Rousseau and Thomas Jefferson." Doctoral thesis, University of Colorado, 2012.

Rommen, Heinrich. *The State in Catholic Thought*. St. Louis, Missouri: B. Herder Book Co., 1950.

Rorty, Richard. *Objectivity, Relativism, and Truth: Philosophical Papers*. Vol. 1. New York: Cambridge University Press, 1991.

Rosenblum, Nancy L., ed. *Liberalism and the Moral Life*. Cambridge, Massachusetts: Harvard University Press, 1996.

Rousseau, Jean-Jacques. *Discourse on the Origin and Foundations of Inequality among Men*. In *The Basic Political Writings*, 2nd ed., ed. Donald A. Cress. Indianapolis, Indiana: Hackett Publishing Co., 2011, pp. 27–92.

Rousseau, Jean-Jacques. *On the Social Contract*. In *The Basic Political Writings*, 2nd ed., ed. Donald A. Cress. Indianapolis, Indiana: Hackett Publishing Co., 2011, pp. 153–252.

Rousseau, Jean-Jacques. *Discourse on the Sciences and the Arts*. In *The Basic Political Writings*, 2nd ed., ed. Donald A. Cress. Indianapolis, Indiana: Hackett Publishing Co., 2011, pp. 1–26.

Rousseau, Jean-Jacques. *Discourse on Political Economy*. In *The Basic Political Writings*, 2nd ed. Edited by Donald A. Cress. Indianapolis, Indiana: Hackett Publishing Company, 2011, pp. 121–152.

Rousseau, Jean-Jacques. *The Confessions*. Translated by J. M. Cohen. New York: Penguin Books, 1953.

Rousseau, Jean-Jacques. *Reveries of the Solitary Walker*. Translated by Peter France. New York: Penguin Books, 2004.

Rousseau, Jean-Jacques. *Rousseau, Judge of Jean-Jacques: Dialogues*. Translated by Judith Bush et al. Hanover, New Hampshire: University Press of New England, 1990.

Rousseau, Jean-Jacques. *The Collected Writings of Rousseau*, Vol. 5, trans. Christopher Kelley. Hanover, New Hampshire: Dartmouth College, 1995.

Rousseau, Jean-Jacques. *The Collected Writings of Rousseau*, Vol. 9, trans. Christopher Kelley and Judith R. Bush (Hanover, New Hampshire: Dartmouth College, 2001.

Rousseau, Jean-Jacques. *Emile or On Education*, trans. Allan Bloom. New York: Basic Books, 1979.

Rummens, Stefan. "Deliberation and Justice." In *The Oxford Handbook of Deliberative Democracy*, ed. Andre Bächtiger et al. New York: Oxford University Press.

Russell, Bertrand. *The History of Western Philosophy*. New York: Simon & Schuster, 1972.

Russett, Bruce. *Grasping the Democratic Peace: Principles for a Post Cold War World*. Princeton, New Jersey: Princeton University Press, 1993.

Ryn, Claes G. *Democracy and the Ethical Life: A Philosophy of Politics and Community*. 2nd ed. Washington, DC: The Catholic University of America Press, 1990; first published in 1978.

Ryn, Claes G. *The New Jacobinism: America as Revolutionary State*. 2nd expanded ed. Bowie, Maryland: National Humanities Institute, 2011; first published in 1991.

Ryn, Claes G. *Will, Imagination and Reason: Babbitt, Croce and the Problem of Reality*. New Brunswick, New Jersey: Transaction Publishers, 1997; first published in 1986.

Ryn, Claes G. *America the Virtuous: The Crisis of Democracy and the Quest for Empire*. New Brunswick, New Jersey: Transaction Publishers, 2003.

Ryn, Claes G. "A More Complete Realism: Grand Strategy in a New Key." *Humanitas*, Vol. 35, Nos. 1–2 (2022).

Sadat, Kosh, and Stanley McChrystal. "Staying the Course in Afghanistan: How to Fight the Longest War." *Foreign Affairs*, November–December 2017. Available at https://www.foreign affairs.com/articles/asia/2017-10-16/staying-course-afghanistan.

Saward, Michael. "Rawls and Deliberative Democracy." In *Democracy as Public Deliberation: New Perspectives*, ed. Maurizio Passerin D'Entreves. New York: Manchester University Press, 2002.

Scheiber, Harry N. *The Wilson Administration and Civil Liberties, 1917–1921*. Ithaca, New York: Cornell University Press, 1960.

Schlesinger, Arthur M. *The Birth of the Nation: A Portrait of the American People on the Eve of Independence*. New York: Knopf, 1968.

Schulz, Gerhard. *Revolutions and Peace Treaties: 1917–1920*. Translated by Marian Jackson. London: Methuen & Co., 1972.

Schulzke, C. Eric. "Wilsonian Crisis Leadership, the Organic State, and the Modern Presidency." *Polity*, Vol. 37, No. 2 (April 2005): 262–285.

Skinner, Quentin. *Liberty before Liberalism*. New York: Cambridge University Press, 1998.

Skinner, Quentin. *Thomas Hobbes and Republican Liberty*. New York: Cambridge University Press, 2008.

Solzhenitsyn, Aleksandr I. *The Gulag Archipelago: 1918–1956*. Translated by Thomas P. Whitney. New York: Harper & Row, 1973.

Sowerby, Emily Millicent, ed., *Catalogue of the Library of Thomas Jefferson*, 5 vols. 1952–1959.

Steelier, Irwin, ed. *The Neocon Reader*. New York: Grove Press, 2004.

Stone, Geoffrey R. *Perilous Times: Free Speech in Wartime from the Sedition Act of 1798 to the War on Terrorism*. New York: W. W. Norton, 2005.

Strauss, Leo. *Natural Right and History*. Chicago: University of Chicago Press, 1953.

Strauss, Leo. "On Classical Political Philosophy" In *The Rebirth of Classical Political Rationalism*, ed. Thomas Pangle (Chicago: University of Chicago Press, 1989).

Talmon, J. L. *Political Messianism: The Romantic Phase*. New York: Frederick A. Praeger Publishing, 1960.

Talmon, J. L. *The Origins of Totalitarian Democracy*. New York: Frederick A. Praeger Publishing, 1961.

Taylor, Alan. *Thomas Jefferson's Education*. New York: W. W. Norton & Co., 2019.

Terry, Patrick C. R. "The Libya Intervention (2011): Neither Lawful, nor Successful." *The Comparative and International Law Journal of Southern Africa*, Vol. 48, No. 2 (July 2015): 162–182.

Thompson, C. Bradley, with Yaron Brook. *Neoconservatism: An Obituary for an Idea*. Boulder, Colorado: Paradigm Publishers, 2010.

Thompson, Dennis F. "Deliberative Democratic Theory and Empirical Political Science." *Annual Review of Political Science*, Vol. 11 (2008): 497–520.

Tocqueville, Alexis de. *Democracy in America*. Translated by Harvey C. Mansfield and Delba Winthrop. Chicago: University of Chicago Press, 2000.

Tucker, Robert W., and David C. Hendrickson. *Empire of Liberty: The Statecraft of Thomas Jefferson*. New York: Oxford University Press, 1990.

Tucker, Robert W., and David C. Hendrickson. "The Triumph of Wilsonianism?" *World Policy Journal*, Vol. 10, No. 4 (Winter 1993–1994): 83–99.

Tulis, Jeffrey K. *The Rhetorical Presidency*. Princeton, New Jersey: Princeton University Press, 1987.

Tulis, Jeffrey K., and Stephen Macedo, eds. *The Limits of Constitutional Democracy*. Princeton, New Jersey: Princeton University Press, 2010.

Tuveson, Ernest Lee. *Redeemer Nation: The Idea of America's Millennial Role*. Chicago: University of Chicago Press, 1968.

UNESCO. *Human Rights, Comments and Interpretations*. Paris: PHS, 1949.

Vico, Giambattista. *The New Science of Giambattista Vico.* Edited by Thomas Goddard Bergin and Max Harold Fisch. Ithaca, New York: Cornell University Press, 1968.

Vico, Giambattista. *The Autobiography of Giambattista Vico.* Edited by Max Harold Fisch and Thomas Goddard Bergin. Ithaca, New York: Cornell University Press, 1944.

Voegelin, Eric. *Science, Politics and Gnosticism.* Wilmington, Delaware: ISI Books, 2007.

Voegelin, Eric. "Ersatz Religion." In *Science, Politics and Gnosticism.* Wilmington, Delaware: ISI Books, 2007.

Von Kuehnelt-Leddihn, Erik Ritter. *Liberty or Equality: The Challenge of Our Times.* Edited by John P. Hughes. Auburn, Alabama: The Mises Institute, 2014.

Von Kuehnelt-Leddihn, Erik Ritter. *The Menace of the Herd or Procrustes at Large.* Milwaukee, Wisconsin: Bruce Publishing Company, 1943.

Wallace, Anthony F. C. *Jefferson and the Indians: The Tragic Fate of the First Americans.* Cambridge, Massachusetts: Belknap Press, 1999.

Walt, Stephen M. *The Hell of Good Intentions: America's Foreign Policy Elite and the Decline of U.S. Primacy.* New York: Farrar, Straus and Giroux, 2018.

Walzer, Michael. *Spheres of Justice: A Defense of Pluralism and Equality.* New York: Basic Books, Inc., 1983.

Weart, Spencer R. *Never at War: Why Democracies Will Not Fight One Another.* New Haven, Connecticut: Yale University Press, 1998.

Weaver, Richard M. *Ideas Have Consequences.* Chicago: University of Chicago Press, 2013.

Weinberg, Albert K. *Manifest Destiny: A Study of Nationalist Expansionism in American History.* Baltimore, Maryland: Johns Hopkins University Press, 1935.

Weinstein, Kenneth R. "Philosophic Roots, The Role of Leo Strauss, and the War in Iraq." In *The Neocon Reader,* ed. Irwin Stelzer. New York: Grove Press, 2004.

Wilson, Woodrow. *The Papers of Woodrow Wilson,* 69 vols. ed. Arthur S. Link. Princeton: Princeton University Press, 1966–1994.

Wilson, Woodrow. "War Message to Congress." Publicly available at the National Archives website, archives.gov.

Wilson, Woodrow. *Leaders of Men.* Edited by T. H. Vail Motter. Princeton, New Jersey: Princeton University Press, 1952.

Wilson, Woodrow. *The New Freedom,* ed. William Bayard Hale. New York: Doubleday, Page and Company, 1913.

Wilson, Woodrow. *Congressional Government.* Baltimore, Maryland: Johns Hopkins University Press, 1956.

Wilson, Woodrow. *A History of the American People.* New York: Harper and Brothers Publishers, 1902.

Wilson, Woodrow. *Constitutional Government in the United States.* New York: Columbia University Press, 1908.

Wilson, Woodrow. *The Public Papers of Woodrow Wilson: College and State.* Vols. 1–2. New York: Harper and Brothers, 1925–1927.

Wilson, Woodrow. "Address on Flag Day," June 14, 1917. This document is publicly available at The American Presidency Project at https://www.presidency.ucsb.edu/documents/addr ess-flag-day.

Wilson, Woodrow. "Address at Cheyenne, Wyoming, September 24, 1919. The American Presidency Project: https://www.presidency.ucsb.edu/documents/address-the-princess-theater-cheyenne-wyoming.

Yarbrough, Jean M. *American Virtues: Thomas Jefferson on the Character of a Free People.* Lawrence: University Press of Kansas, 1998.

Yellin, Mark E., ed. *The Intellectual Origins of Jeffersonian Democracy.* Lanham, Maryland: Lexington Books, 2000.

Zummo, Paul. "Thomas Jefferson's America: Democracy, Progress, and the Quest for Perfection."
    Doctoral dissertation, The Catholic University of America, 2008.
"Mark Zuckerberg and Jack Dorsey Testimony Transcript Hearing November 17,
    [2020]," Transcript Library, rev.com/blog/transcripts/mark-zuckerberg-jack-dorsey-
    testimony-transcript-senate-tech-hearing-november-17.
Zuckert, Catherine H., and Michael P. Zuckert. *The Truth about Leo Strauss: Political Philosophy
    and American Democracy*. Chicago: University of Chicago Press, 2014.

INDEX